Beyond Plymouth Rock

AMERICA'S HOMETOWN IN THE 20TH CENTURY

VO

KA

BEV

Layout and d   *Design*

THE PLYMO   H, MA

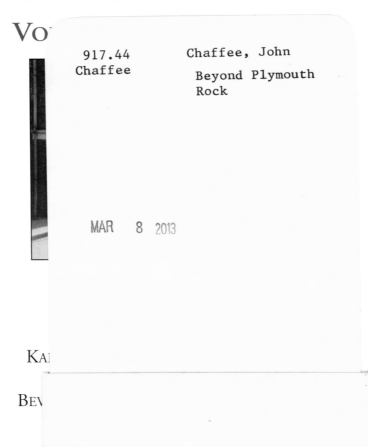

ISBN 0-9725513-0-1

Published by the Plymouth Public Library Corp.
132 South St., Plymouth, MA 02360

Layout, design and printing by Rogers Print & Design
41 Christa McAuliffe Blvd., Plymouth, MA 02360

Library of Congress Catalog Card Number pending
For customer service and orders call: (508) 830-4250
E-mail sales @ plill@ocln.org
Visit us on the Internet at www.gis.net/~ppl

Table of Contents

FOREWORD – FROM THE SHADES OF OBLIVION
Peter J. Gomes 1

PREFACE
John Chaffee 3

1 1900: THE DAWN OF THE 20TH CENTURY
Richmond Talbot 5

What life was like in Plymouth in 1900 and during the early years of a new century.

2 A SMALL NEW ENGLAND MILL TOWN
John Chaffee 9

A walking tour of downtown and North Plymouth at the turn of the 20th century.

3 SUMMER PEOPLE
Joan H. Bartlett..................14
An introduction to the summer colonies of Plymouth.

4 PLYMOUTH: THE TOURIST TOWN
James Baker 15

Because Plymouth was "where it all began," it has long been a tourist destination.

5 SUMMER PEOPLE: THE FORGES
Joan H. Bartlett.................20

6 AS TIME GOES BY
Nan Anastasia 21
Plymouth in 1901 as recorded in the pages of the *Old Colony Memorial*.

7 SUMMER PEOPLE: LONG POND, HIGH CLIFF AND WHITE HORSE BEACH
Joan H. Bartlett 32

8 ROPEMAKERS OF PLYMOUTH
Samuel Eliot Morison 33
A distinguished 20th century historian tells the story of the Plymouth Cordage Co.

9 ALL PLYMOUTHEANS ARE IMMIGRANTS

Laurence Pizer 37
Everyone who lives in Plymouth is an immigrant or descendant of immigrants.

10 LIFE ON A CRANBERRY BOG AT THE TURN OF THE CENTURY

Rose T. Briggs.......................39
Memories from the childhood of a distinguished Plymouthean.

11 PLYMOUTH'S JEWISH COMMUNITY

Karin Goldstein 43
While not as numerous as Italians or Portuguese, Jews were a significant immigrant group.

12 DOWNTOWN POST OFFICE

How Main Street was extended and a new post office was built.....................46

13 HIGH SCHOOL GRADUATION - 1913

Sue Sadow 47
In her autobiography a Plymouth native recalls her local high school when she was 16 years old.

14 PLYMOUTH'S ORIGINAL TOWN HOUSE

Beverly Ness 49
Until 1952 the town's business was conducted in a 1749 courthouse.

15 GROWING UP ITALIAN IN PLYMOUTH

Alba Thompson 51
A daughter of Italian immigrants recalls her childhood.

16 SUMMER PEOPLE: SUMMERHOUSES FOR PLYMOUTHEANS

Joan H. Bartlett..................56

17 PLYMOUTH AND SOME PORTUGUESE

Peter J. Gomes 57
A son of Cape Verdean immigrants discusses their impact on Plymouth.

18 THE CORDAGE STRIKE OF 1916

Samuel Eliot Morison 61
Cordage workers stage an unexpected work stoppage to seek higher wages.

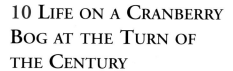

19 OVER HERE: 1916-1918

Karin Goldstein *65*

The impact of World War I on the Plymouth homefront.

20 A 'SPANISH LADY' PLAGUES PLYMOUTH

Herman Hunt *69*

An influenza epidemic leads to a shortage of caskets.

21 TRIAL OF THE CENTURY: LOCAL AMNESIA

Robert Knox *71*

Plymouth has always been ambivalent about local resident Bart Vanzetti.

22 FOREFATHERS' DAY 1920

John Chaffee *77*

A yearlong series of events marked the 300th anniversary of the Pilgrim landing.

23 GURNET LIGHT SINGLED OUT

The twin beacons on Gurnet Point became one in 1924. .... *80*

24 MEMORIAL HALL AND HEDGE HOUSE

The Hedge House was moved so Memorial Hall could be built. *81*

25 PLYMOUTH TROLLEYS

Karin Goldstein *83*

Trolleys were familiar sights on Plymouth streets during the early years of the century.

26 TRIAL OF THE CENTURY: CRIMES, PROSECUTION AND DEFENSE

Robert Knox *85*

Sacco and Vanzetti were foreigners, draft dodgers and murder suspects.

27 FROM POWDERHOUSE TO PORTICO: 1920-21

A series of events marked the 300th anniversary of the Pilgrim landing. *92*

28 PILGRIM TERCENTENARY: 1921

John Chaffee *93*

One day the president and three battleships came to town to honor the Pilgrim settlers.

29 FIRST GRADE AT THE ALDEN STREET SCHOOL

Alba Thompson *97*

Walking from Mill Village to a one-room schoolhouse.

30 TEMPERANCE AND RUMRUNNING

Karin Goldstein *99*

During Prohibition Plymouth had both teetotalers and tipplers.

31 SUMMER PEOPLE: EEL RIVER FARM

Joan H. Bartlett...............*102*

32 TRIAL OF THE CENTURY: LAST DAYS

Robert Knox...................*103*
The local newspaper ignored the case until it was over.

33 CORDAGE FROM COURT STREET

A description of the rope factory when the workday was over. *108*

34 OAK STREET SCHOOL IN THE 1930s

Marie Fehlow *109*
How the school prepared students for life.

35 PLYMOUTH DURING THE DEPRESSION: THE EARLY YEARS

Karin Goldstein *111*
Community ties helped Plymoutheans get through tough times.

36 SUMMER PEOPLE: MANOMET AND MANTERS POINT

Joan H. Bartlett...............*116*

37 TWO THEATERS AND A REEL RUNNER

Philip Forman *117*
Two movie houses provided much of Plymouth's early 20th century entertainment.

38 MEMORIES OF PLYMOUTH

Maggie Mills *119*
A reporter recalls her childhood growing up in downtown Plymouth.

39 PLYMOUTH DURING THE DEPRESSION: THE LATER YEARS

Karin Goldstein *123*
Federal aid helped build a new high school on Lincoln Street.

40 DOWNTOWN PLYMOUTH 1940

A map showing "historic shrines." *129*

41 SUMMER PEOPLE: PLYMOUTH BEACH

Joan H. Bartlett *130*

42 I REMEMBER: PERSONAL MEMORIES OF 20TH CENTURY PLYMOUTH

Twelve longtime residents recall earlier days. *131*

Arthur Ragazzini
Mary Alice Janeiro Post
Jane Brenner Weston
Primo Bastoni
Willard Dittmar
Ramo Bongiovanni

Anita Fiocchi Scagliarini
Pat Farina
Allen Cappella
Arnold A. Blackmur
Jerry L. Rezendes
William S. Franks

43 THE HOMEFRONT: 1941-1945

Bobbi Clark *137*
From Pearl Harbor to V-J Day, life in America's hometown.

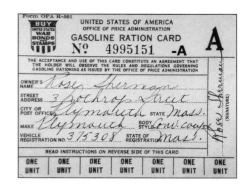

44 MANOMET SHORE PATROL

George W. Carter Jr. *147*
Walking the Plymouth coastline during World War II.

EPILOGUE

Peter J. Gomes *151*

BIBLIOGRAPHY: Sources Consulted *154*

AUTHORS AND CONTRIBUTORS *159*

ACKNOWLEDGEMENTS: Others who helped *161*

INDEX *162*

Foreword
FROM THE SHADES OF OBLIVION

Peter J. Gomes

For many, and for too long, Plymouth's 20th century history has been held hostage to the legendary status of its 17th century past, giving the casual observer the impression that the past had stopped even before the 18th century had begun.

That past history was often burdensome to those who felt excluded and alienated from it, as it made history in Plymouth something for the tourist rather than for domestic consumption. Local history was not quite as local as it might have been when local wags in the 1920s referred to the formidable gray granite temple on Court Street as "Grim Pill" Hall, rather than Pilgrim Hall. And as recently as 1970, as the town prepared to celebrate its 350th anniversary, a selectman named William "Cozy" Barrett — who in his youth made a living as a guide at Plymouth Rock and in later life a successful political career out of Pilgrim-bashing — reportedly said, "It was an ill wind that blew the Mayflower into Plymouth harbor." Such views reflected a populist hostility to the perceived filiopietism which for so long passed as history in and of Plymouth. It would become the work of the 20th century to make the history of ordinary Plymoutheans—an increasingly diverse and cosmopolitan population—the subject of legitimate inquiry and pride.

My own interest in local history began in 1958 when I went to work after school as a page in the Plymouth Public Library, which was then in the handsome Russell building on North Street. I had an aptitude for history which the librarian, Miss Eunice E. Sharp, encouraged. In those days, long before the Internet and the World Wide Web, persons from far away who were interested in Plymouth and its history routinely wrote to the local library. Miss Sharp had little interest in this correspondence and even less in the huge volume of genealogical inquiries, which she regarded with overt hostility. Thus, she assigned a small portion of my 20 hours per week to what for her was the disagreeable task of dealing with what she called "the Mayflowers." I enjoyed the work.

In 1962, at the end of my first year in college, I began a summer job in the library of Pilgrim Hall, thus beginning an association with the Pilgrim Society that continues to this day. There I encountered some of Plymouth's great 20th century local historians, including the director, Miss Rose T. Briggs, and the banker-turned-historian, Allen Danforth Russell, one of Miss Briggs's many cousins. What they didn't know was not worth knowing. Neither was a trained nor professional historian, although each had an eye, an ear, and an aptitude for what an 18th century Pilgrim Society founder, Dr. James Thacher, referred to as "numerous events and incidents of more recent occurrence, which the antiquarian would lament should be consigned to the shades of oblivion."

That ambition of Dr. Thacher's was captured in what is now an obscure little book written in 1968 by the long-time president of the Pilgrim Society, Ellis W. Brewster, entitled *Plymouth in My Father's Time*, which was full of 19th century pictures and local lore. Brewster — the ninth lineal descendant of Elder Brewster of the Mayflower, and as president of the Plymouth Cordage Co., one of New England's leading industrialists — would be the first to describe himself an amateur in history. He was keenly interested in the preservation of local history and not just in that of his ancestors, and he devoted nearly as much of his considerable energy to the Pilgrim Society as he did to the cordage company. He described his little book as, "An informal collection of pictures and anecdotes — authentically Plymouth — assembled as some insurance against their loss in the passage of the years."

My early years at Pilgrim Hall coincided with the Plymouth Redevelopment Authority's urban renewal project at Summer and High streets. No one who remembers that neighborhood will deny that it had long been a neglected and blighted landscape at the very center of the town. Yet in its dozens of houses bounded on the north by Burial Hill and on the south by Town Brook was to be found the heart of nearly two centuries of domestic life, the physical rudiments of which would do honor to any 18th and 19th century townscape in America. Hindsight is always 20/20, but had the area been restored instead of leveled to the ground, we would now have a historic center the equal of Salem or Marblehead or Newport. Such was not to be, however, and so before the wrecker's ball hit, Miss Briggs and her assistant, Dorothy D. Merrick, and I took photographs and measured drawings of every structure in the affected area, the process being animated by Miss Briggs's lively anecdotal knowledge of who lived where and who did what. To the redevelopment people we were a nuisance, I am sure, but to me this was the essential and vital stuff of local history, and all the more important in that it was soon to be lost.

I had a similar experience with Allen Russell who from his splendid ancestral home on North Street wrote in a spidery longhand many detailed monographs of neglected aspects of 19th and early 20th century history. At Pilgrim Hall, whenever we were in doubt or in dispute about facts, the ultimate solution was nearly always to "call Allen." One day he decided that he wished to determine the exact location of all of the 18th century mill privileges on Town Brook from Brewster Gardens to the headwaters above Billington Sea. This was no small project, as the area was thick with undergrowth, paths had long since disappeared, and markers either had been vandalized or had disappeared entirely. A party of young professional surveyors would have had trouble. Allen was then in his late 70s, and with no more assistance than I could provide as his "man Friday," we took several weeks at mid-summer to complete the task to his satisfaction.

What I most remember about Ellis Brewster, Rose Briggs, and Allen Russell was their enthusiasm, in their muted Yankee fashion, in sharing their wealth of knowledge of Plymouth with everybody and anybody, including a young black kid on a summer job. They were and they remain for me the epitome of local history at its best. They understood that history was not just documents, but 'stuff' and people and the recollections of ordinary lives and ordinary times; materials which might be 'below the radar' of professional and formal history, but without which the real life of a town and its people could not be known.

It is in this spirit that I believe this present project of local history is conceived. "*The Less Remembered Years*" is the title of an elegiac essay published by the late Horace C. Weston as a Pilgrim Society note nearly 40 years ago, about the period after the glory days of the Pilgrims and just before 1692 and the end of the Colony. That title might well be applied to the essays in this book, for each one tells us something that very few of the rest of us know. What is so valuable about these essays is that together they reclaim for us all the "less remembered years" of the 20th century, a time through which so many of us have lived but which, until now, has not been time shared. This book is an enterprise not simply in preservation, but in cultural sharing.

We often imagine that history happens to other people in other places and in other times, never to us, and never at home. Yet the genius of local history reminds us that this is our history and our story, and that we are not mere onlookers upon someone else's drama but players in our own play, which is both stranger and stronger than fiction. In addition to the strengths of local authors, this book is enhanced by a wonderful collection of photographs from personal archives, many of which will be seen for the first time. I cannot imagine a greater gift to Plymouth's 21st century future than this lovingly crafted and very personal memoir of its 20th century past. For this labor of love, which rescues precious bits of our 20th century history from the shades of oblivion, the gratitude of the town and its friends belongs to the Plymouth Public Library Corp. and its local history committee. In words of which Dr. James Thacher would approve, may our future ever prove worthy of our past.

Peter J. Gomes
Sometime President of the Pilgrim Society
The Lodge, Plymouth
April 2002

Preface

This is a work of love — love of America's hometown, love of history and love of the Plymouth Public Library. Shortly after I became a library trustee in 1999, Lee Regan, reference supervisor and curator of the library's extensive Plymouth history collection, suggested the need for a history of 20th century Plymouth. The town's story had been often and sometimes well-told from its Pilgrim settlement through the 19th century but not since. As a once aspiring historian and recently retired writer-editor, I agreed to help compile such a work.

With the enthusiastic support of Library Director Dinah Smith O'Brien and the Plymouth Public Library Corp., a small group of us began meeting to plan this endeavor. Initially I was joined by Lee and two of her reference colleagues, Sharon LaRosa and Beverly Ness. Enhancing the library's Plymouth history collection is part of their duties.

Later our team was augmented by the addition of two highly skilled and dedicated volunteers: Karin Goldstein, curator of original collections at Plimoth Plantation, trustee of the Plymouth Antiquarian Society and former curator of collections at Pilgrim Hall Museum; and Wes Ennis, Pilgrim Society secretary, chairman of the town's Historical Commission and staff photographer for Plymouth's weekly newspaper, the *Old Colony Memorial*.

We selected a local talent, Kathleen Branigan of Rogers Print, to craft a layout and design that captured an early 20th century look and feel.

Very early on we agreed to compile a popular rather than pedantic history, told as much as possible by people who had lived it. And so, for readability, we adopted the Associated Press style manual and chose to append an extensive list of references rather than interrupt the text with footnotes. As an aid to both readers and future researchers, a detailed index also has been included.

We are grateful to those who contributed, both as authors and researchers, as well as those individuals and organizations that shared with us their photos and their oral and written memories of an earlier Plymouth.

We are particularly grateful to Robert D. Hale, novelist, editor, former owner of the Westwinds Bookstore in Duxbury and past president of the American Booksellers Association, who shared with us his experience editing and marketing a highly regarded history of Duxbury, published in 1985. Without his wise advice and counsel this book would have lacked many important features.

This volume is but the beginning of a larger story. It tells how a predominantly Yankee town in 1900 became a very diverse all-American town by World War II, thanks in large part to a rope-making company that imported hundreds of immigrant laborers, primarily from Germany, Italy and Portugal. Overcoming many obstacles, the company and the town succeeded in tying everybody together into a common whole. And so, Volume I, *Ties That Bind*, covers only selected aspects of Plymouth during the first half of the 20th century. As we move further into local history in a later volume of *Beyond Plymouth Rock*, we plan to tell not only the story of Plymouth during the second half of the century, but also to include chapters on a variety of subjects, such as the town's villages, churches and personalities that will cover the entire 100 years.

While this may be one of the few histories of Plymouth that was not written to emphasize the town's Pilgrim heritage, we learned in compiling it that Plymouth, to paraphrase the Rev. Peter Gomes, is very much like a pilgrim — constantly moving to an as yet unachieved destination.

John Chaffee
Managing Editor

This book is dedicated to
THE PEOPLE OF PLYMOUTH

1

1900 THE DAWN OF THE 20TH CENTURY

BY RICHMOND TALBOT

The year 1900 was greeted in Plymouth with optimism. In those days people believed in progress, and the new century lay before them like a golden opportunity. The Old Colony Division of the New York, New Haven and Hartford Railroad linked the town to the world as did the wharves along Water Street. Boats and trains brought tourists to admire Plymouth Rock, which rested under its ornate Victorian canopy. Overlooking it on Cole's Hill, the Plymouth Rock House hotel offered steam heat, electric lights, and a long-distance telephone. It was a time when folks shook their heads and wondered, "What will they think of next?"

Then, as now, the Rock was a little disappointing as a scenic wonder, but people were readers in those days. Longfellow, only 18 years dead, had popularized the Pilgrims in "The Courtship of Myles Standish," and even lowbrows knew the story. Not everyone pressed lips to the gray boulder, but most stood in reverence. The Forefathers' Monument towered over the town proclaiming the Pilgrim virtues, topped by Faith.

At the Rock on a quiet summer's day, the clatter of industrial machinery could be heard, for

Plymouth was a town of factories and mills. Attracted by water power, they lined Town Brook almost to the new Morton Park where Plymoutheans could promenade on a Sunday afternoon. As the brook emptied into the harbor, it widened into a marsh, and low tide exposed mud and debris that had been thrown in over the years.

Above a souvenir shop on the corner of Main and Leyden streets were the offices of the *Old Colony Memorial*, which advertised itself: "The leading weekly and recognized 'County Paper' for over 75 years. Nothing objectionable allowed in its reading or advertising columns, so it is always clean, reliable, and welcome in every

Reprinted from
"Turning Back the Pages: 100 Years of Change in Plymouth." A supplement to the *Old Colony Memorial*, May 27,1999.

subscriber's home. Valuable to business patrons because of established reputation and very best classes of circulation. Politics, straight Republican."

Plymouth waterfront in the 1890s with Plymouth Rock under Hammatt Billings' Victorian canopy and the Plymouth Yacht Club on the pier at the left, viewed from Cole's Hill.

OLD COLONY CLUB COLLECTION

The horse was still a favored means of getting around town; and David O. Harvey, who advertised himself a horse shoer, carriagesmith and general blacksmith, had a shop at 101 Summer St. Currier's dining and ice cream room stood at 22 Main St., and news dealer and stationer Charles A. Smith had a store a little way down at number 46. Next door at 44 Main St., Isaac N. Stoddard & Son offered insurance. Funeral directors and embalmers Raymond & Beaman had their office and warerooms at 28 Middle St.. They advertised, "modern equipments" and a "Lady Assistant when desired." Across LeBaron Alley the Plymouth Public Library occupied its new building on North Street.

Things were pretty peaceful, although in 1900 there were 13 arrests for larceny and two for adultery. Of course, both adultery arrests may have resulted from the same incident — the crime statistics don't make it clear. A good deal more was whispered over the back fences of the town.

In North Plymouth along the electric trolley line that connected us with Kingston, the row houses of the Plymouth Cordage Co. were home to workers whose families had come from many European countries and whose politics were often different from the factory owners and the *Old Colony Memorial*. Plymouth was in the midst of a wave of immigration. Twenty years earlier, 90 percent of the population had been native born, but in 1900 that number was dropping and would be only 68 percent by 1910.

Strangers to the United States and often poorly educated, these newcomers needing help adjusting, and, under the leadership of President Augustus P.

Loring, the Cordage was adopting a paternal attitude toward its employees. The newly opened Loring Library contained books in Italian, French, Portuguese, German as well as a few in Polish, and Russian. There were woods, a bathing beach, and athletic fields on the factory grounds, as well as a hall for social gatherings. There was an employee health plan, and in 1900 a kindergarten was provided for the workers' children as a sort of "Head Start" to ready them for the Plymouth schools.

New housing for the workers featured modern bathrooms. As they would be at the other end of the

Twenty years earlier, 90% of the population had been native born, but in 1900 that number was dropping and would be only 68% by 1910.

century, the voters of the town were reluctant to tax themselves for an upgrade to the sewer system, so it was built and paid for by the Cordage. Each housing unit had a yard suitable for gardening so the families could supplement their income with home-grown food. Prizes were given for the best garden and the best kept hen yard. Every Labor Day a fair exhibited output of the gardens and foods from the kitchens of the women, some of whom took cookery classes provided by the company.

The Cordage was a keystone in the economics of Plymouth and produced rigging for ships and twine to be used with the McCormick reaper, but the town was not complacent. Just the previous year in

1899, an organization of businessmen held a meeting on the subject, "Resolved, that Plymouth possesses those attractions which should induce business to relocate here." It was a theme that was to echo through the new century.

Not all laborers in Plymouth were so fortunate as the workers at the Cordage. The going rate of pay on the cranberry bogs was 12½ cents for a 10-hour day. Shortly after the turn of the century, Portuguese from the Cape Verde Islands began to undertake this toil. There was a community of them in Chiltonville where, besides agricultural work, they found employment in mills along Eel River. There was another settlement along South Pond Road. Some of the bog workers were migratory, having winter jobs as far away as the steel mills of Pennsylvania.

In the cranberry industry the modern age was emerging with scoops and snap machines replacing human fingers for picking. In 1900 a steam pump was installed to substitute for old-fashioned gravity to flood and drain a bog. Horse drawn carts rumbled through the dirt roads of the town carrying barrels of cranberries to the railroad station to be shipped.

The leisured classes were finding new ways to enjoy themselves. Golf was first played on the pastures of the Holmes Reservation in North Plymouth, where the newly organized Plymouth Golf and Tennis Association began play in 1903. Three years later the Hotel Pilgrim on the hill overlooking Plymouth Beach established a golf course on its grounds, and on April 13, 1910, the Plymouth Country Club was formed.

The Plymouth Yacht Club, which had been

founded in 1890, had its clubhouse on Long Wharf at the foot of North Street. Sailboats were associated with times gone by, and the forward-looking members cruised into the 20th century under power.

If golf or excursions on the water weren't contemplated, visitors and local residents could take the trolley to Plymouth Beach, where there was a new wooden pavilion that made the beach a fashionable gathering place in the summer. Band concerts were performed, and the more daring might even swim.

By 1909 the Bradford Joint Co., manufacturers of steel fastenings for bedsteads, advertised that they would do automobile and motor boat repairs at their machine shop at 51 Market St. Currier's and Smith's were still going strong. The Stoddard Agency had become Stoddard & McLean, but in the following year it would be bought by the young attorney Harry Talbot.

For the next few years the *Old Colony Memorial* reported storms and fires and now and then an automobile accident. Often on the front page there was a column telling about the activities of Company D of the fifth regiment of the Standish Guards. It was chatty stuff mostly — sports scores, salad suppers, a class in map reading, or the arrival of a shipment of bugles. On June 21, 1916, however, Captain C. H. Robbins received orders to assemble his command. America's neutrality was coming to an end, and we were about to become involved in what everyone was calling "The Great War."

On the 23rd the Company moved out from the railroad station to swelling martial music and a fluttering of flags. Schools and factories were closed for the farewell. There were those in the crowd who had seen such departures for the Civil War and the Spanish-American War, and they knew that not all

1749 COURT HOUSE MUSEUM COLLECTION

Stereo view looking up First Street or Leyden Street in the 1880s.

these young men would return. The big bell on the Puritan Mill boomed good-bye and the band played "The Girl I Left Behind Me," a Civil War tune. The Memorial reported, "Tear wet cheeks, masculine as well as feminine, were numerous, and throats were filled with unswallowable lumps."

There would be other departures, and the paper reported the receipt of letters that showed that the troops had safely passed over the U-boat infested sea. The next year the *Old Colony* sponsored a fund for the purchase of a new Edison machine, "the phonograph with a soul," to send to the boys of Company D. Contributions could be left at the paper or with the local Edison dealer. The Edison Co. was offering these "instruments" at cost, which was $55 and added a collection of cylindrical records for another $20. That was quite a bit, considering you could get a new Ford for under $400;

but people imagined the troops gathering around enjoying the music, and contributions flowed in.

That year in France an officer needed a volunteer. The driver of an ammunition truck and his assistant had been killed, and the vehicle was stalled on blasted ground near Allied lines. There it stood under a barrage of artillery fire with the odds increasing every minute that a shell would ignite the cargo killing the troops around. Sherman Whipple Jr., a young man of Plymouth, stepped forward and accepted the assignment. Toes, knees, elbows, and hands propelled him on his belly through the dirt under enemy fire and the rain of exploding shells. When he got to the truck, he stood and managed to get the vehicle started. At the wheel, he drove it to a place of safety. He was 19 years old.

In 1920 Sherman Whipple Jr. was living in Chiltonville with his wife, Margaret. The War was over and President Warren Harding had gained the White House on a platform of "normalcy." The year was the 300th anniversary of the landing of the Pilgrims, and in Plymouth, a momentous event was planned to mark what was the high tide of interest in the Pilgrims. President Harding arrived on the yacht *Mayflower* and viewed a spectacular pageant with a cast of hundreds on a stage 400 feet wide and 450 feet deep.

Modernity was reflected in the outdoor electric lighting system, which was the largest used up to that time. Fifty lighting units were provided by General Electric, and special 1500-watt bulbs were used in each. There were 50 more "projectors" specially designed for the pageant which could each throw a narrow spot of light. There were 15 miles of rubber covered wire and 5,000 porcelain insulating knobs. In the program special thanks were given to C. F. Gardner, manager of the Plymouth Electric Light Co., and his assistant P. J. Peterson at the power house.

The pageant lacked nothing except talent and brevity. There were Indians, Norseman, and the voice of Plymouth Rock. There was a large band to provide music, and a verse by the young poet Robert Frost was read. There were horsemen representing the Royal Riders of the Progress of King James, and George Washington and Abraham Lincoln had their say at the end. Just about every townsperson who wanted a part got one, and President Harding, who

PILGRIM SOCIETY COLLECTION

The Old Curiosity Shop on Water Street at the base of Cole's Hill c.1910.

secretly preferred poker and hooch to amateur theatricals, made appropriate compliments.

For the occasion warehouses, rooming houses, seamen's taverns, and ships' chandleries that had crowded Water Street were cleared away. The Colonial Dames of America contributed money for the portico over Plymouth Rock that we know today, and the drawing that was made to show how the modern waterfront park would look showed airplanes in the sky. Adjacent to the new park, the marsh at the mouth of Town Brook was replaced by the lovely Brewster Gardens.

The charm of the pageant and the surrounding festivities was in the enthusiasm of participants with names like Tassinari and Carafoli, Howland, and Brewster. Nearly the whole town was involved, and

bunting was everywhere. Modern hoopla was combined with small town simplicity, but innocence was beginning to fade.

In 1921, 13 establishments in town advertised auto repairs, and Arthur S. Nickerson performed "auto truck body building." In the Town Report of the next year the selectmen complained, "It has been necessary to keep officers constantly at several points on the highways, and this will probably be the practice in the future. Auto travel has become so heavy that constant supervision has become imperative.

"The parking situation has also become acute. We unfortunately have no such vacant place in the heart of the business section as some towns enjoy. It has become absolutely necessary to limit the time that a car may stand on the Main Street to 20 minutes and to prohibit parking in other places. Until this problem has been worked out there will be some unsettled conditions." Those conditions continue to this day.

The optimists of 1900 were proven right; in 22 short years the town had changed. We were truly in a new century and a new age. Some residents of Plymouth looked at the crowded roads and shook their heads remembering the good old days, but modern times had come to town. That was the way it was to be — losses and gains. Some would rejoice at the opportunities and others would sadly remember what was gone.

2

A Small New England Mill Town

BY JOHN CHAFFEE

As the 19th century gave way to the 20th, Plymouth was a small but very busy New England mill and factory town with tourism a lesser economic factor than it was to become later in the new century. Most of the town's 9,500 residents worked at one or another of more than a half-dozen mills or factories, the names of which recall a nation in the throes of an industrial revolution: Plymouth Cordage Co., American Woolen Co. Puritan Mill, Edes Manufacturing Co., George Mabbett & Sons Worsted Mill, Ripley & Bartlett Tack Manufacturing Co., Plymouth Stove Foundry Co., Atlas Tack Co., Plymouth Mills Standish Worsted Co.

In 1900, the police chief reported that half the town's population lived north of Chilton Street. That's because at that time the cordage company in North Plymouth employed nearly 2,000 people, most of whom by necessity lived within walking distance of their work.

In 1900, Plymouth had no paved roads. Only one resident was known to have one of the new horseless carriages. To get about within town, people walked, relied on horses or rode the Brockton and Plymouth Street Railway trolley. It entered town from Brockton at the Plymouth-Kingston line and continued down Court Street, through downtown and south along Warren Avenue to the Hotel Pilgrim, which was perched high on the hill overlooking Warren Cove and Plymouth Beach. Within

NEWFIELD HOUSE COLLECTION

The intersection of Market and Mill streets c. 1880s looking north to Town Square with the Gothic spires of the First Parish Church visible at top left. The church was destroyed by fire in 1892. At the top of Market Street can be seen the Odd Fellows Hall that was destroyed by fire in 1904.

Sailboats in the harbor in front of the Plymouth Yacht Club on Water Street c. 1890s.

PILGRIM SOCIETY COLLECTION

town, the fare was 5 cents.

Passengers who wanted to continue on south to the tiny village of Manomet could ride a trolley along the newly opened 4.5-mile line of the Plymouth and Sandwich Street Railway Co. that ended at the Manomet post office. That line ran along Rocky Hill Road.

The downtown waterfront sported a string of wharfs at which both steamships and sailing schooners tied up, primarily to discharge or take on cargo. Plymouth was a working port, ranking second in the state after Boston in customs duties collected. While the new Plymouth Yacht Club had a facility on Long Wharf, recreational boating was an activity for only an affluent few.

Ships coming into Plymouth Harbor steamed or sailed past twin lighthouses and an old fort at Gurnet Point, past Saquish Neck and another old fort at Saquish Head, turned into the harbor between the Duxbury Pier Light and the Plymouth Point Beach Pier and tied up at one of the many wharfs on the downtown waterfront. There was no inner harbor breakwater, so the harbor could be treacherous in heavy weather.

Also on the waterfront was the Brockton and Plymouth Railway powerhouse just below the foot of Winslow Street and, at the mouth of Town Brook near the beginning of Leyden Street, the Plymouth Electric Light Co. power station. Both featured tall brick smokestacks similar to the one at the Cordage in North Plymouth. Both were fueled by coal brought in by boat.

Plymouth Rock, the town's primary tourist attraction and already considered one of the nation's foremost historic icons, rested under a tall, thin granite canopy at the base of Cole's Hill. At the top of the hill overlooking the Rock was the Plymouth Rock Hotel. Just down Carver Street at the south end of the hill was the Universalist Church. The portion of Cole's Hill below the hotel and across Water Street from

Plymouth Rock under the Billings canopy and the Plymouth Rock Hotel at the top of Cole's Hill from Long Wharf c. 1890.

Steamer from Boston at Long Wharf c. 1890. The Boston boat office can be seen at the end of the wharf.

First Baptist Church on Leyden Street near Main Street c. 1900. The church was razed to make room for the construction of a new post office and customs house in 1914, but the church clock was saved and installed in the post office cupola.

the Rock had some years before been cleared of old and unsightly buildings by the Pilgrim Society, which purchased the property, graded it and provided a grassy slope.

Along Water Street south of the Rock was a line of small buildings, most of which were related to activities on the various wharfs but one of which was well-known to residents and tourists alike.

It was the Old Curiosity Shop whose proprietor, a dealer in antiques, had perhaps the most Pilgrim of possible names: Winslow Brewster Standish.

A visitor in 1900 might have walked up Leyden Street, the oldest street in town, passing on the left a Baptist church, which housed the town clock; the printing office of the *Old Colony Memorial*, one of three weekly newspapers in town; and the entrance to the Standish Guards Armory. Later in the century, the church, newspaper office and armory would come down to make way for a new post office and to extend Main Street across Town Brook. At the top of Leyden Street was Town Square, an open area that in 1900 was a very busy area. On the south side of the square was the Town House, built in 1749 as a county courthouse, but after 1820 the home of Plymouth's municipal government, including a fire department hook-and-ladder and police headquarters with three jail cells in the basement.

Across the square from the Town House was the wooden Church of the Pilgrimage, a Congregational church built in 1840. At the top of the square facing east down Leyden Street was the newly built granite home of the First Parish Church, Unitarian, which replaced a Gothic wooden structure that had burned down in 1892.

A pathway up the hill beside the First Parish Church brought a visitor to perhaps Plymouth's sec-

WINIFRED AVERY COLLECTION

Town Brook's mill pond, known as the meerstead, at high tide c. 1900. This view, looking northeast from what later became Brewster Gardens, shows the rear of houses on Leyden Street, the steeple of the Universalist Church on Carver Street and the smoke stacks of the Plymouth Electric Light Co. at right.

ond most popular tourist attraction in 1900, Burial Hill. At a time when Victorian gardens were the rage, Burial Hill provided sweeping views of the town, the harbor and Cape Cod Bay. Here, where Myles Standish directed the Pilgrims to build their first fort, are buried many of the Plymouth Colony's early settlers. And from the heights of Burial Hill a visitor could see south to the Manomet Hills and Chiltonville with its churches and factories, or, closer to downtown, the Plymouth Alms House on a small pond fed by Town Brook. The view to the north would take in Captain's Hill in Duxbury topped by a monument to Myles Standish, military commander of the Pilgrim settlement, and Clark's Island, where the Pilgrims held their first worship service in the New World.

At the corner of Main and Leyden streets, just below the Church of the Pilgrimage, was the Odd Fellows Hall. The next three blocks north made up a 1900s version of an outdoor shopping mall composed entirely of locally owned businesses, no chains. Between Leyden and Brewster streets were three banks, a furniture store, a clothing store featuring "gents' furnishings," the central fire station

Detail from a 1910 map shows points of interest along the Plymouth waterfront from Water Street to the Plymouth Cordage Co.

that later became a restaurant, a florist shop, the Davis Opera House and a department store. Just down North Street toward the waterfront, a new public library was under construction. At the corner of Court and Brewster streets, below the county courthouse, the Old Colony Club had been in its new home for seven years. Across Brewster Street from the club was a Methodist church.

From this point north to the Kingston town line, major features of 1900 Plymouth included:

(1) At the corner of Court and Chilton streets, ***Pilgrim Hall***, home of the Pilgrim Society and site of the nation's oldest museum.

(2) ***St. Peter's Roman Catholic Church***, which had been built in 1873 to serve a growing immigrant population.

(3) ***Samoset House***, at the corner of Court and Samoset streets, a majestic hotel that had been built by the Old Colony Railroad to house summer visitors who traveled to Plymouth from Boston by train.

(4) Just down Park Avenue from Samoset House was ***the terminus of the New York, New Haven & Hartford Railroad's Old Colony Line***, which included a passenger station, freight terminal and roundhouse.

(5) ***National Monument to the Forefathers***. High on a hill on Allerton Street, one block west of Court Street and overlooking the town, harbor and bay, stood an 11-year-old symbol of pride in the town's Pilgrim founders. Topped by a figure of Faith with upraised hand and finger, the 80-foot-high Maine granite monument was financed by popular subscription.

(6) ***Overpass of the Plymouth and Middleboro Railroad Co.***, which branched off the Old Colony Line at Lothrop Street and continued on to Middleboro through West Plymouth, crossing under Standish Avenue in North Plymouth at Centennial Street.

(7) ***Plymouth Golf Links,*** a nine-hole facility on an open field just south of Robbins Lane, which led down to the waterfront site of the Robbins Lumber Yard.

(8) ***Plymouth Cordage Co.***, founded in 1824, became the world's largest maker of rope and twine, and thus Plymouth's largest employer, by far. Its red brick mills and tall smokestack remained a Plymouth landmark throughout the 20th century.

10 **_Seaside_**. Finally, at the Plymouth-Kingston line, down a short street then called Station Street but later renamed Boundary Street, were two buildings of note: the Seaside railroad station and the North Plymouth post office, which actually was located across the town line in Kingston.

So popular and well-known was the name Seaside that during the early years of the 20th century nearly all of North Plymouth was referred to as Seaside.

Plymouth in 1900 was a man's town with women playing a traditional subordinate role. Every public official was male and only men had the right to vote. It was usually the man of the family who worked while the wife stayed home to care for the house and children. It was the man who walked to work in one of the mills or factories every morning, as early as 6 o'clock, putting in a 58-hour week that included working half a day Saturday.

Plymouth in 1900 was a self-contained if not wholly self-sufficient community, much smaller in population, more compact, more Protestant and less worldly than it was to become 100 years later.

9 **_Zion Evangelical Lutheran Church_**, across from the Cordage, which had been founded in 1888 by German families who had settled in North Plymouth to work at the cordage company.

OLD COLONY CLUB COLLECTION

A conductor and others pose in front of a locomotive on the north bound rails at the Plymouth terminal c. 1890.

The Plymouth railroad terminal c. 1900. Trains connected the town to points north and west. The terminal was located at the east end of North and South Park avenues.

PLYMOUTH PUBLIC LIBRARY CORP. COLLECTION

SUMMER PEOPLE

BY JOAN H. BARTLETT

In the early decades of the 20th century, there were distinct and separate summer colonies in Plymouth, inhabited by families who knew each other or were related to each other. These enclaves stood alone. Once you reached your holiday destination in Plymouth, you pretty much stayed there. Your social life, if you wanted one, was in your neighborhood. In general, people in Manomet did not mingle with people in Chiltonville; Boot Pond people did not know Long Pond people, White Horse Beach did not mix with Priscilla Beach. This isolation was not unusual in summer colonies everywhere. What is unusual about Plymouth's summer people, however, is their staying power through the generations. And what is even more unusual is that many of these former summer families had, by the end of the century, become full-time and year-round residents.

For example, in 1908 my husband's grandfather, Joseph Bartlett, bought a fishing shack on the cliff overlooking Warren Cove. Over the years the shack was expanded and made into a summerhouse with porches. My grandmother-in-law called it "camp." By the end of the century, five generations had spent summers in the house. And 10 years before the century ended my husband and I began living there year round. We don't know why the family chose to set up a summer retreat in Plymouth, but we do know the year they did so because the date is carved into the cement kitchen doorstep.

By the middle of the century, sojourners from different summer colonies had gotten to know each other and year-round people. They had begun to play together at the beach club, the country club, and the yacht club. Friendships and marriages bound families together from different parts of town.

Since the only proof of my husband's Plymouth lineage I can dredge up is that cement stoop at the kitchen door, I asked other former summer people for their memories and impressions. We didn't research dates and specifics, so think of these stories as hazy impressions of hot summer days.

PILGRIM SOCIETY COLLECTION
A montage of photographs from a family album depicting Labor Day at the beach, 1908.

Plymouth: The Tourist Town

BY JAMES BAKER

Plymouth, like all Colonial towns, began as an agricultural community in which immigrants struggled to survive by adapting familiar methods to an unfamiliar land. Until the 19th century, farming primarily underwrote the town's economy and identity. In addition to the land, the sea also helped support the town. Fishing was a major occupation from an early date, and the Plymouth fishing fleet provided a hard-won livelihood for many families until modern times. There was some seaborne trade as well, which increased tremendously with the growth of local industry after the late 18th century. By 1890, Plymouth was an active port, second only to Boston in revenues collected in Massachusetts. The Industrial Revolution brought the greatest prosperity that the community had known, and Plymouth could have been just another New England "mill town" — except for the accident of its historic birth.

Plymouth has always had to contend with an excess of history. Not only did the Mayflower passengers actually end up here, but their inspirational story became the shared heritage of all

Plymouth could have been just another New England "mill town" — except for the accident of its historic birth.

New Englanders. Plymouth was "where it all began," at least according to the Yankees. As early as 1689, people like Samuel Sewell were interested in seeing for themselves where New England began. Sewell was required to travel to Plymouth as part of his duties as a circuit court magistrate. On one such occasion, he spent a cold morning consciously tracing the steps of the Pilgrims from the grist mill on Town Brook up to Burial Hill and the meetinghouse, when he could have remained comfortably at the fireside in Cole's Ordinary. Another early visitor with an historical interest in the town was the young James Thacher. In 1775 Thacher stopped in Plymouth on his way from Cape Cod to join the Patriot troops after the Battle of Concord. Despite the urgency of his journey, he made a special point of viewing Plymouth Rock. The Rock's symbolic role as the "cornerstone of the nation" had been enhanced when it was moved to Town Square by local patriots the year before, and Thacher was among the first of a never-ending stream of visitors who came to pay homage to it.

New England enjoyed a veritable monopoly on historical interpretation in these early days of the republic, the "Pilgrim" story beating out Jamestown as the birthplace of Colonial America. However, the real tourist era had not yet

Plymouth Rock under the Billings canopy at right, showing the appearance of the waterfront in a view from Cole's Hill c. 1900.

dawned. Travel was serious business. It was usually dangerous and uncomfortable hard work - "travail" indeed. Most people traveled only on business or for other pressing needs; sightseeing was a secondary aim, if that. There was no such thing as a vacation for the middle classes in Colonial times. The earliest travelers were limited to pioneering souls who sought out places of interest off the established routes. When men such as Timothy Dwight in 1800 or Edward Kendall, 1807, searched out Plymouth for the town's history, they did so while pursuing some larger plan such as writing a book. More importantly, they brought their historical expertise with them. They didn't come to discover the unexpected or be spoon-fed the information they sought. They had done their homework and came to see, in person, locations already familiar to them from historical texts and tales.

Leisure travel in America, or "tourism" as it became known, first appeared in the 1820s. The first tourist destinations in New England — Newport, the White Mountains and Nahant — catered to a small and exclusive audience. Plymouth, which lacked the cachet and amenities of those resorts, was not yet a tourist destination. The town made no special accommodation for non-commercial or educational interests. There was little of an obvious historical nature for anyone to look at; no markers, historic houses or other memorials had yet been set aside for the curious visitor. Before Pilgrim Hall was built in 1824, Burial Hill, Plymouth Rock and the old Colonial records in the court house were the only evident relics of the Pilgrim past.

But it was not just the Pilgrim story that brought early travelers to Plymouth. The present was as much an attraction as the past. Hunting and fishing

Samoset House c. 1920 - Built by the Old Colony Railroad in 1846; it could board up to 100 guests and included dining facilities. It was located on the northwest corner of Court and Samoset Streets, later the intersection of state Routes 3A and 44.

in Plymouth's extensive woods, or visits to the town's churches, mills and factories were of equal interest with historical properties. New England in the early 19th century had not yet assumed the identity of the nation's quaint old attic. As Dona Brown has pointed out in *Inventing New England* (1995), New England was the "Silicon Valley" of the time — the region with the most modern and up-

to-date technology as well as the most progressive and liberal social movements. People traveled from other regions, especially from the agrarian South, to see these marvels. However, Plymouth transport was limited to private vessels, horseback or "shanks' mare" (on foot) until the thrice-weekly Plymouth to Boston stagecoach was introduced in 1796. The only places to stay were inns and "ordinaries" whose primitive arrangements were intended for traveling sportsmen, merchants and workmen, not pleasure trippers. It was highly fortunate, however, that Plymouth had a rich historical past as well as its mills and factories, for the latter supported the community for no more than a century and a half, and then faded away.

It was only later that the Pilgrims and the New England countryside proved to be an inexhaustible attraction and the foundation of the subsequent tourist industry. In November 1845, the Old Colony Railroad opened a line between Boston and Plymouth. Travelers could now get to Plymouth easily, quickly and comfortably. The train took about two and one-half hours from Boston and the fare was $1. The railroad also built and operated Plymouth's first real hotel, the Samoset House, with room for 100 guests, dining facilities and all of the comforts required by the up-to-date Victorian traveler. Other resort hotels followed, such as Clifford House (1852; later, the Hotel Pilgrim) above Plymouth Beach and Plymouth Rock House (1873) on Cole's Hill.

Plymouth slowly began to capitalize on its historical attractions. W. S. Russell published his *Guide to Plymouth and Recollections of the Pilgrims*, Plymouth's first guidebook, in 1846. His book became the basis for related series of pictorial guides that lasted into the 1950s. The Pilgrim Society undertook the construction of a substantial monument to the Pilgrims and a canopy over Plymouth Rock in 1859. In 1872, A. S. Burbank bought a Plymouth bookstore and became the town's most important source of Pilgrim souvenirs, and other dry goods stores followed suit. Steamboats began regular service from Boston to Plymouth in 1880.

The steamer took nearly three hours and charged $1 for adults, 60 cents for children. The Kingston and Plymouth Street Railway made its first run in 1889. The line grew and was extended to Brockton by 1900. The Boston to Plymouth fare was 55 cents in 1907, and the trip took about three and one-half hours with changes. Day-trippers from across the region took advantage of these conveyances to make quick visits to the Pilgrim town. Guest houses sprang up here and there. Families came to stay in

The most important development for Plymouth's heritage business was the increasing interest in the Pilgrim story as the 300th anniversary of the famous 1620 landing approached.

Plymouth during the summer months. Mothers and children enjoyed the sea breezes, bathing and walks in the woods while fathers labored in Boston and joined them on the weekends. In the late summer and fall, men continued to come by themselves to hunt and fish with professional guides. In town, restaurants or ice cream and oyster "saloons" (which served fast food rather than liquor) served local people, casual visitors and the vacation crowds.

While Plymouth never became as fashionable a resort as Newport, New Hampshire's White Mountains or the southern coast of Maine, the steady growth of vacation travel brought a new element to Plymouth tourism. Rather than stay in rented rooms, some visiting families chose to build private summer cottages along Plymouth's shoreline or on the many ponds in the town's extensive woodlands. The most impressive of these were the large estates in the Manomet Ponds and Chiltonville areas, but hundreds of more modest cabins — many built by Plymouth residents themselves — appeared as well.

A fashionable taste for natural resources, rather than Pilgrim history, motivated this new movement. Hunting and fishing had long been one of Plymouth's most notable attractions, but later generations added swimming, sailing and other outdoor sports. The impressive Columbia Pavilion—built on Plymouth Beach in 1883—provided an excellent venue for summer fun, including bathing, sailing, parties, dancing and "shore dinners." Enlarged in 1890, the Pavilion was a center for tourist activity until it was swept away by the "Portland Storm" of November 1898. Plymouth also acquired another venue for natural recreation when Nathaniel Morton gave the town its first public park on property near Billington Sea in 1889.

By 1890, the town had been transformed into a regular tourist destination. A growing interest in antiques, historic houses, and other vestiges of the past accompanied the "Colonial revival" movement that followed the national centennial of 1876. Visitors began to seek out the oldest houses in town as New England's quaint past came to overshadow its earlier reputation as the most technologically and socially advanced region in America. Plymouth held

The new middle class passion for antiques arrived as well. B. F. Goddard had an "antiquities" store in North Plymouth in 1887, and Winslow Brewster Standish turned his Water Street dry goods store entirely over to the antique trade in 1890.

The most important development for Plymouth's heritage business was the increasing interest in the Pilgrim story as the 300th anniversary of the famous 1620 landing approached. Plans for a grand celebration began in 1915, and the recent identification of the Pilgrims with the Thanksgiving holiday brought a flood of publicity to benefit Plymouth tourism. The year-long Tercentenary Celebration began on December 21, 1920—Forefathers' Day (the anniversary of the *Mayflower* landing)—and extended through the autumn of 1921. The climactic event was George Baker's "Pilgrim Spirit" pageant in August 1921, in which an estimated 1,300 Plymoutheans took part. The event was attended by thousands of spectators, from President Harding and other dignitaries who arrived on the presidential yacht *Mayflower*, to the anonymous visitors arriving in Model T's. Pilgrim images and Pilgrim stories pervaded popular culture. The pageant contributed to a greatly increased "Pilgrim presence" in the town. Numerous monuments and historical markers were erected and

Looking up Leyden Street from Water Street c. 1890. The men are standing in front of the M. B. Blackmer Livery & Boarding Stable. The steeple of the First Baptist Church can be seen towering above the houses on the left.

Pilgrim Hall as it appeared about 1880. Note the wooden carved tableau in the pediment of the museum and the wooden columns along the front. At one time Plymouth Rock was behind the fence at the left.

its first historic pageants in 1896 and 1897 to raise money to rebuild the First Parish Church. The Howland Society acquired the Jabez Howland house in 1914, and the Plymouth Antiquarian Society was organized in 1917 to save the 1809 Hedge House.

a new canopy graced Plymouth Rock. Several historic houses were opened to the public for the first time. The unsavory millpond at the mouth of Town Brook was filled in and became the Brewster Gardens in 1924.

The Tercentenary was a climax in other ways. Popular interest in the Pilgrims exploded for a decade or so, but then receded again as cultural fashions do. At the same time, Plymouth industry went into a decline that lasted over 40 years. The pageant itself had been performed on the ashes of the town's old commercial waterfront, which was cleared away in preparation for the 1920 event. The street railway, made obsolete by buses, ceased operation in 1928. Railway passenger service came to an end in 1959. The large hotels closed one by one, replaced by more modest tourist homes and motor courts designed for the short visits dictated by the new automobile culture. By 1970, almost all of Plymouth's mills and factories had closed or moved away.

Before the automobile appeared on the scene, Plymouth wasn't on the way to anywhere. It was the end of the line—whether for the railroad, the steam-

HERRING STREAM, EAST WHITE HORSE BEACH, MASS.

Herring Stream from Taylor Avenue and White Horse Beach, Manomet c. 1910.

Before the automobile appeared on the scene, Plymouth wasn't on the way to anywhere.

boat or the streetcar. Except for those few local excursionists who came for a day or two or for some special event, the summer people had generally remained for the duration of their vacations. With the coming of the automobile, Plymouth became either a day of sightseeing on a circuit that began and ended at home, a temporary destination from which side trips could be taken, or, increasingly, just a stop on a longer journey to Cape Cod.

In the years following World War II, Plymouth experienced an upswing in tourism. Plimoth Plantation, founded in 1947, built a new and vibrant version of the Pilgrim Story. As the last of the old industries faded away, and dependency on tourist income increased, community pride suffered. Families whose identities had been based on the mills and factories rather than Pilgrim descent resented this shift in priorities. Despite efforts to revive manufacturing and to overcome the presence of the past through urban renewal, the town reluctantly and sometimes angrily recognized that tourism was becoming Plymouth's major industry.

19

SUMMER PEOPLE

BY JOAN H. BARTLETT

THE FORGES

Lalla Withington Brewster spent her summers at The Forges, not far from the house on Old Sandwich Road where at the end of the century she lived year round.

"Until I was about 5, we stayed at my grandparents' house, Chilton Hall. There were 52 rooms and 13 bathrooms. It was a big house, but you never felt it—we weren't rattling around. We were a large family; there were 15 grandchildren.

"My grandfather bought The Forges from Eben Jordan in 1910. Jordan had gathered up a lot of small properties to make up his almost 2,500-acre estate. One of them was a little

PILGRIM SOCIETY COLLECTION

Images of outdoor gatherings from an unidentified family album c. 1910.

factory that forged iron for cannon balls, hence the name Forges. Most of the 2,500 acres was forest, but 500 acres was farmland, including the big house, the stables and the casino.

"It was a feudal-like farm. On Saturday nights, "entertainments" were held in the casino for family and friends, and on Sunday morning there was a church service there. The folding wooden chairs in sets of three would face the stage at one end of the hall on Saturday nights, and would be turned to face the altar

at the other end of the building on Sunday mornings. There was an old white pump organ behind a screen and "Holy, Holy, Holy" was written over the altar. The rector from somewhere near Philadelphia would come up once a summer and do all the christenings. During my day we had dances and parties at the casino and those same wooden chairs in sets of three would be stacked along the side walls.

"When I was a child, we pretty much stayed out at The Forges all summer—we really had a haven there. I didn't meet the

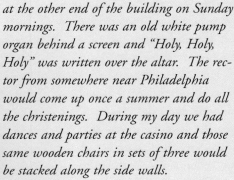

Brewsters until 1934 or so. Those big boys came over and sat right down on the round cement things they have at the beach club and they said hello to us. Three from our family married three Brewsters and became year-round residents."

As Time Goes By —

PLYMOUTH IN 1901

Highlights of Plymouth life in 1901 as reported in the *Old Colony Memorial* and compiled 100 years later by Managing Editor Nan Anastasia.

JANUARY

Plymouth celebrated the birth of the new century on New Year's Eve 1900 with a band parading through the streets, church bells ringing and fire alarm whistles wailing. At midnight a bugler saluted the new century by playing reveille from the top of Burial Hill. "The noise at midnight beat all that was ever made here except, perhaps, on the Fourth of July 1876, and even this is doubtful," the newspaper commented.

A citizens committee planning the new Jordan Hospital agreed that any person subscribing $1 should become a member of the corporation and a subscription of $100 would confer life membership. The committee also agreed to provide hospital privileges to residents of Kingston, Duxbury and Carver "if the people of those towns so desire."

At a meeting of the library corporation it was announced that a permanent home for the library would be provided on North Street, thanks to a gift from the heirs of William G. Russell, a prominent Boston lawyer.

Police raided a barbershop and poolroom on

Court Street and found six men playing cards for money. The owner and five other men were charged with gambling.

FEBRUARY

Two fishing boats ran aground on Brown's Bank during a winter storm

PILGRIM SOCIETY COLLECTION

Studio portrait of Plymouth Fire Dept. Company #1 taken in 1900. Front row, from left, Henry Healy, James Noble, William Flockton, Timothy Downey Jr. and Everett Sampson. Back row: Richard Pickett, Thomas Reagan, Manuel Scott and Michael Downey.

that also washed out sections of Plymouth Beach north of a new breakwater that was under construction.

PLYMOUTH PUBLIC LIBRARY CORP. COLLECTION

Main Street, looking north from Leyden Street following a snowfall. Note the manual snow removal except for the plow on the front of the trolley to help clear the tracks c.1900.

Known as "Jack the Hugger," a tall thin man wearing a coat with a cape that he pulled over his head to conceal his face had been accosting women in town. "Plymouth girls should carry a bottle of ammonia or a revolver and check the actions of the scamp," the newspaper advised.

After a snowstorm, "sleighing parties were much in evidence," the newspaper reported, and trolley service to Kingston was delayed while service to Manomet was shut down completely.

The inner harbor, which had been frozen over for two weeks, cleared enough at the end of the month for vessels to enter and leave the docks. "It seems good to see blue water again," the newspaper said.

People gather in front of the Billings canopy over Plymouth Rock in August 1889 on the day the Forefathers' monument was dedicated.

Court Street looking south from South Russell Street toward Shirley Square c. 1900. The horse-drawn water department buggy is about to pass the 1889 Davis Building on the left, which housed A.S. Burbank's bookstore where a woman is window shopping. The northbound trolley on the right is at rest with the motorman on the sidewalk while a woman and little girl walk toward him.

The corner of Main and Leyden streets c. 1900 showing Lyceum Hall, the building that housed A.S. Burbank's Pilgrim bookstore and the offices of the Old Colony Memorial. *This building and the Standish Guards armory at right were later torn down to create Main Street Extension and to clear a site for a new federal office building to house both a post office and customs office. Note the First Baptist Church at left, also demolished for the new post office building, and the downtown utility lines that were later put underground.*

MARCH

The newspaper reported that the steamer *Cape Cod* would be put on the Boston to Plymouth route in the summer. The 165-foot steamer, built the previous year, could reach a speed of 15 knots, which meant the trip from Boston to Plymouth could be made in about 2 1/2 hours. The boat had accommodations for 950 passengers, including 21 staterooms.

The annual Town Meeting, "attended by a surprisingly small gathering," adopted an annual operating budget of $114,605, including $35,000 for schools, $14,000 for roads and bridges and $6,000 for the fire department, the newspaper reported.

Manila rope made by the Plymouth Cordage Co. was delivered to Bristol [RI] where a boat was being built to defend the America's Cup. "It is made from a very fine grade of manila hemp, remarkably white in color, and smooth and free from protuberances of any kind. Old sailors who examined it at Bristol gave the opinion that it was the finest rope they ever saw," the newspaper reported.

APRIL

The new Manomet Life Saving Station at Manomet Point was nearly complete and the school committee approved plans for a new school building in Vallerville to replace the school destroyed by a forest fire the previous September. The one-story wood-frame building was planned to accommodate 30 pupils. Its estimated cost: $1,500.

The Plymouth Cordage Co. ordered a new hook and ladder truck to improve fire protection at the mills.

Four young Plymouth men pleaded guilty in district court to stealing a horse and carriage from Weston's Stable on Leyden Street, taking it for a spin and returning it in the night. They were fined amounts ranging from $15 to $25.

The board of health established a public dump on Obery Street, described by the newspaper as "near the site of the old smallpox hospital."

MAY

President McKinley's plans to visit Plymouth on July 3 were confirmed in a letter to the Pilgrim Society. He was scheduled to arrive by train at 11 a.m. and during a three-hour visit stop at the Rock, Cole's Hill, Leyden Street, Burial Hill, Pilgrim Hall and the Pilgrim National Monument. An aide said the president wanted no formal public demonstration, parade or escort.

The macadam topping on Main Street was about

PLYMOUTH PUBLIC LIBARY CORP. COLLECTION
From Long Wharf c. 1880, Plymouth Rock and Cole's Hill are visible in the distance at the left while the yacht club was located in the building on the right.

PLYMOUTH PUBLIC LIBRARY CORP. COLLECTION
Close-up view of the canopy over Plymouth Rock c. 1900. Designed by Hammatt Billings for the Pilgrim Society, the cornerstone was laid in 1859 and the structure, delayed by the Civil War, was completed in 1867.

1749 COURT HOUSE MUSEUM COLLECTION
Plymouth Rock under the Billings canopy c. 1900 was located on Water Street near a coal wharf. A companion work by Billings, also commissioned by the Pilgrim Society, was the National Monument to the Forefathers.

23

Robinson Iron Works on Town Brook at Newfield Street c. 1890. A locally owned firm that included a rolling mill and nail factory, it employed 200 men until ceasing operations in 1897 and being destroyed by fire in 1900.

Odd Fellows Hall at the corner of Main Street and Town Square c. 1900. The home of a fraternal beneficiary organization, it was built in 1877 and destroyed by fire in 1904.

Panoramic view of Plymouth Harbor from Cole's Hill c. 1900. The large building on the left is the coal shed for the Plymouth & Brockton Street Railway Co. power station at North Wharf. At the right is the Billings canopy over Plymouth Rock.

*Two young women drink water from the Brewster Spring at the top of Leyden Street next to
A.S. Burbank's bookstore and souvenir shop c. 1890.*

The Spring Hill Restaurant on Summer Street at the corner of Market Street c. 1900.

*Main Street looking south from Shirley Square with the steeple of the Baptist church on
Leyden Street in the distance c. 1900.*

to be renewed and the town had set up a stone crusher at Rocky Hill to break
up rocks for the new surface.

Chicken thieves plagued Plymouth during the month. A Chiltonville man
lost 11 hens and a brood of 12 chicks while a man who lived on Court Street
near Park Avenue went to feed his hens one morning only to discover them
packed into crates near their coop, ready to be carried away.

Jordan Hospital directors chose a lot on Old Sandwich Road as the site of the
new medical facility, "about five minutes walk from the electrics at Jabez
Corner," the newspaper reported.

Ground was broken for the new public library building on North Street.

A boy described by the newspaper as "a young Italian child" nearly drowned
in the harbor. He went into the water at the foot of Leyden Street and floated

Descendants of Robert Bartlett gathered for a reunion photo at the Hotel Crescent at White Horse Beach c. 1890.

William Burns on the step of his grocery store at the corner of Samoset and Court streets c. 1900.

Man with horse and wagon at south end of Main Street near Town Square c. 1890.

up Town Brook with the tide. A former member of the Manomet lifesaving crew who was working on the resurfacing of Water Street saw the boy, jumped into a dory and pulled the youngster out of the water and revived him. The newspaper said it couldn't discover the child's name because his family didn't speak English.

JUNE

The Commercial Club, at its last meeting of the season at the Samoset Hotel, agreed to ask the Old Colony Railroad to build a new downtown station, labeling the existing station as "shabby and inconvenient."

President McKinley's planned visit to Plymouth was cancelled.

The 13 members of the Plymouth High School Class of 1901 graduated during an evening ceremony at the high school on Lincoln Street.

Main Street businessman Charles H. Churchill was knocked down by a horse on Leyden Street.

The steamer *Cape Cod* made its first Boston to Plymouth run of the season, carrying 51 passengers during a trip that took nearly three hours.

William Seaver Danforth, registrar of deeds for 39 years and "one of the best known and most highly esteemed citizens of our town" died at 69 after a four-month illness, the newspaper reported. Born in 1832, the son of *Old Colony Memorial* founder Allen Danforth, he served the town as a water commissioner and member of the school committee. At the time of his death he was also president of Plymouth Savings Bank and an associate justice of the Third District Court.

Odd Fellows Hall at the corner of Main and Leyden streets decorated for the 1889 dedication of the National Monument to the Forefathers. Note the rare 39-star flags produced in anticipation of the Dakota Territory joining the union.

The Unitarian Universalist Church at Town Square, newly rebuilt of stone after being destroyed by fire in 1892. The Town House is at the left.

JULY

There was no official celebration of the Fourth of July, but firecrackers popped, whistles and church bells rang and horns blared, starting the night before, the newspaper reported.

The town was scorched by a 35-day heat wave during which the temperature soared above the 80-degree mark every day and once reached 96 degrees in the shade.

A.S. Burbank of the Pilgrim Bookstore was offering a new souvenir of Plymouth: bottled water from the Brewster Spring.

A weekly concert by the Pilgrim Band drew a crowd of 536 people, the *OCM* reported. "A good many young people were over from Kingston and

farther up the road, brought in by electrics," the newspaper said, referring to the trolleys.

Ground was broken for Jordan Hospital and the outer walls of the new library on North Street were under construction.

Police issued orders to local ice dealers, prohibiting deliveries after 9 a.m. on Sundays.

AUGUST

The U.S. census reported that in 1900 Plymouth had a population of 9,592.

Three runaway horse incidents were reported during the month. A pair of horses pulling a milk wagon ran away on Oak Street; another horse, pulling a load of mattresses, was frightened by a steam roller and ran through Plymouth

Power station of the Brockton and Plymouth Street Railway Co. on the waterfront at the foot of Winslow Street c. 1900. It was shut down in 1918 and in 1920 the buildings were sold to the Massachusetts Tercentenary Commission.

Clifford House, later the Hotel Pilgrim high on a hill overlooking Plymouth Beach, was remodeled by the Plymouth and Kingston Street Railway Co. in 1890.

The trolley John Alden, at rest with motorman Leon Sherman, was one of a stable of Plymouth and Kingston Street Railway Co. streetcars bearing Pilgrim names that traveled between Kingston and the Hotel Pilgrim in the 1890s.

The Old Curiosity Shop on Water Street at the base of Cole's Hill sold a variety of antiques and other objects of historic interest c. 1890.

Town Square looking east from the steps of the Unitarian Church with the Town House barely visible at the right. The north-bound Plymouth and Kingston Street Railway Co. trolley is making the turn from Market into Main Street c. 1890s.

Shirley Square looking east down North Street with the historic Winslow-Warren House on the right c. 1890. The house was built in 1726 by Gen. John Winslow, who gained infamy for evicting the Acadians from eastern Canada on behalf of the British during the French and Indian war of 1755-1763.

Center; and a Carver man and his grandson had to jump out of their wagon on Summer Street when the undercarriage gave way and the horse bolted. The boy wasn't hurt, but the man opened up an old Civil War leg wound.

The *OCM* described the site of the new Jordan Hospital: "…located on a lot on the westerly side of Cole's Lane at Wellingsley, and the situation is well-chosen, the high land assuring plenty of light and air and good drainage. At the same time, the ascent is not too sharp to be easily made on foot or by carriage."

In a collision with an electric trolley, a Plymouth doctor was thrown out of his buggy on Warren Avenue one night and the horse broke a hip and had to be destroyed.

Assessors set the town's property tax rate at $16.80 per $1,000 of assessed value, an increase of $1.60 from the previous year. The assessed value of real estate in town rose to a total of $6,022,750.

Selectmen set a speed limit of eight miles an hour on any street or highway in town, with a penalty of a $20 fine for each violation.

SEPTEMBER

The steamer *Cape Cod* made her final run of the season, bringing about 200 passengers from Boston.

Plymouth schools reopened for the new school year and, the newspaper reported, "as usual most of the school rooms are overcrowded, as the crop of children seems to come right along whether or not the town makes provision for them." Because a new school on Court Street hadn't been completed, double sessions were held at the Burton School near Burial Hill. The death of President McKinley was reported in great detail after he was shot in early September, clung to life for a week and finally died from his wounds. During

Guy Cooper's General Store at Jabez Corner with the Wellingsley School at the left c. 1900.

Cranberry pickers on a bog with six-quart tins for hand-picking and wooden shipping boxes at the right c. 1900.

the national day of mourning, every Plymouth business was closed, all flags were at half-staff and prior to a union memorial service at the Davis Opera House, the fire alarm and church bells tolled for an hour.

OCTOBER

The schooner *Angelina* took in 350 barrels of fish off the entrance to the Plymouth harbor channel, just north of Gurnet Point, and landed them at the T Wharf in Boston, where the catch of 38,000 fish sold for 8 cents apiece.

At a firefighters field day, the parade included a steamer from the Plymouth Hackney Stud Fire Dept., a private company from E.D. Jordan's stud farm in Chiltonville. "The machine was a beauty," the newspaper reported, "in full nickel plate and had a fine four-horse hitch, which attracted a good deal of attention."

Two boarders in the house of a 53-year-old North Plymouth woman are suspected of murdering her after her bloody body was found on Atlantic Street.

One of the boarders was arrested the next day in the cellar of the woman's house. The other boarder was chased by police into woods in Manomet and disappeared.

Services in English were planned at the German Lutheran Church in North Plymouth on two Sundays every month. All other services were in German.

The Plymouth & Sandwich Street Railway Co. was laying rails to extend its trolley service from the car house in Manomet to Fresh Pond.

NOVEMBER

Construction of the breakwater at Plymouth Beach was completed. The *OCM* reported, "The wall is about a mile in length, reaching from just a little way from below the 'turn of the channel' to a spot just above the footbridge at Manter's Point. It is very solidly built of heavy granite blocks ranging from one to five tons in weight…it is unlikely that the sea will break through again at any point along the line."

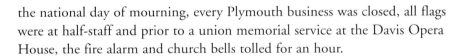

The school committee voted to name the new school on Court Street near Atlantic Street the Frederick N. Knapp School after a former longtime school board chairman.

A bull being towed into town sat down at the corner of Market and Leyden streets and refused to move for several hours, despite repeated efforts to get him to move. "When he was good and rested he got leisurely upon his feet and started on his journey," the newspaper reported.

The temperature in Plymouth on Thanksgiving morning was 14 degrees. A few days later a northeast gale struck and the newly finished breakwater at Plymouth Beach got its first test, the waves washing hundreds of tons of sand against the stone barrier, filling in the crevices.

A fire in the trolley company's coal shed at North Wharf burned for a week.

DECEMBER

The school committee voted to require that all pupils be vaccinated for smallpox. Meanwhile, a farm on Stafford Street was under quarantine after a 23-year-old woman came down with smallpox, the first case reported in the town in 30 years. Later that month the woman died and was buried the same day at Vine Hills Cemetery.

The new Russell library building was nearly complete. "The edifice is a tasteful feature of North Street," the *OCM* reported, "standing back of the row of big lindens." Library trustees voted to purchase furniture and book racks.

The Plymouth Electric Light Co. was replacing incandescent street lamps with new arc lights from Samoset Street to the northern corner of the Training Green. The new lights will remain on all night, the company said.

Plymouth County's lobster catch led the state. The *OCM* reported that 155 boats were engaged in lobster fishing and that during 1900, 765,291 pounds of lobster were caught in South Shore waters, with a total value of $63,553.

The Lend-A-Hand Club provided coal and 11 large Christmas baskets "filled with articles of comfort and cheer" to elderly women living alone and widows with small children.

A rare flash photo of Ichabod Morton inside his gristmill and grain depot on Market Street c. 1900.

Fire Department horse-drawn pumper in front of the old post office at the corner of Main and Middle streets c. 1890.

SUMMER PEOPLE

BY JOAN H. BARTLETT

LONG POND AND SHIP POND

Brooks Barnes, at the end of the century, remembered:

"In my great grandfather's day at the end of the 19th century, a number of men in Boston came to Plymouth for hunting and fishing, bringing guides who set up things for them. Some of these men, like my great grandfather, built cottages for their families to stay in for the summer months. One year my great grandfather built a racetrack at Long Pond. You can still see the oval of that track from an airplane. I'm not sure if this track was meant to be a business enterprise or just a sporting arena for gentlemen drivers.

"When they were first married, my grandfather and grandmother lived in Boston and went to a cottage at Ship Pond in the summers. Later grandpa had cranberry bogs and he and the family would make a long season of it. They would arrive in the early spring and return to Boston in late November after the cranberry harvest.

"In 1901, when my mother's sister was 5 years old, my grandparents built a house in town so they could stay year-round and their children could go to school. My mother grew up in Plymouth and married a Plymouth man. Gradually my family had become year-round residents."

HIGH CLIFF

At the end of the century, Rich Botieri lived in a house that was built as a summerhouse for one of the Plymouth Cordage Co. executives.

"Each executive had a house on Holmes Terrace and and all five of those houses had a summerhouse on the nearby cliff. They lived year-round on Holmes Terrace and went to their summer places just across the street.

"These houses on High Cliff were built in 1905. They are the only beach houses in North Plymouth and are well sited. If you go to the center of Plymouth Bay and look to the west, with Duxbury on your right

The houses were insulated with seaweed

and downtown Plymouth on your left, High Cliff is directly ahead, looking straight out at the Bug Light.

"After the Cordage closed, all five High Cliff houses were bought by one family. One member of this family was a school teacher. She lived in what is now our house and she was a little eccentric. The story goes that she and the lawn man, who was about 30 years younger, had a romantic relationship. When she died she left him the house.

"The lawn man was in a poker game in Boston and lost the house for $1,500 to a man from Connecticut. The man from Connecticut came to Plymouth to see the house that he had won. He stopped at my grandfather's jewelry store for directions and told him the story and said he didn't know what to do with the house. My grandfather said he would buy it for $1,500.

"The houses were insulated with seaweed. The seaweed is still there and it's very good insulation."

WHITE HORSE AND PRISCILLA BEACHES

Mary Jane Calhoun and her husband John spent many summers in Plymouth before settling here year-round. As she recalled at the end of the 20th century:

"I started coming to Plymouth before I was born. My mother's family used to rent at White Horse. I spent all my summers there and after I was married, my husband and I continued to do so with our children. In 1969 we saw a house for sale at Priscilla Beach. We bought it, tore it down and took it to the dump. We had seen a house in Florida that we loved and we wanted to copy it and have it built here. When we finally tracked down the architect in Florida it turned out his name was Miles Standish. We figured that was a good sign and he designed this house for us.

"My family first came to White Horse in 1928. A number of people from Worcester spent summers there. In those days there was a White Horse Beach Hotel. Many of the families living here now, like us, first rented then bought summerhouses and later moved here full-time after they retired.

"Most of us at White Horse knew each other. The houses were built at about the same time in the 1920s. People at White Horse came from Worcester, Cambridge and Arlington. Having the chapel was a draw and I think it is why so many Irish and Italian people settled here. You didn't have to go over the Pine Hills and into town for Mass."

Ropemakers of Plymouth

BY SAMUEL ELIOT MORISON

Ever since large-scale manufacturing began in New England, there had been two schools of thought and action respecting labor policy. In the Fall River and New Bedford area, complete laissez-faire prevailed. Employees found their own housing, had little or no help from employers in case of accident or sickness, and whatever education they received was provided by the community. In the Boston and Essex County area, on the other hand, a semi-paternal policy was initiated after the War of 1812. Francis C. Lowell, who had studied Robert Owen's experiments at New Lanark in Scotland, appreciated the fact that to keep working people healthy and happy something must be done by management to ease the transition from farm to factory; that a manufacturing company had a social responsibility for the welfare of its employees. Until the 20th century the state intervened largely to prevent grosser exploitation of workers by excessive hours or conditions dangerous to health; state welfare programs involving sickness insurance, retirement pensions, adult education and recreation are of very recent growth. Before the New Deal, such things were provided, if at all, by manufacturers who followed the Lowell rather than the Fall River tradition. Among such firms, the Dennison Manufacturing Co. of Framingham, and the Plymouth Cordage Co. have outstanding records of social service.

Plymouth stood midway between the two con-

KENNETH TAVARES FAMILY COLLECTION

Aerial view of the Plymouth Cordage Co. c. 1940. Note the Old Colony Railroad line bisecting the vast North Plymouth complex of mill and storage buildings, plus, at right, a deep-water pier.

trasting areas. As long as the Spooners were dominant in management, the laissez-faire system prevailed, except for the original and necessary housing of 1825. North Plymouth was never a dreary mill town, but a pleasant and salubrious site equal to those shores of Plymouth and Duxbury Bays which have been taken up by summer homes of well-to-do Bostonians. And the Cordage labor force for many years was composed largely of independent Yankees

who could take care of themselves.

As the 19th century drew to a close, the need for a change became apparent, especially to Boston directors like the Lorings who were allied by marriage with the Lowells and shared their feeling that corporations must do something for the workers' welfare. The presence in the Cordage working force of several hundred Germans and Italians, people of a high type morally but ignorant of the English language and American ways, brought "welfare" to the front. The company decided that it must assist the incorporation of these people into the general stream of American life.

Caleb William Loring, third president of the corporation and grandson of the first treasurer, on the occasion of his last visit to Plymouth before his death in 1897, remarked that "he wished to do something for the operatives, something to make them happier." This pious intention was translated into action by his son Augustus Peabody Loring, who had been clerk of the corporation since 1884 and was advanced to the presidency in 1897. Gideon F. Holmes, the self-made man who had actually managed the plant since 1875, fell in with Loring's views, and appointed the superintendent of grounds and buildings, William E. C. Nazro, to take charge of welfare work. He remained at the head of it for 28 years; since 1910 as the head of a special department. Nazro, an architect by training, had been reading Ruskin. He believed that wage-earners like other people had a yearning for beauty and for betterment. He regarded industrial welfare work as "the seed for one of the greatest educational processes the country has ever known."

In seeking motives for the welfare program we are about to describe, a cynic or a Marxian would say that it was a shrewd move to keep the proletariat contented with low wages. And everyone must admit that employee benefits did pay the employer. Plymouth Cordage could not raise wages above those paid by its many competitors and survive; but it could and did withhold from profits the modest sums necessary to give its employees greater happiness and security. Yet there was a lot more to it than mere calculation. The present writer, who knew

Augustus P. Loring, has no hesitation in declaring that his natural benevolence, and his recognition of the essential worth of the working man, were the main motives behind the numerous welfare activities at Plymouth. A portly, ruddy, jovial man who reminded one of Dickens's Mr. Cheeryble, Loring exuded cheer and goodwill to friends, neighbors and employees alike. He had many charitable interests, notably Near East Relief of which he was a director and a prominent contributor; he would talk for

> *The presence in the Cordage working force of several hundred Germans and Italians, people of a high type morally but ignorant of the English language and American ways, brought "welfare" to the front.*

hours to anyone who would listen, about welfare in Plymouth or rehabilitation of displaced persons in Greece. Except for sailing, in which he delighted, Loring took no part in the clubs, sports or other social activities common to Bostonians of family and wealth; next to his own family, the Plymouth Cordage employees were closest to his heart. Even in his old age, in the depth of the Great Depression, he was more concerned with the welfare of the employees than with that of the company.

The Loring Library, presented in 1899, one of the first evidences of the new social policy at Plymouth, was wholly paid for by Augustus P. Loring and stocked with some 3,000 books by himself and his brother and sisters. They saw to it that good selections of German, Italian and Portuguese literature were included, so that employees in the course of their Americanization would not forget their native culture.

The jubilee year 1899 marks the real beginning of welfare at Plymouth. Number 2 Mill, built that year, was provided with restrooms and a ventilation and heating system which was as close as engineers 50 years ago could attain to air conditioning. And the first large housing program was started.

From time-to-time since 1825 the company had built tenements of the normal mill-village type for its workers, but in 1899 it started an ambitious housing program of very different and superior quality, with 21 two-family homes of the architecture then vaguely called "colonial." Each family unit comprised five to seven rooms and a cellar, a modern bathroom, a front lawn with place for a flower garden, and a back yard big enough to grow vegetables and raise poultry. Electric lighting and central heating plants were installed a few years later. The company also laid sidewalks and a sewage system at its own expense, since the town would not. The rents were very moderate. And, more important, the appearance, finish and accommodations of the houses were of the sort then sought after by the younger business and professional men with incomes much larger than any factory operative could earn, so that to live in them gave an employee's family self-respect and standing in the community.

The company encouraged emulation among its

tenants by giving annual prizes for the best-kept garden and the best poultry yard; annually it held a fair on Labor Day, at which prizes were given for vegetables raised by the operatives and for cakes, embroidery and the like made by their wives.

As demand increased, more houses were built between 1910 and 1920, so that by 1924 the company owned 125 dwelling houses, containing 351 tenements (including the original ones then almost a century old), renting from $1.20 to $4.50 per week; the whole was appraised at about $2 million and originally returned 2.5 to 3 percent on the investment. In addition, land was procured and lots were sold at cost to employees who wished to build for themselves, and building loans were made by the company at a very low interest.

After housing came educational activities. The earliest was a free kindergarten for employees' children, opened in 1900; a special building was constructed for it later, and the enrollment reached 90 or 100. A carpentry school was opened for boys and classes in sewing, dressmaking and millinery, basketry and drawing, for women and girls. A cooking school was opened by the company in 1901, "to teach young girls how to prepare good food economically"; the

average attendance between that year and 1927 was between 50 and 100. At various times, classes in canning and preserving were held.

For 75 years the company's employees went home for their meals if they lived nearby, or brought their

The imported raw materials for making rope and twine being unloaded from a ship tied up to the Plymouth Cordage Co. pier.

lunches in the traditional dinner pail, which was supposed to be full only when the Republican Party was in power. In 1902 one floor of the superintendent's office was fitted up for the men to eat their lunch in. First hot coffee was provided, then sandwiches and fruit were added, at the request of bachelor workers who had no one to fill a dinner pail for them. These earliest quarters were too small to accommodate more than a fraction of the employees, but this innovation was so successful that before the end of the year Edward R. Harris, the largest stockholder of the company and son of the second treasurer, built Harris Hall at his own expense. This was a company restaurant where light refreshments could be had, a complete dinner was served for 25 cents, or a worker could eat his own lunch. Harris Hall had to be enlarged twice before 1920, and by 1949 served an average of 225 dinners a day in addition to about 525 sales of light refreshments. An additional cafeteria in No. 2 Mill served meals for the force in that building, and there was a traveling milk and sandwich service brought to the workers at their machines.

The earliest service of a medical nature provided was a nutrition clinic established by Augustus P. Loring at his own expense around 1900, where children of employees could be examined and their parents advised about diet. Some years later he was immensely gratified when a state inspector declared the Plymouth Cordage employees' families to be unusually well

◆ In 1900 the United States had 75 million people in 45 states. One-third of the population was foreign-born or the children of foreign-born parents. Sixty percent of the population lived on farms or in communities of less than 2,500 inhabitants.

◆ In 1900 William McKinley was re-elected president while New York Gov. Theodore Roosevelt was elected vice president. In 1900 Boston's Symphony Hall – the first acoustically-designed building in the U.S. – opened to the public.

◆ In the 1900 Olympic Games in Paris, the U. S. finished second with 20 gold medals behind France with 29 gold medals.

◆ In 1901 President McKinley was assassinated.

◆ In 1901 Gillette Safety Razor Co. was formed.

◆ One of the most popular songs of 1902 was "Bill Bailey, Won't You Please Come Home."

◆ In 1902 the Woman Suffrage Alliance was formed.

◆ In 1903 Wilbur and Orville Wright made the first successful flight in a heavier- than-air machine at Kitty Hawk, North Carolina.

◆ In 1903 the Boston Red Stockings defeated the Pittsburgh Pirates five games to three in the first baseball World Series.

◆ In 1904, 25,000 textile workers in Fall River went on strike.

nourished for factory workers. Following a scarlet fever epidemic in 1903, the company engaged two visiting nurses to be constantly in residence. They conducted a clinic and classes in nursing and infant care, and later a resident doctor was engaged to direct the clinic and the nurses. An informal pension system to long-term employees, at the discretion of the management, was established before 1900. The stipend was $6 per week, until 1916 when it was raised to $7. By 1921 this informal system was made available to all employees, and put on a "sliding scale" basis - 1 percent of the last annual pay, multiplied by years of service.

In 1920, when the Pilgrim Tercentenary was approaching, the company built an auditorium where visitors to Plymouth could be entertained. The celebration passed but the auditorium remained as a place where concerts, lectures and theatricals could be given by and for the employees. A gymnasium class was organized there, and equipment provided. Even earlier a community bathhouse had been built on the beach owned by the company, within easy walking distance of the operatives' homes; by 1924 there were sea-bathing facilities for 750 persons a day, with a swimming instructor provided by the company. Instruments and uniforms were provided for the Plymouth Cordage Band, an excellent outlet for the musical tastes of the employees, and a community asset. A nearby colonial farmhouse was purchased in 1921 and fitted up as a men's club with bowling

By 1924 there were sea-bathing facilities for 750 persons a day, with a swimming instructor provided by the company.

alleys, pool tables and other apparatus for indoor sports. Membership in this Cordage Club was available to all male employees at very moderate rates.

It would be hard to exaggerate the pride that the directors and officers of the company showed in these welfare activities. They felt that they were indoctrinating immigrants in the "American way of life" and enabling them to be self-respecting citizens. Plymouth Cordage put on welfare as well as production exhibits at the St. Louis World's Fair of 1904 and the Lewis and Clark Exhibition the following year; and each welfare exhibit was awarded the gold medal. In 1905 the Company received first prize for its solution of a factory housing problem in a contest held by the International Exposition at Milan. Another compliment to the company was a request from the Panama Canal Administration to borrow its welfare director, Nazro, to start welfare work among the canal employees. He willingly went, but gladly returned to Plymouth.

When the history is written of that great social movement which, for want of better terms, is called employees' benefits or workers' welfare, Augustus Peabody Loring and William E. C. Nazro will doubtless stand high. As the latter predicted, and as William Bradford had predicted of the Plymouth Colony three centuries earlier: "Thus, out of small beginnings greater things have been produced."

9

All Plymoutheans Are Immigrants

BY LAURENCE PIZER

In America it is a cliche to call a town a place of immigrants. The only real issue is the era when groups and individuals began to arrive. For Plymouth the phrase at once reveals and obscures.

All who live in Plymouth are immigrants themselves or descendants of immigrants. Even the most famous symbol of the town is an immigrant: Plymouth Rock traveled to Plymouth from foreign origins some three million years ago.

The history of the town is dominated by the story of the first European settlers, who traveled great distance in a well-documented trip before erecting their dwellings near a Rock and Town Brook. However, archeological evidence demonstrates that Native Americans had been in the area for at least seven millennia before the arrival of the Pilgrims in 1620. Most likely, Wampanoag habitation was seasonal. When the Pilgrims arrived they found cleared fields and no inhabitants.

The Mayflower Pilgrims, with the help of Native Americans, succeeded in establishing a colony, and immigration from Europe, primarily but not exclusively from England, continued throughout the 17th century.

The largely English makeup of the town remained throughout the 18th and early 19th centuries as Plymouth receded from its early position of important European outpost to the status of a small coastal town serving mainly its own inhabitants.

Leyden Street, Plymouth, Mass. The first street in New England.

WINIFRED AVERY COLLECTION

Postcard view looking down Leyden Street c. 1900. Note the dirt roadway, sidewalks, electric streetlights and, at the bottom of the street, waterfront structures that were demolished in 1920.

When Plymouth's harbor proved inadequate for the town to compete with cities like Boston and New York in international trade, Plymouth residents were forced to consider other ways of earning a living. Yankee ingenuity and the presence of waterpower along the brooks and rivers of the town encouraged the development of small factories.

What would become the major employer for Plymouth was the Plymouth Cordage Co., established in 1824 along a small brook in North Plymouth. Its success outstripped its ability to find workers, and even before the Civil War, the owners encouraged German artisans to move to Plymouth as ropemakers. The new employees founded a church in North Plymouth, Zion Lutheran, and settled in as citizens of the town. Also evident in the years before the Civil War was the increasing number of Irish and Canadian settlers.

By 1889, the continuing success of the rope company demanded a new and much larger source of workers. Turmoil in northern Italy exposed a well-trained workforce interested in new opportunities, and the company recruited from the area around Bologna and nearby Ferrara during the years leading to World War I. Within the first decade or two of the Italian presence in North Plymouth, their institutions began to dominate the area as these newcomers committed to forming a community within the town.

More than 100 years later, large numbers of Plymouth residents still can trace their families to Bologna or the Emilia-Romagna region surrounding that city.

As Italy solidified its economy during the early years of the 20th century, the Cordage could not fill its employment rolls, and it turned to the Portuguese for the final large group of employees before the company's demise after World War II. Unlike the Italians who tended to emigrate from Italy to Plymouth, the Portuguese were recruited from already established groups in such American places as New Bedford and Provincetown.

A second industry of importance to the Plymouth economy, cranberry cultivation, also attracted Portuguese workers, both from the homeland and from associated islands like the Azores and

PILGRIM SOCIETY COLLECTION

Workers who built the "new" Plymouth Rock canopy in 1920-21 pose on the steps of Pilgrim Hall.

Cape Verde. Also, during the late 19th and the first half of the 20th century, textile mills and some smaller metal-working firms prospered in Plymouth, providing employment for other immigrants, again frequently Italian or Portuguese.

Children and grandchildren of the immigrants who came to work in the cordage factory and in the mills of downtown Plymouth later filled the ranks of small businesses and local professions. A late 20th century list of insurance agents, dentists, and teachers includes many of Italian and Portuguese descent.

A study of Plymouth politics reveals that a changing relationship between the older, mostly English population in town and the 19th and early 20th century newcomers, largely Italian and Portuguese, did not occur until the latter half of the 20th century. Only in the 1930s did Plymouth residents of Portuguese or Italian descent begin to get elected to major local offices. The first to do so were Amedeo Sgarzi to the board of selectman and David Cappannari to the school committee.

Political control of the community evolved slowly, but inexorably, as population numbers shifted.

PILGRIM SOCIETY COLLECTION

Cornish School pupils assembled on the school steps c. 1910.

10

Life on a Cranberry Bog at the Turn of the Century

Reprinted from
They Knew They Were Pilgrims,
copyright 1971 by The Pilgrim Society.

BY ROSE T. BRIGGS

Life on the cranberry bogs has changed drastically since 1900. In my childhood a 10-hour day was normal, and the current rate for day labor was 12 and one-half cents an hour. In 1910 the foreman got 40 cents, semiskilled labor 20 cents, and day labor 16 and two-third cents an hour. In 1903, when scoops and snap machines were beginning to come in, the rate for that work was 25 cents an hour. Picking was always paid at a higher hourly rate than day labor.

There were no automobiles in 1900, and our berries had to be carted 10 miles from Manomet to the railroad at Plymouth and everything we needed, from hay to yeast cakes, hauled 10 miles back. The result of lower wages and slower transportation was that we did on the place nearly everything that would now be done by hiring someone with specialized equipment. We lived in a completely unmechanized age. We didn't even have gasoline engines till after 1900. There was a pumping engine at one of our bogs, but it ran by steam. Like most of the older bogs, ours were built so they could be flowed by gravity. Frosts and pests were controlled by flowage. Spraying and dusting for pest control were still in the future. Weeds were rooted out by hand, perfectly practical at the wage scale then current. Sanding was done with wheelbarrows and shovels. The earliest bill I can find is for 20 iron wheels for wheelbarrows.

With transportation what it was, we expected few services from outside, and no mail unless we went for it. We had a mail bag where letters accumulated until someone went to town. There was no telephone so far from Plymouth, and of course no electricity. The town kept up the main roads. That

PILGRIM SOCIETY COLLECTION
Pencil drawing by Rose T. Briggs of cranberry pickers in a Manomet bog c.1915.

is, the town engaged someone who had men and horses available to do it. We maintained the roads in our area. It took experience to build a good dirt road that would not be too sandy in summer, nor too muddy in winter. The road material had to be a happy proportion of gravel and loam. Test holes were dug, and my father decided that one lot would do, and another lot was worthless.

The responsibility for fire fighting was distributed in the same way. The town paid the bills, and someone in each area who had a horse and wagon was issued a rack of extinguishers and made a fire-ward. My father was firewarden in our area, and a big red fire wagon was kept at our place. It belonged to the town, but it was moved by our horses and manned by our men, and my father had charge of the fire, and whatever volunteers turned up to fight it. Those were the days when fires were fought with backfires, while men with shovels and extinguishers held the lines. Whenever smoke appeared on the horizon, my father had to go, and if my brother and I were with him, we went too.

The transportation problem made a lot of horses and wagons necessary. There were a pair of driving horses, trained both to double and single harness, and two or three other horses as well, any of which my father used in an open buggy or a meadowbrook cart to drive around the bogs. There was also a quiet horse

for my mother to drive, and a couple of utility horses. At picking time we usually added some extra work horses to take picking crates down to the bog and bring the berries back to the screen-house.

All these horses had to be fed, which meant that we grew corn, mowed what grass we could raise, and sometimes bought standing hay and went with our men and equipment to cut it. Even then we bought

Women sort and separate cranberries in a Carver screen house c. 1900.

oats and baled hay by the carload, and the horses that ate it hauled it home.

The horses had to be shod, the wagons kept in order, the flume irons made, windmills kept working, etc., so a blacksmith was necessary. He was

wonderful to children, and let us hang round the forge, and even hammer out things ourselves. But he only let us use cold iron, not the lovely cherry-red stuff that came out of the forge, and bent so beautifully on the anvil, and gave out such fascinating showers of sparks.

We made most of our own barrels, buying staves and hoops by the carload, so we had to have a cooper. His work was as absorbing to watch as the blacksmith's. After the Great Fire, we produced our own barrelheads. We bought a lot of standing white pine which had been scorched but not burned, logged it off, dumped it in the reservoir, bought a sawmill and milled out the lumber for the buildings we had to replace after the fire, and for barrelheads and crate stock. The sawmill was run by a stationary gasoline engine, the first we had on the place. We installed several such engines at the bogs at about the same time.

We raised sows, pigs, chickens, vegetables, and fruit, bought flour and sugar by the barrel, and most of our meat. A fish peddler brought fish from Ellisville, three or four miles away, but there was more choice in Plymouth, if anyone was going to town. We had a boarding house for the unmarried help who lived on the place, and there were shanties of various sizes for married help and for the pickers.

You may think I date everything from before or

40

after 1900. I do. This is the date of the forest fire when all our buildings were burned. It took place in picking time – Sept. 12, 1900. We still picked by hand in those days, and most of the pickers were Cape Codders not yet Cape Verde Islanders. The Cape Codders came with their whole families, and camped out in the shanties which every bog provided for its help before the days of the automobile. The fire swept down on us with a sudden change of near-hurricane wind. My father, with the fire wagon and all the men who had any firefighting experience were already out fighting it. The shift of wind put the main fire between them and home. Of the people on the place, some took refuge in a sand hole; the rest, including my mother and five-year-old brother, in one of the flumes. The fire swept over the place, and finally into the sea at Ship Pond. No one was hurt, but when my father and the men got back, nothing was standing but the hen house and the cow barn. Fortunately the picker's shanties were in a little hollow, and the fire skipped over them. That night we ate half-baked apples off the scorched apple trees. There was nothing else.

We had other excitements beside the fire. There was an elopement. The young people stole the girl's father's horse and buggy, and made off down the road, with the father panting and swearing after them. Some wild young men stole green corn at Ship Pond. The owner sat up for them with a shotgun. One got peppered with birdshot, and had to be driven to the doctor in the middle of the night. Fortunately he was more scared than hurt. Children fell into ditches, and were hauled out before they drowned in the mud. Babies were put to sleep in cranberry crates and got stung by hornets. About

> *Those were the days of hand-picking. We used a six-quart tin that had a lovely reverberation when the first berries were dropped into it, but took so long for a child to fill.*

that time the Syrians came, one of the most colorful groups we ever had. They put on a sort of fire dance at night, dancing around, and finally over a small fire, hand-in-hand, in a long line, behind a leader who swung a knotted handkerchief in his free hand and made a great play of stamping out symbolic sparks as he leaped over the fire. There was a sort of wild chant that went with it, and the little boys marked time by thumping on the bottom of their tin picking pails.

Those were the days of hand-picking. We used a six-quart tin that had a lovely reverberation when the first berries were dropped into it, but took so long for a child to fill. Then you proudly lugged your tin up to the tally keeper, called out your number, emptied it (another satisfying sound) and returned to begin another. The bog was laid off in rows with section-line, so each picker or family had its own row, and no one could hog the best picking. The man in charge of the gang had an eagle eye for dropped underberries and for thin spots neglected, and the tallykeeper rejected measures that were not properly full or had vines stuffed into the middle!

In 1900 snap machines were beginning to come in. They took some skill to operate, and of course

were much faster than handpicking. The men who operated them were paid by the hour, not the measure. In 1903 it was 25 cents an hour. Scoops were also coming in, and with them the Cape Verde Portuguese, who soon were the characteristic labor force on the bogs. The scoop was their distinctive harvest tool, as the shovel and wheelbarrow were the tools of those who stayed for the winter sanding. They often worked their way over from the Islands on some sailing vessel. They were amphibious, as the whaling captains knew, who had hired them as whalemen, and taught them the way to New Bedford. They would pick cranberries in the fall, blueberries in the summer, and cranberries again when the harvest season came around. Their labor built new bogs and sanded old ones. Sometimes they got winter jobs in Providence or even in the steel mills of Pennsylvania but they all came back for the picking. Even in wartime, they would leave better jobs to join their cousins — they were all cousins — on the bogs.

They arrived and left in neat store suits, each carrying a suitcase and a furled umbrella. Every few years they would return to the Islands for the winter — to get married, or perhaps just to visit. One of them told us about his wedding.

"Well, where's your wife, Jock? Didn't you bring her with you?"

"Oh no, Mr. Briggs! I left her home, take care of the cow!"

A few years later. he went home for good. He told us his wife would come down from their village to meet him, leading a donkey. Jock would ride back in state, and his wife would follow, carrying the baggage on her head. What he counted on to make the biggest sensation with his friends was a deckload of lumber with which he was going to make a wooden floor for his house. I don't know how he planned to get the lumber home, but it was to be the only wooden floor in the village!

When immigration was put on a quota basis, all this commuting to the Islands came to an end, and settled Portuguese communities grew up in this country. They too came picking.

During World War II energetic women, Portuguese and others, operated as scoopers, which had always been considered strictly a man's job. The type of picking machine now in use is often operated by women. The big gangs of scoopers have gone. What strikes one now in looking at a picking crew, is the small number of people involved. Sometimes the tenders outnumber the pickers.

Our screen houses have become mechanized, too. Our shipping containers are different. Barrels went out of use long ago; shipping boxes have followed them. The final packing is done at a central plant,

SUFFRAGE MEETING IN MANOMET

Women in the United States didn't get the right to vote in local, state and national elections until 1920 after a 72-year battle that included hunger strikes and picketing the White House.

A woman's suffrage meeting in Manomet in 1914 was attended by about 75 people, "including Manomet residents, summer visitors and Plymouth people," according to a lengthy report in the *Old Colony Memorial.*

The speaker was Mrs. Wenona Osborne Pinkham of Boston who told of living in the West where women often had the right to vote. "People in the West do not consider woman suffrage a subject for debate," she said.

Her appearance in Manomet was part of a statewide campaign to enact woman's suffrage legislation in 1915.

"What we need is the vote of the country people, the good old New England stock," Pinkham said. "There are many foreigners in the city," she noted, "and the men regard their women as so much property."

At the conclusion of her talk, according to the *OCM*, "A committee was appointed of both permanent and summer residents who will see to it that the suffrage work is continued in this locality."

The 19th Amendment, which was passed by Congress in 1919 and ratified by the states the next year read: "The right of citizens of the United States to vote shall not be denied or abridged by the United States or any State on account of sex."

During World War II energetic women, Portuguese and others, operated as scoopers, which had always been considered strictly a man's job.

not at the home screen house. Much of the crop goes in bags to the cannery. Where the grower's team once carted his berries to the railroad, huge trucks now come from outside to transport the crop. Sanding and other bog work is done, increasingly, by experts with specialized equipment. The work force comes in automobiles in the morning and goes home at night. Cranberry growing is still a colorful business, but the days of self-sufficiency are over.

Plymouth's Jewish Community

BY KARIN GOLDSTEIN

While it's well-known that Plymouth industries recruited large numbers of Italian and Portuguese immigrants, less prominent ethnic groups were attracted to the town as well. These included Germans, Finns, and Jews. Jews arrived in Plymouth shortly after the Italians and formed a substantial community. In fact, at the end of the 20th century, Plymouth boasted the oldest synagogue on the South Shore still in existence.

> ... at the end of the 20th century, Plymouth boasted the oldest synagogue on the South Shore still in existence.

Like the Italians, Jews were part of an immigration movement of people from eastern and southern Europe who came to America between 1880 and 1920 searching for a better life. Many Jewish families were fleeing persecution in Russia, particularly after the assassination of Czar Alexander II in 1882. These immigrants came to Plymouth because of opportunity. With the Plymouth Cordage Co., American Woolen Mills and tack factories, Plymouth had a wide range of jobs to offer new immigrants.

Probably the first Jews to settle in Plymouth were the Resnicks, who arrived from Lithuania by 1890. A Resnick appears in the town's 1893 street directory as a "junk dealer." David Resnick had a concession to collect all the scrap from the Plymouth Cordage Co. Louis Resnick was listed as both a grocer and a peddler at his house on South Street.

Another early Jewish family was named Toabe. Max Toabe came from Shepetovka (Ukraine) in the 1890s. At the Port of Boston, he announced his name to the immigration officer as Mottel Toib. The man considered and said, "Here's your name, Max Toabe." Toabe tried factory work, but only lasted two days. He saw a man with a pack on his back, asked for whom he worked, and got started in Boston as a peddler. His route eventually took him to Plymouth, where he found several Jewish families, including the Resnicks, the Bergs, the Orentlichers, the Cohens and the Sadows. Max Toabe first appeared in the Plymouth street directory in 1899, at 15 Howland St. Max did well as a peddler, and soon sent for his family, including father, sister, wife and two sons. When they arrived in Boston he went to

MURIEL SWARTZ COLLECTION
Max and Fannie Penn, 1893

MELVIN KLASKY AND HARRIETTE MINSKY COLLECTION
The Shriber Family, c. 1900

meet them. Everyone was there except his wife, who had died on the way. Toabe went to a marriage broker to find a wife to look after him and his sons and soon remarried. His son, Mitchell Toabe, remembered hearing how the entire family lived in two crowded rooms on Howland Street, near the gas works. The parents slept in the room down-stairs, and everyone else slept in the loft above.

The Toabes soon moved to a house on Cherry Street in North Plymouth. Max peddled pots and pans until he was approached by Luigi Cortelli (L. Knife), who owned several buildings in North Plymouth. "Why don't you sell your pots and pans in one of my empty stores?" Cortelli proposed. Max protested that he didn't have enough money to pay rent. "Don't worry," Cortelli coun-tered. "You can pay me rent when you earn enough money." One day a man at the railroad station showed Max a load of damaged goods. "Why don't you take these," he suggested, "and have your family fix them to sell in your store?" This is how the Toabe family started a hardware business, which eventually grew to several stores all over the South Shore, from Duxbury to Cape Cod. For many years during the 20th century there was a Toabe hardware store at the corner of Leyden and Main streets in downtown Plymouth.

ROSE SHERMAN GELLER COLLECTION
Michel Toabe, c. 1905

Many Jewish people started as peddlers and soon owned their own businesses. Joseph Berg first appears in street directories in 1893, listed as a peddler. By 1896 he had purchased his store, selling dry and fancy goods, at 395 Court St. in North Plymouth. The Bergs lived above the store for several years, until they purchased a separate house up the street.

Plymouth was not usually the first destination for Jewish immigrants. Some families, like the Shribers, came from outside New England. They came from Odessa via Philadelphia. Many families, like the Brodys and Penns, landed in Boston and settled there. Max Penn and his wife Fannie Brody Penn lived in Boston until she took ill. Their doctor advised them to move to the country. Max's brother worked at the flower market, and asked about nearby towns. A customer suggested that Penn look south of the city. Penn boarded the train at South Station and traveled south. He got off the train at the last stop, which was Plymouth. Not only was it a country town, but there were several Jewish families! The Penns moved to Plymouth. Sadly, Max died soon after, leaving Fannie with two children to raise. Her husband's family invited her back to Boston, but she vowed to stay and support them. "As long as I have two hands," she said, "I can feed my family." Fannie became a peddler, selling aprons door to door to support her children. Her son later went into partnership with the Maccaferris and opened Puritan Clothing Co., a mainstay in down-town Plymouth for much of the century.

> *Many Jewish people started as peddlers and soon owned their own businesses.*

By 1910 there were enough Jewish families to undertake building a synagogue. That year the newly-founded Beis Jacob Society purchased land at the foot of Pleasant Street.

The new synagogue, constructed in 1912, was built in the Orthodox tradition with the bima in the center, surrounded by seats. In the early years, these were folding seats given by the Old Colony Theater. Men and boys sat downstairs, while women and girls sat upstairs in the gallery. Rose Sherman Geller remembers how she and her teen-age girlfriends received many stern looks from below. Below the sanctuary was a mikvah, or ritual bath.

Before there was a synagogue, the community rented public meeting space, such as the Town House and Red Men's Lodge on Middle Street, for services. Sarah Toabe Sherman kept the Torah in her house between services. Plymouth's Jewish community had only about 40 families and no permanent rabbi. Kosher food was hard to obtain. Some families sent to Boston for Kosher meat, which was brought to town on the train. Rose Sherman Geller remembers going to Boston with her father one day a week to buy Kosher meat. Sometimes a member of the community was a shohet (ritual slaughterer). Many families brought chickens to shohet Jacob Steinberg, who lived across from the synagogue. When traveling, Jewish people usually stayed with other Jews so they could eat Kosher food. Ida Sherman Padlusky, who was known as a wonderful cook, kept a spare room to rent to Jewish peddlers who were traveling through town.

The community purchased Jewish breads from the Millers, who ran a bakery, and foods such as fish and bagels from Joseph Cohen, who ran a grocery store on Summer Street. Most families adjusted to American living and kept their businesses open on Saturdays. At the end of the century, many older

> ### While most had been brought up Orthodox, Jews in Plymouth came from a variety of places — Russia, Lithuania, Poland — each with its own traditions.

residents of Plymouth remembered gathering at Cohen's store on Saturday — more of a social occasion than a shopping expedition!

While most had been brought up Orthodox, Jews in Plymouth came from a variety of places — Russia, Lithuania, Poland — each with its own traditions. Mitchell Toabe remembered tailor Simon Orentlicher, a Chassid, dancing at services. Other families had been socialists in Europe, and had less interest in religion. People interpreted religious law differently. Mitchell Toabe recalled his elder brothers' stories about how their grandfather, Michel Toabe, had a liberal and considered interpretation of the Jewish law. When the boys asked their father if they could go skating on Saturday, the Jewish Sabbath, he automatically said no. Carrying skates on the Sabbath was considered work, as was cutting the ice with the blades. When they asked their grandfather, who also served as the community teacher, he said, "Let us consider the situation. If you should happen to go to services and have your skates with you... and you should go to a frozen pond that other people have skated on so no matter how much you skate, you aren't cutting the ice... that's not so bad."

Most of the Jews lived in central Plymouth, on Sandwich Street, South Street, Summer Street and High Street. A few lived in North Plymouth. Many families ran businesses in North Plymouth, including the Toabes, the Shermans, the Shwoms and the Steins, all of whom dealt in a combination of furniture, dry goods and hardware. The Sherman Building and the Shwom Building, built in the late 1920s on Court Street,

ROSE SHERMAN GELLER COLLECTION
The Sherman Family, c.1908

survived at the end of the century.

Plymouth's Jewish people lived alongside Gentile neighbors, both Yankee and immigrant. These were their neighbors, customers and friends. At the end of the century, older residents remembered growing up without experiencing prejudice. "If we could get along today as well as we did then," mused Rose Geller, "the world would be a better place." Plymouth's Jews enjoyed the town's Pilgrim heritage. Sarah Toabe and Abraham Sherman received a picture of John and Priscilla Alden as a wedding present in 1905. As a boy, Bobby Shoman, son of immigrant tailor Samuel Shoman, made pocket money by giving tours of historic Plymouth to day trippers who arrived on the steamboats. Mitchell Toabe carried a torch in the 1921 Tercentenary Pageant

The community averaged 35 to 40 families, most of whom had come between 1890 and 1915. A few arrived later — the Arons, Rices and Dr. Waterman in the 1920s, the Winokurs in the late 1930s, and the Policows and Kellers just before the war. The community stayed tightly knit and slow growing, until after World War II, when an influx of new families arrived and the synagogue gradually became more Reform.

DOWNTOWN POST OFFICE

The red brick building at the corner of Main and Leyden streets downtown was built in 1914 as a federal office building. A Baptist church on Leyden Street was demolished to provide space for the new post office, which fronted on an extension of Main Street that ran from Leyden to a bridge over Town Brook that had been built a few years earlier. In these photos we see the construction of the bridge looking up what would become Main Street Extension with the church still standing in the background, then the new post office building as it neared completion. The clock atop the post office came from the church steeple.

MAGGIE MILLS COLLECTION

HANOLD OBRIEN CO. INC.
PLYMOUTH POST OFFICE
DEC. 1 1914.

RICHARD MELCHIN COLLECTION

From CRANBERRY RED, *a novel by* Old Colony Memorial *Editor Ted Garside, published by Little, Brown and Co., Boston, 1938. In the novel, Baytown is based on Garside's knowledge of Plymouth:*

"Keith Bain climbed the dimly lighted, thin marble steps to the second floor of the Baytown post office, built during the uncertain, symptomatic days of the Harding administration. Weak and puffing, he arrived at the level of the customs offices and the National Reemployment Bureau, the level of cigarette butts, splattered brass spittoons, and of bold, growling young Italians and Portuguese and older, shift-eyed, gone-to-seed Yankees, all milling around the corridor, bumming smokes, discussing fornication and absorbing free steam heat."

13

High School Graduation - 1913

In 1961 at age 65, Plymouth native Sue Sadow, a Simmons College graduate and long-time nutritionist for the United Nations, became the first senior citizen volunteer for President Kennedy's new Peace Corps program. After serving two years in West Africa, she was appointed senior nutritionist for Project Head Start. In 1992, her autobiography, Can Do (Said Sue)*, was published by Beaumont Books, Inc., Denver. Her memories of the Plymouth High School graduation in June 1913 when she was 16 years old recall the conventions of early 20th century America:*

"At last I was ready. I waited impatiently for the arrival of the horse and carriage my father had hired for the occasion. I was dressed in white from head to toe. My thick, dark chestnut brown hair was combed up into an adult-style bun on the nape of my neck. It was so uncomfortable that I was in constant fear it would loosen and drop below my waistline. I wore long white kid gloves (a school requirement) up to my elbow. When the carriage arrived, my family peered out of the parlor window. Tibbie (Morton, her best friend) was already seated, as it had stopped first at her door. Hurrying out our front door, I carefully took our stone steps one at a time to the sidewalk. Mr. Watson, the owner and driver, helped me pull myself upon the blackleather footstand into the seat beside Tibbie. I was careful

not to scratch my white slippers. Mr. Watson, who had known us all our lives, constantly gave me compliments as we drove along, which embarrassed me.

"My mother and the children stood at the window until we waved good-bye. The high school was not even a mile from home. How often we used to run all the way in order not to be late for school! The horse and carriage started off on this important journey. People we knew greeted us warmly and waved as if we were off on a honeymoon.

"When we reached our destination, Mr. Watson alighted first. Carefully he placed a huge, heavy metal disc attached to a sturdy rope under the feet of the horse; it was to keep the horse from running away when left alone. He helped each of us onto the school steps at the girls' entrance and wished us luck.

> ## High school graduation was considered the event of the year in Plymouth.

"As the graduates assembled, we entered the building. We were very silent, not even greeting each other. It was a solemn moment. We all marched quietly into the main hall, which had been specially arranged: All the desks had been removed, and the hall was now filled with wooden settees to

accommodate the townspeople gathered together every June to witness this great occasion. High school graduation was considered the event of the year in Plymouth.

"After a marching drill, the girls and boys went once again into our respective cloakrooms. There was no mingling of the sexes in those days! The crowded, stuffy dressing room was stifling. The temperature and humidity were merciless that day, and there was no air conditioning. My hands sweated inside the white kid gloves, and I could feel the moisture build up under my armpits.

"We could hear the townspeople arriving and the scuffing of feet on the wooden stairs. I was in a panic, fearing my parents might be late. The store (her family's business) was closed that evening and my father had promised to come with my mother, which rarely happened as both could not be away at the same time. I kept wondering where they would be seated. They had never been inside the high school before. Would they know how long it would take to walk there?

"Finally, after what seemed an eternity of waiting, the teachers in charge of the graduation exercises gave us final instructions on marching in and taking our seats on the platform that the teachers and our principal, Mr. William Whiting, used each day to introduce the day's activities and make announcements.

"This evening we sat in their places. As the orchestra struck up a familiar tune, we marched in:

the girls from the left and the boys from the right. The boys were really sweating it out in their prescribed dark navy woolen suits. The audience applauded vigorously as we marched in and stood before our assigned seats. We waited for the signal to sit down in unison. I didn't look out at the audience because I feared that my parents were not there yet.

"The guests in the audience and each of us received a small white cardboard card as the program. On one side was printed the order of the exercises and on the other was the list of graduates. I noticed a small star beside some names. By the star at the bottom of the program was written in tiny letters: "honor students." I looked for my name and was flabbergasted to find a star beside it. I could feel the blood rushing to my cheeks; I was trembling all over. There had been no preparation for this surprise!

"The exercises began. A number of prominent men in the town made speeches. Members of the board of education spoke about the experiment (to select 10 above-average children to skip a grade and see if they could finish high school more quickly), mentioning that all 10 were sitting on the platform as graduates. We were all asked to stand up. This also was unexpected, even to the teachers. We did

Plymouth High School at 11 Lincoln Street as it appeared a few years after being built in 1891 to accommodate 200 students. In the 1930s it was replaced by another high school on the other side of Lincoln Street and remained vacant for many years before being refurbished into a town house. Since 1953 it has been the seat of Plymouth's local government.

not know what we ought to do until Mr. Whiting said to us, smiling, "You may stand now, for you are the youngest graduates. All of you proved what the board of education hoped, and your parents can be proud of you."

"We all stood up and the audience clapped and clapped. Other graduates were not as pleased because they felt it was unfair to feature us. After all, we were graduates just like the rest. The orchestra played between speeches.

"Mr. Whiting, the principal, whom we all loved, made the final speech. He praised all of us for studying so diligently all four years. It was a proud moment in our lives. As diplomas were awarded, one teacher stood on his right holding a huge bunch of long-stemmed American Beauty roses for the girls, and another teacher stood on his left holding a basket of buttonhole red roses for the boys. As Mr. Whiting called out each name (alternating between boys and girls), there was mighty applause. With one hand we girls accepted the diploma and the other the long-stemmed rose. The boys had only to accept the diploma; the teacher pinned the rose in the buttonhole of their jackets

"As each of us honor students marched up to accept our diplomas, there was a pause as Mr. Whiting made a short speech about us and told our class rank. I was third on the list. The applause seemed thunderous for us honor graduates. I felt my eyes filling up with tears and was determined not to make a spectacle of myself. I felt the blood rushing to my cheeks and was so angry that I never could control blushing. My brother remarked later, "You were as red as a beet.""…"

(Reprinted by permission of the publisher.)

14

Plymouth's Original Town House

By Beverly Ness

In 1635, the French forced Capt. Thomas Willet from the Pilgrim trading post in what is now Castine, Maine. He returned to Plymouth, married Mary Browne and built a house on his assigned lot at the upper end of Leyden Street, later called Town Square — the identical lot that at the end of the 20th century was occupied by the 1749 Court House. This property, despite its seemingly humble beginning, has earned the distinction of being both the oldest wooden courthouse and oldest municipally owned building in the country.

By 1660 Willet had moved to Swansea and had surrendered his lot on Town Square to the colony, as required by laws governing real estate at the time. The colony court ordered that this "country house" be converted to lodging for delegates of the colony's legislature, which at the time convened in the old Meeting House on the north side of Town Square. Until 1683 the Meeting House served as church, courtroom, council hall for the governor and a place for town meetings. Then the character of Town Square began to change. First, the church body, or First Parish, built a church of its own at the head of Town Square and then, in 1685, the Plymouth Colony was divided into three administrative centers — Plymouth, Barnstable and Bristol Counties. The newly created Plymouth County Court used the rooms in Willet's house to hold its judicial sessions.

Spurred by population growth, the county court realized the need for a larger facility, so in 1749 the former Willet house was torn down and a new two-story courthouse was built. Probably the curved 40 x 30 foot ceiling over the second floor courtroom was disassembled from the earlier structure and then reassembled over the new building. At the end of the 20th century, the courthouse stood exactly as it was built.

Arrangements were made for the town to conduct civic business at the 1749 courthouse between court sessions. With the eventual increase in both town and court business the county acknowledged the need for a separate court facility. In 1815 the

> **Arrangements were made for the town to conduct civic business at the 1749 courthouse between court sessions.**

town provided the county with a site in the "Great Gutter," the area between Russell and South Russell streets where a new courthouse was built.

In 1820 the town of Plymouth purchased the old courthouse from the county for $2,000 and officially the 1749 courthouse became Plymouth's Town House. The selectmen met and stored their records

there and the assessors occupied a small space, but it appeared the town had no definitive plans for the use of the building. At that time, boards and committees of the town were few. There had been a committee for the poor, a school committee and a board of assessors since very early days. The town clerk, called a secretary, dated back to 1637. Taxes were collected by the constables and turned over to the treasurer, whose office was often at his home. However, as more committees and boards were instituted and records began to accumulate, the building became more utilized.

By the mid-19th century, two first floor jury rooms had been converted to schoolrooms. The second floor criminal's box, grand jurors' seats and the sheriffs' boxes had been removed and a stove was procured to better accommodate town meetings. The courtroom on the second floor had stayed intact; no change would be made there for some years.

A farmers' market, which had operated for more than a century on a little piazza at the east end of the building, by this time had become a nuisance. Overcrowded with stalls, parked wagons and vendors who blocked not just Town Square (or Market Square as it was becoming known) but also the traffic on both Market and Leyden streets. Eventually rent receipts dwindled and the market was abandoned in 1863.

In the southwest corner of the courthouse's main

floor, the town housed the hand-drawn and hand-pumped fire engine Torrent No. 4, exiting when necessary through the west wall of the building and rounding into Town Square. Town meetings continued to be held in the Town House through the late 1800s. Due to overcrowding, the meetings were then moved to the Davis Opera House and for the most part were held there, in the Odd Fellows Hall, the armory or Lyceum Hall until Memorial Hall was built in 1920. Several churches conducted services at the Town House until congregations could be gathered and church buildings built. A police lock-up was built in the basement in 1874. Even the public library occupied the second floor for a short time. By 1889 the building had become so overcrowded that recommendations were made for enlarging and rearranging the offices. Though the proposal was discussed at great length, a decision was indefinitely postponed by a town meeting vote of 222 (opposed) to 39 (in favor).

Prior to the turn of the 20th century, the Excelsior Hook and Ladder No.1 had replaced the Torrent No. 4 fire engine at the Town House. In 1904 the Excelsior was moved from the basement to outdoors in Town Square, much to the annoyance of fire department personnel who needed to clear it of snow and ice after every winter storm. The following year the Central Fire Station was converted from wood to brick and enlarged and the Excelsior

was moved there. This created additional space in the Town House for the police lock-up. By this time, the selectmen acknowledged the overcrowded conditions on the upper two floors and the devastating conditions in the lock-up and some renovations

PILGRIM SOCIETY COLLECTION

Located on the south side of Town Square, the 1749 courthouse building served as the seat of Plymouth's local government from 1820 to 1952. This is a view from the 1890s.

were made. An old brick vault was removed from the building and a new vault was built outside at the west end between the Town House and the old Churchill house that later became the water, school and engineering departments. Other offices were repartitioned. The board of health moved to the Bradford block and the sealer of weights and measures to the Old Chapel, just up the hill from the water department. The selectmen took over the vacated space and used an additional old caucus

room for public hearings.

By 1911 the State Board of Health had condemned the police station in the basement, citing unsanitary conditions, poor lighting and lack of ventilation. The following year the town accepted an offer from the county to rent the old jail on Russell Street for a police station.

With the jail gone, the need for public restrooms was finally addressed and facilities were built in the basement in 1913. These were the last structural changes worth noting. Over the years many new departments and committees came into being, but all were squeezed in somewhere in the building or their needs were met elsewhere.

The building continued to serve as Plymouth's Town House until 1952 when an abandoned high school building on Lincoln Street was renovated and all town departments and offices relocated to the new facility.

In 1953 the 1749 courthouse building was declared structurally unsound. It sat abandoned until the late 1960s, in danger of being demolished. Because of its historical significance, however, the town, the federal government and public contributions provided funds for the building's restoration. The restored building was reopened as a museum in 1970. As the 1749 Court House, it is listed in the National Register of Historic Places.

15

Growing Up Italian in Plymouth

BY ALBA THOMPSON

My mother stood at the kitchen window. She was looking out beyond the Forefathers' Monument and the cupola of the Plymouth Memorial Building to the harbor, to a strip of Long Beach, and farther away, to Massachusetts Bay. She turned to me, her fifth child of six, and asked "Do you know why that ocean is so full of water?" At 10 years of age, I already sensed some wisdom was about to be passed to me.

"It's full because I cried all the way from Italy to America."

In these few words, she conveyed to me all the fear, the pain, the loneliness of a young immigrant bride leaving all she knew behind her and journeying on to a land whose very language was alien and where no family waited.

I now live in that same house whose kitchen looks eastward. That same ocean view is now framed by a large picture window. The lesson remains. There are some who came to America aching and afraid.

My mother, Lisa Malaguti, once of Crevalcore, Reggio Emilia, did not make a return voyage until 1939, more than 30 years after she had left Italy with her husband, Luigi Martinelli of the neighboring village of Rovereto sul Secchia. And in those 30 years, Mama and Papa had received so many of those labored letters in Italian telling of the deaths

of brothers, sisters, parents.

From an early age I remember helping to construct those sad returning messages as my mother sat wiping the tears away. In that way, I learned of uncles and aunts I had never met. Of Arturo, who died in Africa fighting in one of those endless wars that Italy waged to hold on to some ravaged, colonial possession that only made her poorer. And of cousins, shot as they walked down a village street because they had whispered contemptuous anti-Mussolini words to someone who later betrayed them. And young Velia and Reclus, partisans and brother and sister. It was Velia who carried messages in her apron into the woods where she pretended to be gathering mushrooms. And it was Reclus who joined other young men hiding and hitting the fascists from those same woods during World War II.

All the misery of an inept king and an impoverished country seeped through those pages, so laboriously written from the Malaguti and Martinelli

PLYMOUTH PUBLIC LIBRARY CORP. COLLECTION

Water Street looking south c. 1915. The man holding the little girl's hand is pointing out to the harbor while the Mabbett mill building, later a restaurant, is visible behind the man at the right.

families. Later, in some cautious way, the letters reflected the brutality of Mussolini and his Black Shirts as they strangled all democratic expression.

So I knew, and yet I did not know, that I was

Aerial view of the George P. Mabbett and Sons mill on Water Street c. 1935. The photo was taken after the construction of the sea wall, a WPA project during the Depression.

children — and no washing machine.

Papa worked briefly in the Plymouth Cordage Co. and then for the small Downey Construction Co. He moved his family from the north end of town to the more central Wood Street. That must have been a deliberate act of separating himself from the warmth of North Plymouth's large Italian population. Broccoli's market, the sociability of the Amerigo Vespucci and the Christoforo Columbo clubs where he

New Haven & Hartford Railroad tracks in central Plymouth. The Old Colony Line of that august railroad linked Boston to Plymouth, ending in a great roundhouse, freight buildings and a spectacular brick depot where later the A & P Supermarket and still later, the Citizens Bank were to be built.

Mama was a burler in the mill, pulling many heavy yards of fine men's wear woolen cloth over a large table and locating small knots in the weaving. I still have and treasure her burling-iron, precise steel tweezers made in Sheffield, England, which she had used to do her job.

Papa became the night watchman in that same mill, and later took and passed examinations to get a license as a stationary engineer. When I carried his lunch to him on Sundays (in a big blue and white spatterware pot filled with handmade tortellini in a chicken broth), he proudly showed me the clean roaring furnaces and the huge steamdriven pistons whose brass was polished every day. I could clearly feel the throb of that energy rising in a tremble from the oil-soaked floors.

Somewhere in that time, Papa moved his family from Wood Street to one of the duplexes owned by the American Woolen Co., which it rented only to its own employees. You can still see that complex of two-family houses and a few larger tenements (never called "apartments") that made up "Mill Village". It stretches along the north side of the late 20th century shops of the Village Landing.

I was born at 202 Water St., the third daughter and the fifth Martinelli child. The Garuti family

related to those people in the few photographs that came. I understood that both my mother and my father had come from farming families who fought hunger and who constantly worked to pay the owner, a padrone, with two-thirds of the wheat crop and whatever else they could manage to grow on their small farms. And the young died young or sometimes reached 20 years and thought of some escape, perhaps to South America, perhaps to North America.

Very little of that struggle was made known to the six children born in Plymouth. The new life demanded all energy. Mama and Papa, I was told, lived first in North Plymouth. They had one bedroom and shared a kitchen with another young couple. In less than five years, Mama had had four

The weave shed at the Puritan Mills of the American Woolen Co., which was located in the heart of Mill Village west of the railroad tracks between the Plymouth railroad terminal and Lothrop Street.

played briscola, a card game, and drank the lambrusco wine of Reggio Emilia. No women members, of course.

Later both he and Mama began working in the Puritan Mills of the American Woolen Co. which stretched on the Court Street side of the New York, lived next door. The Vermieres, a French family, shared our duplex until they left, and the Strocchis moved in. There were more families named Garuti, Pelligrini, Gavoni and Vacchino in other houses. The Bedards and Carliers were among the few French families who also lived in Mill Village. Many of the men and women were skilled weavers. All took an enormous pride in the fine woolens they helped produce.

What an exciting place Mill Village was when I was a little girl. All the families kept a stern eye on the teenagers. Many of the stay-at-home mothers tended the small child of a working mother along with their own babies.

Older brothers and sisters were responsible for the younger children. The police asked the parents to discipline those who had pitched stones at the street lamps. This discipline was fast and was applied to the rear end. Law and order prevailed.

Best of all, the ocean lapped at the east side of Water Street. The land where the state boat ramp, East Bay Grill and the town's sewage treatment plant are now located is all "fill," earth that was trucked in. But when I was a little girl, always with my dog Blackie, I played on the great granite blocks of the breakwater that protected that part of the harbor on which our houses fronted. On some days, I would poke my head into one of the low windows and watch the ladies gutting fish in the basement of the clam factory or swiftly packing sardines into cans. The clam factory, of course, later became part of the Ocean Spray cranberry headquarters building. And if the factory was quiet because the fishing

boats had not come in with a catch, then I joined my father at Lacey's Boatyard where every spring he scraped and painted our wooden in-board motor boat. That boat carried us all to the dunes of Plymouth Beach where we ate picnics of thick slices of salami, chunks of Italian bread and apples.

WESLEY ENNIS COLLECTION

Market Street looking north toward Town Square c. 1930. The Peoples Market, a neighborhood grocery, on the left, was later the site of a hotel parking lot.

Summer was an endless delight of swimming or rowing the dory.

I was a part of a loving neighborhood that fished together, churned ice cream on the small back porches on Sundays, and tolerated each other's small sins. The adults often gossiped good-naturedly about those peccadilloes in the dialect of their Italian provinces, believing that the children did not understand since they were rapidly "Americanizing."

I learned all about Mr. I's occasional drunkenness and Mrs. T's abortion attempt as well as Sylvia's new sailor boyfriend when the ladies visited each other.

My little sister, Marie, was also born at 202 Water St., joining Bruno, Sylvia, Cleofa, Horace and Alba — six who spanned a period of almost 20 years of Mama's childbearing years.

Maybe Marie's birth jolted my father. For whatever reason, he purchased his first home in 1929, one month before the stock market crash. This in no way affected his immediate situation since he never, in his whole life, purchased any stock. The mortgage was placed, not with a bank, but with an Italian businessman who had an Italian grocery store in the north end. Every dollar was paid in good time. Again, my father effectively removed his family from an Italian neighborhood. Did he do that deliberately to speed up the process of Americanizing the family? I have no idea.

I had already discovered in one awful moment of revelation that Mill Village was considered the wrong side of the railroad tracks. That disclosure was made calmly in school by a teacher who herself was one generation removed from Ireland. Back then I was embarrassed to have lived there, but age has taught me that there are some who enjoy spitting on those who come after them. Did my father want us to move to the "right side" of the railroad tracks? We'll never know.

Our Westwood Road house was on a dirt road that dead-ended at an oak woods. Here Papa raised chickens successfully, chinchilla rabbits unsuccessfully and had a huge garden that gave us luscious tomatoes, Swiss chard, full ears of corn, and fat cucumbers. We were supposed to sell the chinchilla fur at a high price, but maybe the ladies stopped wearing chinchilla, for we ended up eating rabbit when inwardly we were slightly nauseated with the thought of those gentle creatures.

Each morning Mama made a big pot of hot milk lightly seasoned with coffee. Everyone, including the growing children, helped themselves from the white porcelain-coated coffeepot that was kept warm at the rear of the big gray Glendale stove. Each one made his own toast until the kitchen had a smoky haze from slightly burned slices. Mama walked down to the mill at 6:30 a.m. and all the children dashed out thereafter, the older ones to work, the younger ones laden with schoolbooks. We all walked, since the Model A Ford, our family car, driven only by the older brother, had long since disappeared. I wonder if the cut glass flower vase, part of the original car, survived?

In the early morning, the streets were filled with people hurrying purposefully to work and school. The kids from North Plymouth saved the 5-cent bus fare that would have taken them along Court and Main Street to the high school, later the town hall, on Lincoln Street. The boys, especially, chose to walk, and I often met some of them at the bottom of Samoset Street where it joined Court. Their family names were echoes of the waves of migration of the early 1900s that brought their grandparents or parents from Europe. Poluzzi, Brigida, Baietti, Pederzani, Rezendes, Costa, Valente and Borgatti — a determined stream of innocent kids on their way to the terrible discipline of Principals Kate O'Brien and Mary Dolan, them-

selves the children of an earlier Irish migration. There were no teachers with Italian or Portuguese family names in that junior high. Dolores Guidoboni and Iris Albertini, the pathfinders, were still in college. David Cappannari had not yet been elected to the School Committee. Nor did any selectman have a name ending in "a" or "i" or "o".

We students were separated rigidly into levels designated "Bright A-1" down to "Awful B-3" by some classification that seemed miraculously to place children with old English names in the upper classes. The place was a well-run jail with swift punishment for "talking in line" or doing poorly on a math test. The stress level was so high that now and then some sensitive little girl would vomit at the end of the day

Like many others, I worked weekends as a clerk at McLellan's Store or Woolworth's for 26 cents an hour.

as we stood in silent classes in the dark hall waiting to be dismissed to the blessed sunlight. I did that once.

A kinder principal, Wayne Shipman, ruled the high school. I know he encouraged me to think of college even when the Great Depression lingered and my dresses were made over from an older sister's hand-me-downs.

We were all poor, I suppose, but we were poor together, with strong, hardworking families. For the most part, we studied hard (French, Latin, history, English, math for me), played basketball madly, did household chores, and danced vigorously.

Like many others, I worked weekends as a clerk at McLellan's Store or Woolworth's for 26 cents an hour. Many of my classmates worked every day after school at whatever brought a few dollars to their families. How did they manage to do their school-work?

My four older brothers and sisters were working at full-time jobs in the mills, the telephone company, or the small shops. They brought home their pay envelopes and handed them to my father who returned a dollar or two of spending money to each of them. Their contributions to the household later permitted the two younger children to go off to school, me to Bridgewater Teachers College and Marie to Quincy Hospital Nursing School. It was common for some of my classmates in the high school to drop out to go to work. A handful went on to higher education. But some of the brightest never made it to additional training. There simply was no money.

In my case, and Marie's too, we were supposed to bring home report cards full of As and maybe one B+. Failure was never contemplated. Success was expected but not particularly rewarded. It just was. Unconsciously, I believe we knew that movement upward was predicated on hard work. In our family, anyone sitting down to rest before 6 p.m. was suspect. You were supposed to be in fruitful motion.

My father was the traditional old-world patriarch, in firm control, the enforcer of rules and behavior. One of the family's mysteries was how our sweet, gentle mother endured his tyrannies and often was able to brush past them to restore some measure of peace. Mama never read a book on psychology, but each of us grew up believing we were her favorite child. Even in tight times, she always found an extra dollar or two to answer some child's pressing need. Like all good Italian wives, at the end of her life she truly believed she had had a happy marriage. Her children remembered plenty of lightning and thunder.

We also remembered Caruso and Gigli from the big black records played carefully on our Victrola, which was my father's only extravagance. To this day, I can sing along with the great arias of classic opera. I can still recall Papa's impassioned views on politics, too. It may not be wrong to think of him as a revolutionary Garibaldi, striking at icons and enjoying the noise of an argument, which he believed he always won. And he never failed to vote. It was the ultimate expression of his American citizenship. And he wore his best suit to the polls.

The days were studded with inviolate family hours. Dinner came at 12 noon.

Invariably, it was pasta, maybe lasagna, macaroni, ziti, spaghetti, or rotini, with a tomato and meat sauce. Sometimes, there also was a green salad with an olive oil and vinegar dressing made at the table. There were no desserts.

Supper came promptly at 5 p.m. At an early age, every girl had learned to fry the pork chops or veal cutlets and to prepare a dinner for a family of eight. I never heard of pizza until many years later. No one taught us how to cook. We just grew into it. Likewise, all of us could do the big family wash in the early Maytag washer with the rollers through which we threaded all the clothes. ("Don't break the buttons!") Then sometimes, as the wet sheets froze on winter days, we hung them on the backyard clotheslines. We placed towels up front with the sheets to hide the panties and bras that were placed on the back lines. Who was it that ever went into our backyard to ogle the underwear? How things looked was very important. It had something to do with family reputation.

So we grew up resilient, knowing we were quite a bit different from the Murphys, the Brewsters, the Broadbents. I don't recall using the term "Italian-American" and, to this day, I'm no fan of such hyphenated proper nouns. I have come to understand that some of us got an extra measure of strength because of our inheritance of peasant or immigrant blood. Certainly, the crude epithets of bigots or the intolerance of the established Anglo society hurt some of the kids. Some of that survives today in more subtle forms.

On balance, growing up Italian in the small town of Plymouth prepared us for the bigger arena of life. We might have soothed ourselves with charming connections to Puccini, Michelangelo, della Robbia and Marconi, but we didn't. We knew then that we are what we are, what we have earned or abused. Even Myles Standish would have to agree.

Our real problem is passing on to our well-educated and comfortable children and grandchildren some understanding of where their families came from — and maybe some small inkling of the courage and the pain that filled the Atlantic with tears.

America may have been the land of promise, but it was hard-won by the Luigis and the Lisas, latter-day Pilgrims to Plymouth.

In 1914, speaking at her Plymouth High School graduation, Mary Cappannari said, "Ellis Island is only another name for Plymouth Rock!" Brava, Maria!

MEANWHILE ...1910-1920

◆ Between 1910 and 1920 the population of the United States increased from 91.9 million to 105.7 million.

◆ Americans benefited from mass production, buying some 10 million passenger cars during the decade – many of them Model T Fords.

◆ Life Savers candy and Oreo cookies made their debut in the American market.

◆ Throughout the decade, Massachusetts Republican Sen. Henry Cabot Lodge warned that a million new immigrants a year would cause "a great and perilous change in the very fabric of our race."

◆ In 1910, illiteracy in the U.S. hit a new low – 7.7 percent of the population, a decline of 3 percent from 1900 and of 12.3 percent from 1870.

◆ In 1912, New Mexico and Arizona became the 47th and 48th states.

◆ When Woodrow Wilson won the presidential election in 1912, he became only the second Democrat to be elected to the presidency since the Civil War.

◆ On its maiden voyage in April 1912, the British liner Titanic struck an iceberg off the coast of Newfoundland and sank, killing about 1,500 persons

◆ As the gross national product rose from $30.4 billion in 1910 to $71.6 billion in 1920, labor unrest became more prevalent — in the first six months of 1916 alone there were more than 2,000 strikes and lockouts.

SUMMER PEOPLE

BY JOAN H. BARTLETT

SUMMERHOUSES FOR PLYMOUTHEANS

An entirely different breed of summer people were those year-round Plymouth families who saw no reason to go out of town and, like the Cordage executives, had summerhouses right in Plymouth. They did not feel the need to go great distances because Plymouth, with its ponds, ocean beaches, gentle hills and woodlands had it all. Helen Belcher and her family are part of this tradition. As she recalled at the end of the 20th century:

"About all the mingling I remember with summer people was at the mending club my mother belonged to. Eight or 10 women got together each week and brought their baskets. They darned socks and mended clothes. It started in the 1920s and lasted until my mother died in 1979 when just a few of them were still hanging on. They had long since given up mending but would come for dessert and Canasta. A couple of the women were summer people. They would disappear in September and go back to where they lived.

"As a teenager, my father and his next oldest brother and a couple of friends used to love the ponds. They would hire a wagon as soon as school was out and take two tents and cooking gear up to South Pond and camp on the beach. They went up there for several summers, roamed around and fished and

had a great time. I never heard my father say that they had any permit or paid any rent. They just plain camped out on the beach.

"After he had a family, my father wanted us to have a little place in the woods. Myles Standish State Forest was created somewhere around 1917. My

Man wearing a duster and driving cap takes part in a roadside picnic c. 1917.

father heard that they were going to lease lots on Curlew Pond. You could lease the lot for $1 a year and build a house. You would own the house, but never the land. He and three or four other people that he knew leased adjoining lots. He designed a little place, barely a bungalow. There were three rooms, a big front porch and that's where we lived. The

walls were one board thick. We were very happy there and we were much freer there than we were at home.

"We lived in a house in downtown Plymouth that my mother inherited, with antique furniture and knick-knacks everywhere. We had to mind our P's and Q's and behave in town; at the pond my mother would relax.

"We would go on a Friday night. My mother would have everything ready and packed in the car. My father would come home at 5 p.m. and we'd drive to the pond from downtown. On the way we'd stop at the iceman on South Street – Robbins Ice Co. My father had ice tongs so he could heft the ice. He would bring a burlap bag to put the ice in. It would be put in between the fender and the hood of the car, wrapped up and tied onto the car. Since there was always the question of how many days we were going to stay, should he get 35 or 50 pounds of ice? When we got to the pond he'd get the hunk of ice off the car, wash it off and put it into the ice chest.

"We ate differently at the pond. We would get up when we pleased, which was not the way it was downtown. We'd have a fried egg and bacon sometimes, which we never had in town. And we'd have blueberry pancakes. We slept on cots in the living room with an oil lamp. My mother would read us stories at night. I thought that was heaven!"

Plymouth and Some Portuguese

BY PETER J. GOMES

Reprinted from
They Knew They Were Pilgrims
copyright 1971 by the Pilgrim Society

We can never arrive at a meaningful sense of Plymouth's history until we have dealt with the immigrant groups who in the 19th century and the early decades of the 20th century exposed an insular town to the corners of the world.

In order to understand them and hence understand ourselves better, we must look at the "old country." We must ask such questions as, "Why did they come here?" "What did they do when they got here?" "What contributions did they make to the culture, the economy?" "In what ways are they similar and dissimilar to the people that preceded and succeeded them?" "Where are they now?"

My subject is the Portuguese in Plymouth. In the very first book I read in preparing for this assignment, I came across this sentence on the first page: "Our study has shown, the writer believes, the danger of hasty generalization as to the Portuguese."

JESSE FAMILY COLLECTION

Azorean fisherman Marion Teves with a large catch in front of a fishing shack on Atlantic Street c. 1915.

Undaunted, I continued my researches, always mindful of that initial dictum. The title upon which I finally decided for this paper reflects my prudence. I could not possibly discuss all Portuguese; the sociological analysis alone would take too much time. I would not discuss just any Portuguese because of my desire to be relevant. So I have narrowed the discussion to what I can recollect of my immigrant ancestors, their friends and associates. Hence my topic: Plymouth and some Portuguese.

We are concerned with those people who find their immediate origins in those little salt and pepper islands named the Cape Verdes about 100 miles off the Portuguese mainland. And of these islands, two are of immediate concern to us: Fogo and Brava, volcanic peaks thrusting out of the Atlantic from the floor of the sea.

Throughout the 16th and 17th centuries, these islands were used as fueling stations by the Portuguese in the slave trade. Many Negroes became part of the population and intermarriage produced the Negroid racial characteristics of the islanders. Sociologists tell us that there has always been a strong Moorish influence on these islands and this, together with the African miscegenation serves to complicate the racial typology of the islanders.

My father, a native of Brava, tells me that one could walk the entire length of the island in one day. It was a place suited to limited agriculture on the one hand and maritime activity on the other. Children swam in the deep shore waters almost before they could walk, and fishing was a way of life. Because of the extraordinarily heavy surf and powerful currents, the fisherfolk of the island were of necessity seamen of the first order. They knew the peril of the sea as well as any native of Gloucester or New Bedford or Nantucket, for they took their livelihood from it—and it more often than not would take their lives from them.

Life on the islands was simple and quite rugged. Families were large with the hope of many sons, and villages were quite close and fraternal. While there were some schools, most of the islanders were illiterate. My father was fortunate in being able to attend a school which would be roughly equivalent to our high school. The pedagogical methods of the school were most enlightening. It seems that at recitation time one pupil would recite his lesson aloud while another watched with a birch rod in his hand. Each time the pupil made an error his mentor would be allowed to whack him one with the rod. As it usually worked out, the slower pupils were the big bruisers who regularly pummeled the smart fellows with the rod. And when the smart fellows declined to hold the rod over their slower adversaries, the master often took the rod to both parties.

As a Portuguese possession, there was quite naturally a Catholic church on the island. But as the number of clerics was small and the churches on neighboring islands many, the priests "rode circuit," coming to the island perhaps once or twice a year to celebrate Mass, baptize, and solemnize marriages which had been contracted since the last visit. There were times when the priest could not get to the island for one, two or even three-year periods. When he did, however, he was besieged with baptisms and weddings. It was not uncommon for a person to miss his own baptism as an infant and to receive the sacrament when well along into adolescence or even later. It was not unusual to hear of a man baptized one day and married the next.

Funerals and weddings were great occasions for the gathering of communities; both involved long and colorful processions and much eating and visiting.

One discovery which was a surprise to me was the fact that there was a Protestant church on the island—and a Baptist one at that.

Apparently founded by missionaries, it ministered without hindrance from either the Catholic church or the government. To this day there is a Portuguese Baptist church in New Bedford which carries on its work in two languages.

Unlike Irish immigration and the potato famine, no single catastrophic event explains Portuguese immigration to the New World. We do know, however, that Portuguese seamen were recorded as shipping into New Bedford as early as 1830. Many Portuguese came to America not to settle, but as crewmen in Yankee whalers which had stopped off

Immigration was also prompted by relatives already established in America.

at the islands to take on provisions and seamen.

The literature of Cape Cod and southeast Massachusetts is filled with references to these old Portuguese salts who spent many more years than seven before the mast, and some of whom even became masters of their own vessels.

It was natural for some of the folk to settle in the first port they entered, and that was, of course, New Bedford. That city from that day to this became the principal port of entry for Portuguese immigrants in general and our Cape Verdeans in particular.

This fact accounts for the Old World Portuguese flavor in that city today. It is said that the only trace of the New World known on the islands was "New Bedford."

But what was it that made people leave the old country for the New World? One obvious reason was the lust for adventure and the hope for a better

life. The islands were overpopulated and one's future pretty well determined at birth. The New World offered better economic opportunity. Another reason, not so often talked about, was escape from military service. Portugal required military training of all males at age 18 for three years. Inspectors from Lisbon would make the trip to the islands and gather the young men for the training camps on the mainland.

Low as the economic status of the Portuguese peasant was, he did not look upon three years of compulsory military service at 8 cents a day less the cost of his uniform as an attractive substitute for toil. During the height of immigration, the Lisbon government required a deposit from each immigrant to pay a substitute should he fail to return for military duty.

Immigration was also prompted by relatives already established in America. Those who could write would send letters back to the Islands describing life in the New World. Such inducements could hardly be ignored even if they could not always be followed. While the streets were more often paved with clam shells rather than gold, New Bedford must have seemed not unlike the New Jerusalem to the residents of our islands.

The decision to immigrate might be made on the spur of the moment. My grandfather went down to the waterside to see off an old friend for the New World. As he was about to return to his house in the village, his friend shouted that there was room for one more in the crew due to a sudden loss. After solemn calculations lasting some two minutes, [my] grandfather embarked for New Bedford.

I shall leave the technical discussion of the development of the cranberry industry in this area to

Rose T. Briggs and other competent authorities on the subject, but I shall allude to the immigrant contribution to that industry. Sea people by necessity and farmers by habit, the Portuguese immigrant was able to adapt his skills to the opportunities offered by the New World.

From New Bedford they spread over the Cape and southeast coastal region, shipping out and tending to agriculture and odd jobs between voyages. As the whaling industry declined during the last two decades of the century, the Portuguese, like his quondam employer, the shipmaster, had to seek out other means of livelihood.

He found it in the cranberry industry. Bogs needed to be built; and there was good labor left in the backs of the Portuguese. Unlike the immigrants who had preceded them, the Germans, Irish, and Italians, the Portuguese never adapted well to urban living. They lived from and by the sea whenever possible. The next best alternative was agriculture. They were thus "naturals" for the budding cranberry industry.

The bogs in Manomet were brought into production as far back as 1908, and there my grandfather and my father worked.

As a small boy I can recall the thrill of a Saturday trip "down the bog" as we called it. We'd rumble down Bartlett Road till we came to that huge expanse of dull red and brown turf, neatly divided by the canals. Past the rambling screen-houses, we'd enter the "Village," a wagon's-width dirt road, on each side of which were one-room shingled shanties, each with a little vegetable garden and the largest squashes and cucumbers about, and its pile of firewood. As Father and I would walk along this thoroughfare, we'd stop at each house, and on the stoop

there would be an ancient man whose age I guessed approximated Methuselah's. He and father would talk as I looked and poked about.

Often the illiterate ancient had just received a let-

PETER GOMES COLLECTION
The author at age 2 with his father outside their Plymouth home in 1944.

ter from the old country, and my father would read it aloud and write a reply. To a boy seven or eight years old, this seemed to take nine hours, but it couldn't have, as father managed to perform the same chore at nearly all our stops. Usually, these ancient weathered men would shake my hand and talk about me to my father in a language I did not understand; and sometimes. with their firm hand-

clasp they enclosed a shiny dime or even a quarter. Those who did not so grease my palm usually let me have one of the largest tomatoes to take home.

At mid-century, these men were in their 70s, 80s and up! They were the last of the first cranberry men. Most of them were too old to do anything but prepare for death, but nearly all talked about going back to the old country. They had spent all their adult lives in this region, never having ventured below New Bedford and above Marshfield.

In fact, the story is told about the ancient Portuguese who had never been off the bogs. Some friends chipped in and decided to treat the old man to a train trip to Boston to see the big city before he died. Our friend got aboard at the Plymouth depot and kept his eyes glued on the windows as the countryside whizzed by. When he got to South Station, he got out and roamed through the huge terminal, taking in all of the sights. At 5 p.m. he boarded the southbound train and was met at the depot by his friends. When asked how he liked the big city, he raved about all the things he had seen, and remarked that he thought it wonderful that a roof extended over the whole city!

The life of the Portuguese on the bogs was harsh. It was bitter and grueling work for starvation wages. Cheap labor was needed and they were it. Uninitiated into the ways of collective bargaining, and filled with a rural naivete, they were easy marks for the speculators and exploiters who were rife.

There would be the used clothing and furnishing salesman who extended credit to the point where the immigrant's wages for the next 20 years belonged in the merchant's hand. There would be the straw boss who suffered delusions of grandeur at the expense of the immigrant bog workers under his charge. And perhaps most insidious of all, there would be the enterprising immigrant of some years experience in the country. He spoke the language and broke the greenhorns in to the "American way," taking them, his own countrymen, "to the cleaners" as he did it.

The story is told of one of these enterprising rascals who boarded a vast number of newly arrived immigrants. He also kept a store and served as their legal counsel. When they were paid, he took their wages and deducted various fees for his services, leaving the men dependent upon his benevolence until next payday. This fellow often ran afoul of the law, and one of the first English phrases he taught his greenhorns was, "John not here" as a reply to any inquirers at the door.

Life in America for any immigrant group was difficult at best, and we can only suspect that it was even more so for the most recent arrivals. And like their predecessors, the Portuguese tended to cluster together in small communities—ghettos we would call them today. There was, of course, a major community on the Manomet bogs. There was a thriving community in Chiltonville, the workers divided between Forges Farm and the various mills located in that area. South Pond Road was also the site of a small community.

Other major areas in the country included the region of Marshfield known as Greenbush and various sections of Carver. Nearly all the Cape towns had their Portuguese, Wareham and Falmouth being principal centers.

In this country, as in the old, social life often revolved around what a theologian has termed the "Hatch-Match-Dispatch" syndrome. Islanders from all around would gather for a christening and a wedding. And like the Boston of the late George Apley, everybody loved a good funeral.

The connections with the old country were kept up as far as possible. Those who could write did so, both for themselves and for the host of their countrymen unable to do so. On the day letters were to be written, the old people flocked to the house of their scribe and dictated their messages. It was not normal dictation but a running, one-way conversation, filled with the gestures and remarks one would make in talking to a person.

The scribe was not only stenographer, he was editor and at times censor as well! When a packet of letters arrived from the old country, all involved would gather at the home of the scribe, who read them to the crowd. In this way, families separated by the Atlantic kept in touch.

The role of the old country was indeed a vital one. Most people endeavored to send something back once they had made good here. Packets from New Bedford destined for the Islands were laden with rope, poultry, household wares, tools and the like for the folks back home. On occasion an immigrant would return to the old country for one of two purposes—to fetch a wife, or to die. To this day, this is still the custom of many of the older generation.

The effect of the Cape Verdeans on Plymouth and its environs is not easily demonstrable. They have established no lasting institutions. No area of town nor building therein is associated with their name or nation. They are indeed but a minority of a minority in this land and have not yet fully passed through the fabled gates of "Three Generationdom" when the assimilation process is supposedly completed.

Their number has always been relatively small.

Until the first decade of this century, the number was so small that it was probably lumped with other miscellaneous groups in the town clerk's designation: "Other Nationalities." In 1915 the town census revealed that there were 959 persons of Portuguese extraction; from that number subtract the mainlanders, the people from the Azores, and the small remainder might well be Cape Verdeans.

And so we find ourselves at the present day. We see a simple seagoing people who came to this land by accident as it were. They worked very hard — often for very little. No riots followed in their wake, but neither have lasting institutions.

Their history is transmitted via oral tradition alone, and even that is obscured by a language barrier. There are few written documents; journals and diaries are practically nonexistent. They are the last major immigrant group to this area, and their place at the bottom of the ladder is being rapidly filled by the migrant Puerto Ricans, not really immigrants, but not quite Americans either. The older pioneering generation is dead or dying out, and their progeny born on these shores seem to know little and care less about the old days and ways.

Perhaps it is much too premature to assess fully the place of these islanders in the ongoing stream of our history. Yet though our documentation is skimpy and our primary sources few, their story has a naively brave and somewhat familiar ring to it. It could very well be that, like their immigrant predecessors of the 17th, 18th and 19th centuries, they too have built better than they knew and have left a numerous posterity grateful for their labors and confident in their hope.

18

The Cordage Strike of 1916

BY SAMUEL ELIOT MORISON

World War I, breaking out in August 1914, created at first a business depression in the United States which shortly gave way to a war boom, in which Plymouth Cordage shared. The increased purchases of wheat by the Allies stimulated the demand for binder twine, and the ships that took food and munitions to Europe needed rope. In October 1915 the company issued 5,000 shares of new capital stock, which sold at 50 percent premium, adding

> **It is a safe guess that the Plymouth worker of 1894 to 1900, with $8.10 a week, had much better real wages than the 1916 worker with $9 a week.**

$250,000 to its surplus account. It was paying dividends of 8 percent per annum on the par value. Fiber costs, however, were high. Manila became scarce and henequen, now controlled by the Mexican government, rose too. As Canada entered the war with her mother country, many of the workers at the company's Canadian plant in Welland joined the armed forces or migrated to better paying munitions plants so that, despite the urgent demand for binder twine in the Canadian West, that plant could no longer be run at capacity. Then suddenly, without warning, a strike exploded in the Plymouth plant Jan. 17, 1916.

The management at the time seemed to be completely mystified by this strike; and no wonder, since there was no warning in the shape of previously presented demands, no organization, and for several days the company could discover no demand except a 33 percent increase of wages, which seemed preposterous. At that time the German secret service was instigating strikes in American factories that were producing for the Allies, and it was naturally suspected that this was another case of the same sort. But it is now reasonably certain that the 1916 upheaval was, purely and simply, a strike for higher wages at a time when the workers were being hard pressed by a rising cost of living…

There is, I believe, a general agreement

among economists that real wages declined in the United States during the 15 years following 1900; certainly that was true of New England factory labor. Unrestricted immigration, mutual suspicion among the various racial elements that prevented organization, lack of interest by the American

KENNETH TAVARES FAMILY COLLECTION

The Plymouth Cordage Co., founded in 1824 by Bourne Spooner, was the world's largest and best-known producer of rope and twine in the era of sailing ships and beyond. c.1880.

Bales of raw material for rope and twine production are weighed in and added to inventory at the Plymouth Cordage Co. c. 1900.

Federation of Labor in the unskilled, and other factors as well, combined to keep wages from rising with the cost of living…

It is a safe guess that the Plymouth worker of 1894 to 1900, with $8.10 a week, had much better real wages than the 1916 worker with $9 a week.

Another imponderable factor entered into the situation. Through the power of advertising and the circulation of newspapers and magazines new wants had been created, and the factory worker of 1916 was no longer content to live like his predecessor 30 years before. His wife wanted nice clothes for the children and various modern household gadgets; he wanted a small second-hand car or a motorcycle. It was "unAmerican" to be without such things.

American business created these wants, but common workers who demanded the wherewithal to satisfy them were apt to be told that business could not stand the strain. Wage statistics for Massachusetts industries in 1910, at the time of the great strike in the Lawrence textile mills, indicated that Plymouth's rate of 16.6 cents per hour — the rate of 1912-16 — was slightly lower than wages paid in the textile industry (17.8 cents) and well below those paid in the boot and shoe (28.2 cents), the electrical (26.3 cents) and other industries; the Plymouth Cordage rents, however, were much lower than those charged by company and non-company houses in other industries.

Nobody claimed that a worker could raise a family in 1916 on wages of $9 a week, even with a low rent. It would be necessary for the wife and one or more of the children to have a job. That was what textile operatives had come to — whole families working but there were few jobs for women and less for minors in Plymouth Cordage, and opportunities to earn wages elsewhere in the Plymouth area were not very numerous.

For once the Plymouth Cordage management had been caught napping. There had been no labor trouble in the plant within the memory of man. The recent welfare developments and the apparent gratitude of the employees for them seem to have given management the illusion that Plymouth Cordage was one big happy family. And to a considerable degree it was so; witness the lack of violence in the strike, and absence of bitterness after it was settled. But the company had not taken cognizance of the fact it was paying insufficient wages for people to live on decently.

The thing that touched off the strike, it seems, was an unfounded rumor that the company would raise wages on Jan. 1, 1916. On Sunday the 16th, a self-constituted committee, the membership of which was never disclosed, including some men in the company's employ and some who were not, went around to workers' homes urging a general strike next day and threatening them with violence

For once the Plymouth Cordage management had been caught napping.

if they reported for work. Next day, Monday, Jan. 17, trouble started among some of the younger and unskilled ballers — the men who operated machines which wound binder twine into balls — in No. 2 and No. 3 mills. The foreman could not persuade them to return to work, or learn of any grievance except that they wanted more money.

Although none but the ballers stopped work on Monday, there were jeering crowds of pickets at the gates, and stone-throwing, on Tuesday; and on Wednesday, Jan.19, so few workers reported that the plant was closed down. Additional police were called in, from as far as Boston, but there was very little violence at any time.

The strike began without any organization, and a curious feature of it was the repeated refusal of the strikers to let themselves be organized by the American Federation of Labor or the Industrial Workers of the World, who were ready and eager to do so. The strikers appeared to regard this as a domestic issue between themselves and the company, in which they did not care for outside intervention. The first concrete demands were made at a mass meeting of strikers at the Plymouth Armory on the night of Jan. 18. They decided to demand a $12 a week minimum for men and $8 for women. Augustus P. Loring and Francis C. Holmes sent a message offering to meet a committee of the strikers and consider their grievances. Accordingly the mass meeting chose a committee, representing the several nationalities employed, which met Loring and Holmes. The president and treasurer offered to refer the whole matter to the organization already provided by the Commonwealth to handle such matters, the State Board of Conciliation and Arbitration; to abide by its recommendations and, in the meantime, to grant a wage increase of 5 percent. When the committee reported this offer back to the mass meeting, it was received with "choruses of negatives in three tongues." The committee was promptly discharged, leaving the strikers again with no organization; and about 1,200 of them staged a parade that afternoon.

It would be tedious to relate the day-by-day progress of negotiations. They were slow because a large number of the strikers were Italians, Portuguese or Germans who understood no English and had to have everything explained through interpreters. Three successive committees were appointed to deal with the management, but every proposal of AFL organizers or IWW agitators to take charge was hooted down. The strikers held out for $12 a week minimum; management repeatedly offered its 5 percent increase and to abide by what the state board recommended as fair. On the company's unilateral request, hearings were begun by the state board in the Plymouth Armory on Jan. 27. The workers had ample opportunity to air their grievances, almost all of which were low wages; except that it was evident that the piecework bonuses were unpopular, and that some of the younger

men wished to abolish welfare as a tax on them for the benefit of married employees. The company claimed it was paying better wages than in most mill towns and that a 5 percent increase was all it could afford; but it promised to abide by findings of the state board. On Feb. 1, the company's offer was again voted down by the strikers, but they were beginning to weaken. Hearing that large numbers wanted to return but were prevented by intimidation, the company blew the whistle for work two days later. Few then responded, but more came through the picket lines next day and about 125 reported for work on Feb. 7. No. 1 Mill was back in

In the upper photo, a nurse provided by the Plymouth Cordage Co. examines a young girl in her home. The lower photo shows the kind of housing provided by the cordage firm for its workers in North Plymouth. Housing and medical care were but two of many services rendered employees and their families by the paternalistic company.

partial operation on the 8th; on the 14th most of the Germans were back on the job, the Portuguese followed and finally the Italians. On Feb. 15 the strikers voted to accept the company offer, and on the 16th, less than a month after the work stoppage, the plant was in full operation. All strikers who desired re-employment got it. Nobody was discharged because of his part in the strike. The state board communicated its decision on April 5. The company, wishing to make a settlement that left no scars of ill will, bettered the award…

It so happens that the 1916 strike has received a notoriety beyond its deserts, through the reputed connection with it of Bartolomeo Vanzetti, who with Nicola Sacco was executed in 1927 for the murder of a paymaster and his guard at South Braintree in 1920. The present writer, who followed this world-famous case at the time, is convinced that both men were innocent of that crime; and that Vanzetti was also innocent of a holdup at Bridgewater, for which he had previously been found guilty at a session of the superior court in Plymouth. This is not to say, however, that his statements about the Plymouth strike are correct…

In a pamphlet written after his conviction for the South Braintree murder, Vanzetti said: "I had participated in the strike of the Plymouth Cordage Co. workers in 1915 [sic]. This company is one of the greatest money powers of this Nation. The town of Plymouth is its feudal tenure. Of all the local men who took a prominent part in the strike, I was the only one who did not yield or betray the workers… But of all the local men who had taken a big part in the strike, I was the only one who, instead of being compensated, was blacklisted by the company, and subjected to a long, vain and useless police vigilance…"

Apparently nobody in the company ever heard of him as a strike leader until he became otherwise famous; and he was certainly not blacklisted, as the company blacklisted nobody. The probability is that Vanzetti was one of the unnamed members of the self-constituted committee which went about to workers' homes on the Sunday preceding the strike, urging the work stoppage by threats and intimidation, and that he continued violent agitation throughout the strike, and was opposed to the settlement. According to his own testimony at the trial

> **By the time the men had returned to work, Plymouth Cordage was overwhelmed with orders-especially rope for ships and twine for wheat.**

he was working on various odd jobs in Plymouth at that time. As an anarchist, whose object in life was to break down government and capitalism, Vanzetti may well have thought it his duty to start with Plymouth Cordage. But whatever his part may have been in the strike, [it] has no bearing on his guilt or innocence of the murder for which he was executed.

By the time the men had returned to work, Plymouth Cordage was overwhelmed with orders — especially rope for ships and twine for wheat. The whole plant ran at full capacity during the day, and

No. 2 Mill ran nights as well. Production in 1916 reached a new high despite the loss of a month. Management, having learned a lesson about labor the hard way, set up a new personnel department headed by a manager of industrial relations. But there was an unprecedentedly large labor turnover, owing first to the American preparedness program of 1916 attracting workers to the munitions plants, and, after the United States declared war in April 1917, the draft. Manila fiber continued to rise in price and the better grades became scarce, while in Mexico the Carranza government established a government monopoly in henequen which, in the opinion of American consumers, went pretty far. One may add, however, that the Comisz'on Reguladora del Mercado de Henequen defeated its own ends, as it led to extensive planting of henequen and sisal in Haiti, other Caribbean countries, East Africa and the Dutch East Indies.

All such difficulties were intensified when the United States entered World War 1; yet Plymouth succeeded in substantially increasing production. The plant was officially declared to be essential to the efficiency of the Navy, which exempted a number of key men from the draft. As a leading producer of binder twine, Treasurer Francis C. Holmes was chosen one of the six members of the sisal committee of Herbert Hoover's Food Administration. Rope sales for the fiscal year ending July 31, 1917 were the largest to that date and were not again attained until World War II; binder-twine deliveries have never been equaled since. The factory ran 21 hours a day. Rope was manufactured not only for the Navy and the merchant marine but for particular war needs — the lighter-than-air "blimps," Army observation balloons and Navy kite balloons…

19

Over Here: 1916-1918

By Karin Goldstein

"Impossible is Un-American"—the motto of Plymouth High School's class of 1917 reflected the country's mood. That momentous year signaled the end of years of isolationism and neutrality as the United States entered World War I. Although war was not declared until April 6, the country had been preparing for it for many months.

By mid-1916, the local National Guard unit—the Standish Guards—had been called to active duty in anticipation of the country's involvement in war. The whole town turned out to give the local boys in khaki an appropriate sendoff. The night before the troops left town, they were served dinner in the Samoset House, and the next morning, 69 men marched to the railroad station. According to the *Old Colony Memorial*, "Both sides of all ways leading to the station were lined with automobiles, trucks and carriages, while the intervening space was filled, like the vehicles, with humanity. Mills and factories had closed and public schools also…"

In the fervor leading to the declaration of war, Plymouth held a recruiting rally for D Company (the Standish Guards). Enlisted men in full uniform marched with their rifles through the center of town. Guest dignitaries included Capt. Charles Doten, who had led the Standish Guards in the Civil War. Sherman Whipple summarized the reasons for going to war: "We are confronted with one of the gravest crises this nation ever knew. What will

we citizens of Plymouth do…Will we enforce our rights or will we lie down and be a doormat for the other nations? There can be but one answer to this…[the] duties of world leadership come to every part of the United States and especially to Plymouth because of its wonderful traditions…"

In Plymouth, the homefront effort was coordinated by the Committee on Public Safety, a 15-member group established at the March 1917 Town Meeting. The effort involved all residents—men, women and children. As early as 1916, a local branch of the Red Cross Society had been organized, and townspeople banded together to offer their support.

By June 1917, Plymouth pledged to raise $10,000 in a collective Red Cross Week effort. Local businesses led the campaign—$1,000 from the Plymouth Cordage Co. and $500 each from both Standish Mills and Mabbett's Mills. Individuals

PLYMOUTH PUBLIC LIBRARY CORP. COLLECTION

Soldiers from Plymouth's own Company D, the Standish Guards, march through town prior to shipping out for World War I.

could join for a dollar. "Do your bit now," urged an ad in the *OCM*, "every dollar contribution…will be a blow at the Germans." The Red Cross North Plymouth branch raised money through a food sale and tea, with entertainment provided by the cordage company band. One of the most unusual fundraisers was a minstrel show, held at the Forges estate in Chiltonville.

In addition to raising money, women and girls worked to make surgical dressings and clothing for the troops. Finished goods were gathered at the Red

Cross headquarters in the three-year-old Post Office Building on Main Street Extension and sent to Boston. Red Cross Week netted 27 dozen hospital shirts, seven dozen face cloths, a dozen pajamas and eye bandages, a half-dozen stockings, wristers and nurses' mitts, and five mufflers. Jeanette Morton Holmes remembered going to the Red Cross headquarters above the post office to volunteer. "A group of four or five of us girls would go in and roll bandages after school. We knitted scarves and helmets. The helmets were tricky." Doris Gerard Woolson recalled knitting stockings. "I remember cases of yarn, getting those socks out," she said.

Another way to aid the war effort was to help pay for it through the purchase of Liberty Bonds and War Saving Stamps. An advertisement in the *OCM* urged readers to "Buy Liberty Bonds—It is your duty. If you do not come across, the Germans will!" Plymouth High School students and the local Girls' Club held bond-selling

Company D Standish Guard soldiers in bivouac on the grounds of the Nathaniel Morton School c. 1916.

drives. Bonds were available in $50 and $100 denominations, and local banks offered to store the bonds free of charge for purchasers without safety-deposit boxes.

America in 1917 had a large percentage of foreign-born residents, who were often suspected of anti-Americanism and lack of patriotism. German-Americans in particular were scrutinized. Karl Muck, the conductor of the Boston Symphony Orchestra, was fired and interned. Across the country, German measles was renamed "liberty" measles, hamburger became "liberty steak" and sauerkraut was dubbed "liberty cabbage."

Foreign-born residents were required to register with local authorities. In Plymouth, Police Chief John Armstrong posted notices around town informing "enemy aliens" of the law requiring them to turn in any weapons or explosives that they might possess.

As the *OCM* noted, "'Enemy alien' may mean nothing more than that some worthy resident of foreign birth has by carelessness rather than intent neglected to comply with the requirements which would have cleared him of all doubt as to his good intentions regarding the country in which he is an adopted citizen but not yet a full-fledged one…"

Beginning in January 1918, the selectmen acted in accordance with federal government instructions and established a waterfront zone ranging from the railroad

station south to Town Brook from which "enemy aliens" were barred.

Yet while the presence of many unnaturalized immigrants caused concern in other cities across America, tensions between the old guard and newcomers were relatively few in Plymouth. Community leaders stepped up efforts to acquaint new immigrants with American values. The Chamber of Commerce formed a committee on Americanization, "in the interests of our alien population." Numerous flag-raisings and patriotic rallies were held at local mills and businesses, including a flag-raising at Sadow's woman's shop on Court Street, featuring a nine-piece band.

Shortly after war was declared, Patriots' Day in Plymouth provided an ideal forum for what the *OCM* called "the greatest…showing of sentiment that the old town has ever seen." The parade included the Committee on Public Safety, troops,

Red Cross nurses and aides on the steps of the downtown post office c. 1917.

police and sheriff's deputies, Boy Scouts, Camp Fire Girls, fraternal organizations, and ethnic clubs — notably including the Bavarian Benefit Society and Franco-Prussian Veteran Society.

In July 1918 the *OCM* reported on a "Win the War Community Rally" at the Plymouth Cordage Co. where a crowd of 3,000 heard a "leading Portuguese patriot" call for a united effort against Germany. The speaker, Dr. Adelino d'Abreu of Fall River, was escorted to the field by a Portuguese band and a number of local ethnic organizations. Later that year, the cordage company Labor Day festival focussed on Americanization. The *OCM* reported that "fully 10,000 persons were present" to watch a parade through North Plymouth, participate in patriotic songs, folk dances and "national airs sung in Portuguese, Italian and French."

"American, British, French, Italian, Belgian and Portuguese flags flew in the light wind from off the bay, which tempered the heat just enough to make the day a perfect one…" the *OCM* noted, adding, "…it was one of the biggest and earliest efforts ever made thus far in history by a corporation to amalgamate the different foreign-born citizens into real Americans."

Less than a year after war had been declared, the *OCM* reported in March 1918 that Plymouth had 450 men enrolled in military service, 160 of whom were in France. According to the newspaper account, the local Red Cross chapter contributed 9,705 surgical dressings, 264 sweaters, 225 pair of socks, 216 mufflers, 162 hospital shirts, 144 helmets, 120 pair of wristers and 37 pair of pajamas in the previous month.

As the war progressed, shortages of money, labor, goods, fuel and food developed. The town suspended all major capital projects and fuel shortages seriously impacted Plymouth's transportation systems. Fuel shortages and safety concerns combined to cut back dramatically on harbor traffic. The Boston ferry suspended service, and goods like coal came into town by railroad rather than by barge. The Brockton and Plymouth Street Railway, plagued by high fuel costs and labor shortages, was forced into receivership by 1919.

James J. Storrow, the state fuel administrator, ordered stores, saloons, banks, office buildings, theaters and dance halls to close their doors at 10 p.m. and to reduce the heat in buildings while they were closed.

Food shortages probably hit Plymouth the hardest, affecting every resident. Joseph Busi remembered the shortages as miserable. "Everything—food of all kinds—was scarce." Sugar, wheat flour, and eggs in particular were in short supply, he said.

As director of the federal food adminstration, Herbert Hoover began a national food conservation campaign. Pledge cards were available at the post office and at Red Cross headquarters. Cards in French, German, Italian and Portuguese could be obtained at the Loring Library in North Plymouth. "There can only be food enough if America provides it, and America can only provide it by personal sacrifice…" urged one notice from the U.S. Food Administration.

Housewives were encouraged to learn how to substitute ingredients and eliminate waste. The food administration's public service announcements urged thrift and provided recipes for breads and cakes using other kinds of flour, vegetable fats, no eggs, and alternative sweeteners like molasses. By November 1917, bakeries were required to make

War Orders Rushed

THE magnitude of the great war in which we are now engaged, has necessitated unusual preparation. Mighty forces are marshalling great stores of food and munitions are being gathered, and the energies of the nation are focused on problems incident to the war.

At the very beginning of the war, the whole Bell System was placed at the disposal of the Government. No nation has entered the war with such a comprehensive and efficient telephone service.

As our military establishment grows, the demands of the Government upon the Bell System are bound to increase and always they must take precedence over all others.

Increased activity in commerce and industry as the result of larger demands for food and munitions from our allies and for our own use, means more need of telephone service by private business.

But private business must always be subordinated to the Government service.

Each individual American will co-operate in this patriotic service, and submit cheerfully to inconvenience or delay in his telephone service, when he understands how vital it is that Government service shall take precedence over all else.

**NEW ENGLAND TELEPHONE
AND TELEGRAPH COMPANY**
W. H. PARSONS, MANAGER

"war bread" with no sugar, milk or shortening. The *OCM* reported "the sound of the sugar scoop not heard in the pantry." Grocers began to run out of sugar. In December, the public safety committee rationed 2,400 pounds of sugar by ticket at the Court House on Russell Street, limited to one pound per person. The lines extended around Russell Square to Court Street. Orderly at first, the situation deteriorated into a mob scene when a group of men who got off the trolley on Court Street pushed through the line and the crowd rushed the Court House doors.

One way to avoid food shortages was to grow your own at home. Cultivating war gardens (later called victory gardens) was encouraged, especially among school children. Jeanette Morton Holmes remembered the town plowing land that had not been cultivated before. Children could look after gardens at home or at school. Joe Busi recalled working for 15 cents an hour in victory gardens in his Lincoln Street neighborhood. Many young children grew potatoes, cabbages, beets, turnips, corn and beans. One boy, Arthur Fihelly, singlehandledly grew 60 bushels of potatoes during the summer of 1917! Busi won third prize at a garden exhibition that year for his beans. Town Square regained its former function as a marketplace for surplus produce. Starting in August 1917, markets were held on Wednesdays and Saturdays.

Another food-producing scheme was the Pig Club. To help avoid the shortage of meat and fat, children ages 10 to 18 were encouraged to raise a pig. "The boys and girls can help out a lot, secure a profit for themselves and learn a number of lessons which are likely to prove of great utility," the *OCM* said. Plymouth National Bank gave piglets away to children who were willing to raise them. Joe Busi remembered the Pig Club, but he didn't participate because, "My father didn't want pigs around the yard."

The ongoing shortages and rationing were punctuated by more vivid reminders of war. The sighting of a U.S. torpedo destroyer boat off Gurnet Point in May 1917 was notable. As more men enlisted, the sight of soldiers drilling became quite common. Joe Busi recalled seeing men training across from the high school on Lincoln Street, later the playground of the Nathaniel Morton School. Men also drilled on the old Training Green near South Street, first set aside for that purpose in 1711.

While some American soldiers arrived in France as early as June 1917, Plymouth troops didn't leave the States until mid-September. The *OCM* encouraged residents to join parades forming at Town Square to give them a good send-off.

Mitchell Toabe remembered seeing off one of the young men from his father's housewares store. "He picked me up and hugged me and went into the train," Toabe recalled. Residents sent "comfort packages" and Christmas boxes to the boys overseas. One soldier, Lewis Covell, criticized French tobacco, and was sent American pipe tobacco. "I got two boxes...last week and believe me, they were good," he wrote.

The war officially ended Nov. 11, 1918, with the signing of an Armistice. "The town went crazy. People didn't know what to do," recalled Joe Busi. On Monday, Nov. 11, bells rang, "horns brayed, and cowbells jangled...Automobiles and bicycles trailed strings of empty cans...One group had an effigy of the Kaiser...[which] was burned in Town Square," reported the *OCM*. The mills released workers, as it was hard to keep them at their jobs.

Gov. Samuel W. McCall proclaimed Tuesday, Nov. 12, as Victory Day. Buildings, cars and even animals were decorated with flags and crepe paper ribbon. Here in Plymouth, Myer and Bessie Markus named their newly-born daughter Miriam 'Victory' Markus. Just as they had done at the start of the war, most of the town's residents showed their support by marching in the parade, which extended for two miles from downtown to North Plymouth. Americans had proven the impossible was possible.

1917 TOWN REPORT

Arthur Fihelly poses with some of the 60 bushels of potatoes he grew during the summer of 1917 as part of a nationwide grow-your-own-food campaign.

20

A "Spanish Lady" Plagues Plymouth

BY HERMAN HUNT

On Sept. 9, 1918, a 20-year-old Plymouth native came down with what he thought was a common cold. He went to bed in his family home at 12 Washington St., but a week later Geoffrey D. Perrior Jr. was dead, the victim of a deadly flu virus that came to be known as the "Spanish Lady."

Perrior, a 1917 graduate of Plymouth High School and a veteran of the local Standish Guards military unit, was the first of 73 Plymouth residents who would fall victim to an epidemic unprecedented in 20th century local history. Indeed, the "Spanish Lady" flu – so called not because it originated in Spain, but because that country, not being involved in World War I, had an uncensored press that reported on the ravages of the epidemic – was unprecedented in world history, infecting half the world's population at the time and killing more than 40 million people, more than any other disease in human history.

Before September 1918 had run its course, Plymouth Town Clerk George B. Howland would record the deaths of 12 other influenza victims in Plymouth. These included Florence B. Craig, 31, on Sept. 22 and her sister, Gertrude J. Peters, 33, six days later.

Other Plymouth families who bore the fatal burden of the "Spanish Lady" more than once

INFLUENZA BULLETIN

Issued by the

MASSACHUSETTS STATE DEPARTMENT OF HEALTH

To keep well, keep clean.

Wash your hands before each meal.

Don't go to crowded places.

Avoid the person who sneezes.

Smother your cough in your handkerchief.

Keep out of dirty restaurants.

Warmth is necessary. Be well clothed.

Soda is unnecessary. Why run the risk of infection from a dirty glass?

Safety lies in boiled dishes.

A common towel is only for filthy people.

You wouldn't use my tooth brush. Why use my drinking cup?

Sleep well. Eat well. Play well.

DON'T WORRY.

SHARON LaROSA COLLECTION

Influenza bulletin issued by the state Department of Health in 1919.

included: Luigia Borghesani, 53, wife of Gaetano Borghesani, who succumbed to the killer virus, followed by their teen-age son, Henry, 16; also, Ralph K. Jennings, 24, and, a few days later, his 6-year-old daughter, Annie; and John D. MacLean, 38, and his wife, Katherine, 35.

Even expectant mothers were not spared. A premature Baby Zammarchi died only five minutes after being born, followed by its mother, Adaline Vincina Zammarchi, 28, the wife of Eugenio Zammarchi.

Gertrude Alger of Milford traveled to Plymouth to be with her mother, Jennie Hobbs, when her baby was born. But the baby, Flora Mae Alger, died after only one day of life and her mother succumbed a short time later.

On Sept. 27, the *Old Colony Memorial* reported that the local board of health had ordered "theaters, churches and the announced Liberty Loan meeting closed until the epidemic of influenza is a matter of history."

The *OCM* also reported that the public schools had been closed and quoted a board of health member as saying it was the intention of the board to prevent indoor gatherings of people in crowds, "but when it came to open-air concerts and similar reasons for a congregation of people there seemed to be no reason why they might not be held as usual."

While World War I continued to rage in Europe, more Plymoutheans would fall victim to the "Spanish Lady" than to German bullets, shells or poison gas in the trenches of France.

"Influenza made such havoc in school attendance (40 percent being out from nearly every school in town) that it was deemed wise to close the schools," said Dr. Helen F. "Nellie" Pierce, the acting school physician.

When schools reopened, Dr. Pierce said, "As careful supervision as possible was kept, and all children in whose family there was a case, and all children showing symptoms of such trouble, were barred from school.

> ## *More Plymoutheans would fall victim to the "Spanish Lady" than to German bullets.*

"In this way," she added, "we hoped to lessen the spread of the disease." There were few Spanish flu deaths among schoolchildren, Dr. Pierce reported, "but Miss Shaw, one of our Knapp (School) teachers died from pneumonia following influenza."

In 1918, the school nurse, a beleaguered Susie MacDonald, R.N., reported 503 school visits, 565 home visits, 894 treatments in school, 126 contagious cases found in schools, 72 contagious cases found in homes, 5,185 pupils inspected and 43 referred to physicians.

The next year, Dr. John Holbrook Shaw, who

had returned from military service to resume his duties as school physician, reported: "Soon after the opening of the fall term, our faithful nurse, Miss MacDonald, was obliged to give up work temporarily on account of ill health…"

On Oct. 4, 1918, as the epidemic neared its peak, the *OCM* advised readers to go to bed and remain there "at the least suspicion" of having caught the deadly flu virus. Then it offered more detailed advice: "Take a laxative. Drink much plain water. Take plenty of simple, light food, milk, eggs, toast and similar things. Have plenty of fresh air. Send for a doctor. Stay in bed at least 48 hours after you think you are well. Gargles and sprays are liable to irritate and injure the linings of the mouth and nose, which nature has arranged to arrest and destroy germs, and so invite infection."

The article also described how to deal with coughing, protection in the presence of an infected person and how to protect oneself by avoiding situations where one comes into contact with others. The chief protective agent, the paper advised, was a gauze mask used to cover the mouth and nose, obtainable from the local Red Cross.

A week later, the *OCM* reported a shortage of caskets: "Word came from some of the principal fur-

OLD COLONY CLUB COLLECTION

Jordan Hospital c. 1918. Built in 1902 and named for its major benefactor, Eben Jordan, who summered in Plymouth. The nurses' quarters are to the left since for many years the hospital had a nurses' training program.

nishers of burial caskets on Saturday to funeral directors here that all price lists were cancelled and that the demand for burial caskets far exceeded the facilities of the casket factories, the unpopular epidemic being a factor in this action…" Because of the epidemic the board of health banned indoor funerals, recommending instead that services be held in open-air cemeteries.

In December, *OCM* readers were urged to conserve coal and burn wood instead because the epidemic, which raged throughout the nation, had stricken so many coal miners that production had been curtailed.

Nationally, the devastating epidemic, which petered out in 1919, killed more than 400,000 people in 46 states, some 300,000 more than the number of Americans who died in World War I.

21

Trial of the Century:
LOCAL AMNESIA

BY ROBERT KNOX

It's paved today, but Suosso Lane is still a narrow public way off Court Street in North Plymouth, where Valente's Florist sits on the corner. Across Court Street are neighborhood fixtures like Charlie's Hardware store. St. Mary's Church is just two short blocks north. Suosso Lane is a short street, cut off almost immediately by High Cliff, the bluff that Bartolomeo Vanzetti and his North Plymouth neighbors climbed in order to look to down on the seashore. At the end of the 20th century, the solid wood-frame house that Vanzetti lived in with the Brini family was still there, perhaps not much changed on the outside at least, from the nineteen

Plymouth has always been ambivalent about Vanzetti.

teens. It's a two-story shingled house with a wood-railed front porch and shutters framing the windows. There's an old garage behind it on one side of the lot and a garden area on the other side — maybe the same garden where the Brinis grew vegetables and Vanzetti, their boarder, pulled weeds. At the street's dead end, railed concrete steps lead

upward to a townhouse-style senior housing complex. The view from the bluff is still magnificent, though screened by trees. Parked cars in a black-topped lot take up space across the street from the Brinis' house; the unpaved lane would have seen few cars when Vanzetti came to live there in 1913.

The Amerigo Vespucci Hall, "the social center of Plymouth's Italian Colony" was across the street in those days, though neither the club nor a colony exists today. The lane would likely have been filled with kids when school let out. Here, or on a neighboring street, Beltrando Brini, then age 13, chased a ball into a neighbor's vegetable garden on the last day he spoke to his friend as a free man. Vanzetti told him — very gently, Brini recalled, not to trample people's gardens or speak rudely to adults.

Plymouth has always been ambivalent about

WESLEY ENNIS PHOTO

35 Cherry St., where Vanzetti lived when he was arrested.

Bartolomeo Vanzetti

Vanzetti, a defendant and arguably the central figure in one of the most famous criminal trials of the 20th century. By the end of the century even long-time Plymouth residents had largely forgotten that he lived here among us, at 35 Cherry St. when he was arrested on a Brockton streetcar in 1920. But for many years, the name of Vanzetti was known throughout the world. People who had never heard of John Alden, Gov. Bradford or Myles Standish, or who may not have known much else about America in the 1920s, nevertheless knew who Nicola Sacco and BartolomeoVanzetti were — the revolutionary workers who were framed and executed for their opposition to capitalism.

While the two Italian immigrants languished in jail in the 1920s, waiting for legal challenges to their convictions to be heard, the case's notoriety gained momentum — in Europe, South America, Mexico, South Africa, Australia, wherever a workers' move-

> **For most of Plymouth, the case had little to do with "us."**

ment could draw a crowd for a rally. Strikes and demonstrations protested the persecution of what workers of the world saw as two innocent working men. Unions passed the hat to support the defense; donations came in from all over the country and all over the world. In Europe the international Communist Party turned out the masses and used the case as an organizing tool for its own ends.

When the sentence of death was at last pronounced in April 1927, reaction was immediate and worldwide. Pleas for a new trial or a pardon swamped the governor's office; they came from Albert Einstein, the French premier, the Vatican. European newspapers referred to the sentence as "political judicial murder." When the executions were finally carried out on Aug. 23, 1927, rioting shook the French government. A general strike brought Paris to a halt and the American embassy was guarded by tanks. American property was destroyed in Switzerland, demonstrators took to the streets in Germany, a riot broke out at London's Marble Arch.

Mass meetings took place in cities as widely separated as Mexico City and Sydney, Australia.

America was more divided by the case that many still regard as "the trial of the century." Support for Sacco and Vanzetti came from the radical labor movement and from intellectuals who felt the trial had not been fair. From Felix Frankfurter to Edna St. Vincent Millay, the roster of Sacco and Vanzetti protesters is a virtual who's who of 1920s American intellectual and artistic life. As worldwide denunciations of its system of justice grew in intensity, the Massachusetts legal and political establishment closed ranks around the verdict. Mainstream Massachusetts opinion hardened against the defendants. There were demonstrations in Boston, but not the riots that police feared. Protestors were arrested for carrying signs in front of the State House, but no enemy confronted the fortified positions established by police on the night of the electrocutions. After the executions, 100,000 mourners came to view the bodies of the electrocuted men, and tens of thousands paraded afterward through Boston in "the most spectacular funeral the city had ever seen."

"All quiet here," Plymouth's local newspaper headlined a story on Aug. 26, 1927, about the night Vanzetti was executed. Extra police had been ordered to watch the courthouse, registry of deeds, Town House, county jail, Jordan Hospital, and "the homes of various of the more prominent court officers" the nights before the execution. Even Pilgrim Hall took precautions, the *Old Colony Memorial* reported, "where basement lights were kept burning all night." But the night passed quietly. After locals heard on the radio that the executions had been carried out, there was a "general

feeling of relief," the newspaper reported, "that the whole case was now a closed matter."

For most of Plymouth, the case had little to do with "us." Vanzetti may have been living in Plymouth, but he was not one of "us." *OCM* articles refer to "the Italians." "The Italians laugh," one story notes, at the idea that Vanzetti drove the getaway car in the South Braintree payroll robbery; they knew that Bartolomeo Vanzetti, the fish peddler, did not know how to drive. But what they knew meant comparatively little in the Massachusetts courts. For Plymouth Yankees, North Plymouth was a different world; as the author John Dos Passos would write in *USA*, his study of American society written after the case: "We are two nations." If you were an Italian immigrant you were likely to believe that the court was prejudiced against the two Italian defendants.

"The people on Cherry Street supported him at the trial. The Italian community wanted them to be

> **By the end of the 20th century, Plymouth had forgotten Vanzetti...**

found innocent," long-time Plymouth resident Harold Boyer recalled.

"In North Plymouth the Italians were afraid to even talk about the case," Beltrando Brini recalled in 2000 when he was 93. "The Yankee community acted as though the trial and Vanzetti didn't exist," he added.

Native-born Americans simply assumed that "the Italians" would stick together, which was precisely what the prosecutor wanted the jury to think. "That came under the umbrella of listening to the immigrant," local resident Alba Thompson said. "They're anarchists — or terrorists."

More telling than the prejudice against Vanzetti was the disrespect shown to the witnesses who testified on his behalf, when Vanzetti stood trial on the charge of taking part in a failed hold-up in Bridgewater, the first of two crimes he was accused of committing. When his neighbors testified to the North Plymouth fish seller's whereabouts on the day of that crime, the prosecution made insinuations about their reasons for appearing on his behalf. What was their relationship to Vanzetti? What were their political beliefs?

"There's a lot to be ashamed of," noted Ken Stein, whose family-owned business in North Plymouth was founded in 1915.

"The neighborhood people around here thought he got railroaded," said boat-builder Ted Jesse Sr. His father, Frank, was a witness at the second trial; when defense witnesses placed Vanzetti in Plymouth on the day the Slater and Morrill factory payroll was robbed and a paymaster and a guard were shot dead in South Braintree.

"My father said he was down here at the boatyard but he couldn't say what day it was," Ted Jesse recalled. Jesse says he remembered Vanzetti himself. "He was a little fella, about five-six or seven inches, about 160 pounds. He was a nice quiet fella."

By the end of the 20th century, Plymouth had forgotten Vanzetti, just as it had forgotten the days when prejudice against immigrants from southern Europe was common and acceptable. The house at 35 Cherry St. was still there, but there was nothing to indicate it had been the home of the defendant in one of the most famous trials in American history. The house on Suosso Lane, where Vanzetti lived with the Brini family from 1913 to 1917, was similarly unmarked. Nothing there told a visitor, or a new generation growing up in North Plymouth, that Vanzetti lived here, and that he and Vincenzo Brini and others — immigrants, political radicals — stayed up late talking politics in an era when factory

Revisiting Sacco and Vanzetti opens a window on Plymouth's early 20th century history.

workers made $9 a week, Social Security had yet to be invented; the Wagner Act, which legalized collective bargaining, was still 20 years in the future and there was no law to keep owners from firing workers who talked about unions.

Unlike Suosso Lane, Cherry Street became a busy street. Number 35 would fit in any American town: a neat American farmhouse style dwelling with a brown-shingled facade and a porch in front. It's set among streets such as Cordage Terrace, where the characteristic worker housing of the early 20th century could still be found 80 years later. These low, box-like houses were home to the 2,000 workers who worked at the cordage company at its peak.

Revisiting Sacco and Vanzetti opens a window on Plymouth's early 20th century history. It's a history that has little to do with Pilgrims and has everything to do with immigration, labor history and the struggle of daily life in an industrial town.

In 1919, the year of the attempted payroll truck hold-up in Bridgewater — the crime for which Vanzetti was first tried — the 18th Amendment declaring Prohibition was ratified. The foundation of the Plymouth Honor Roll, including the names of the 625 Plymouth men who served in World War I (Vanzetti not among them), was laid on the courthouse lawn, and the town held a celebration when Plymouth's Company D came home from the war.

In 1920, the year of the South Braintree payroll robbery and murders and Sacco and Vanzetti's subsequent arrest, Prohibition went into effect, Warren G. Harding was elected President on a platform of normalcy, unemployment was high. The Massachusetts Tercentenary Commission announced that Plymouth harbor would be made over for the celebration of the 300th year of the Pilgrim landing. The town's attention — the old town, the Pilgrims' town — was on the tercentenary, but what would that event have meant to the factory workers and their families in North Plymouth? North Plymouth was another place; another country. In the summer of 1921, while Sacco and Vanzetti sweated out their trial in a Dedham courthouse, Plymouth Rock was placed on a new foundation, and re-enactments of the famous landing took place on a daily basis.

In an *OCM* story written in 1992, a Cherry Street resident is quoted on growing up in North Plymouth. "We lived in a ghetto and never knew it," said Mary Cash. "We weren't poor. There wasn't crime. But it was a Catholic, Italian-Portuguese ghetto. We were isolated. We had everything we needed and there was no reason to go to Plymouth or anywhere else. Almost everyone worked at the cordage company. We had our own stores and a movie theater and schools."

Retired postal worker Bob Viella grew up on Suosso Lane. He said his mother, Margaret Christofori Viella, used to clean Vanzetti's room as a young girl. His mother's older sister, Esther Christofori, was one of the many local residents who testified in Vanzetti's defense at his Plymouth trial. Still, he does not recall much talk about the famous case or the infamous anarchist. "My mother mentioned it once in a while," he recalled in an interview at the end of the century. "Reading between the lines, when they talked about it they thought he was not guilty for what he was tried, that both [Sacco and Vanzetti] were scapegoats." Then he made the salient point about the case's place in local memory. "The man you want to talk to," Viella observed, "was my father."

But his father, Antonio Viella, who would have been in his 90s, had died. The generation that shared North Plymouth with Vanzetti was mostly gone. Bob Viella said his father knew all about the case and believed the government's prosecution of Sacco and Vanzetti reflected the anti-Italian prejudice of the time. "Even when I was in high school, they said, 'stay in North Plymouth,'" Viella recalled. "Now I live in Chiltonville. You can drive around here now and see all the Italians who live in Chiltonville."

As a very young child, Alba Thompson — a former town selectman and Air Force officer — heard her father talk about the trial and got the impression that the grownups felt there were serious questions about the government's case. "You would hear things as a child, lighting the candles or pouring the wine," she says. "They weren't at all sure that the facts of the case were being honestly distributed. Also, it was the 20s. It was the Red Scare. Anybody with an immigrant name was suspect..." But while her father was an Italian immigrant, the family lived near downtown in Mill Village, not in North Plymouth, and Vanzetti was not really regarded by her neighborhood as a Plymouth man. She remembered hearing talk of the case afterwards. "People talked about it, but not with the kind of passion you might think there was." Their energy, Thompson recalled, went to other demands. "Everyone was working so hard, so

Eighty years later Plymouth still kept a low profile on one of the biggest stories of the 20th century.

intent on Americanization and doing it successfully. They hardly had time to think about things like Sacco and Vanzetti."

For immigrant families trying to assimilate into American society, radicals like Sacco and Vanzetti — regardless of the justice of the case against them — were hardly good role models. Vanzetti and his anarchist comrades did not want to Americanize; they wanted to change America.

In the early 1920s, when bizarrely detailed racial theories were still influential, Italian immigrants were seen by Yankee New Englanders as belonging to a different "racial" group. The prejudice against immigrants endured long after the racial theories were discredited. As late as World War II, when thousands of Americans of Italian descent were fighting for their country, the families they left at home faced wartime restrictions. In 1942 about 600,000 Italians were labeled "enemy aliens" and required to register at post offices; their travel was restricted to five miles from home. The father of baseball hero Joe DiMaggio was one of these "enemy aliens"; as a result he couldn't visit the family restaurant at Fisherman's Wharf in San Francisco.

As assimilation progressed, prejudice against immigrants from southern and eastern Europe faded, but Americans were slower to recognize the injustices of the Sacco and Vanzetti case. In 1947, 20 years after the executions, Eleanor Roosevelt and Albert Einstein offered Massachusetts a bas-relief plaque of Sacco and Vanzetti, but the offer was rejected by the state's governor. Official opinion on Sacco and Vanzetti shifted slowly. On Aug. 23, 1977, Gov. Michael Dukakis proclaimed "Nicola Sacco and Bartolomeo Vanzetti Day," but even this proclamation was narrowly framed to avoid offending the institutions that had condemned them and the individuals who still believed in their guilt.

Leaving aside the question of guilt or innocence, the proclamation stated that "the atmosphere of their trial and appeals was permeated by prejudice against foreigners and hostility toward unorthodox political views" and questioned the trial's impartiality. The point of proclaiming a day for the defendants of that trial (without exonerating them) was that "simple decency and compassion ...require that the fate of Nicola Sacco and Bartolomeo Vanzetti be pondered by all who cherish tolerance, justice and human understanding." Dukakis also proclaimed that "any stigma and disgrace should forever be removed" from their names.

Eighty years later Plymouth still kept a low profile on one of the biggest stories of the 20th century. More than a criminal trial, the case became an international story because of what it said about life in the newly industrialized world. Sacco and Vanzetti "revealed the whole anatomy of American life with all its classes, professions, and points of view and all

Nobody was closer to Vanzetti than the Brini family of Suosso Lane.

their relations," literary lion Edmund Wilson pointed out, "and it raised almost every fundamental question of our political and social system."

It also became an international cause because of the personality of Bartolomeo Vanzetti.

Nobody was closer to Vanzetti than the Brini family of Suosso Lane. Beltrando Brini, born in 1907, was the star defense witness at Vanzetti's Plymouth trial. His family took in boarders, and since his father, Vincenzo, also was an anarchist the two men became friends. In a 1987 interview with historian Paul Avrich, Beltrando Brini recalled his childhood in North Plymouth, "the Italian and Portuguese quarter of Plymouth, where the Cordage was located. The Italians were despised by the Yankees," he told Avrich, "who treated them as second-rate citizens, as the Negroes were treated in the South." Young Beltrando had a close relationship with Vanzetti, who lived in his house from 1913 until 1917, and who regarded the boy as his "spiritual son." Brini has warm memories of Vanzetti as a

THE BOSTON GLOBE VIA MERLIN-NET.COM
Vanzetti in handcuffs on the courthouse steps.

supportive, parental figure: "[He] made me feel proud of myself, something my father never did." Vanzetti encouraged him in his efforts to play the violin, he took an interest in everything the boy did. He "was like a father to me," Brini said.

"There were no guns in our house," Brini also recalled. He never saw Vanzetti with a gun; nor did Vanzetti have any interest in money. "I cannot even conceive of his doing anything violent," Brini states. Beltrando not only told his tale in the Plymouth courtroom. He told it to the governor; he told it to Upton Sinclair and to Dos Passos, major novelists of

the time who were trying to bring documentary rigor into their work, and to the philanthropist nephew of Henry James, Edward Holton James. Brini believes that Vanzetti's philosophical absolutism — "he believed in the perfectibility of human nature" — was "his blind spot," but 70 years later he remained true to his boyhood experience. "He was my ideal," he told Avrich. "For some boys it was Ty Cobb, but for me it was Bartolomeo Vanzetti."

Vanzetti didn't drink, smoke or play cards, Lefevre Brini Wager, Beltrando's older sister, recalled in her interview with Avrich in 1987. "He was a studious man. At home he liked to sit and read. But he also loved the outdoors... We went with him to gather mayflowers and violets, blackberries and red berries on Castle Hill, or walked with him on the beach or along the railroad tracks picking up pieces of coal." Faye Wager tells a tale of Vanzetti's nursing a sick kitten back to health. "There was not a bit of meanness in him. I never saw him angry." She tells the incident (recreated in Sinclair's novel, *Boston*) of his giving away his boots to a family man he worked with who didn't have boots of his own. The family was "stupefied" by Vanzetti's arrest, she recalled. "He helped people, not hurt them. Never! Besides, he was in Plymouth. We knew he didn't do it."

Before Vanzetti's first trial, the Brinis visited him every day in the Plymouth jail, bringing flowers, cookies, newspapers, books. Both of the Brini children point out that the other witnesses to Vanzetti's whereabouts were not anarchists. Good Catholics, they were a little embarrassed at being associated with the atheist Vanzetti.

A few years before the century's end, Plymouth reference librarian Lee Regan recalled someone from the Italian embassy contacted the Plymouth library in an effort to find out where Vanzetti had lived. There was nothing to do in Plymouth to honor his memory, she discovered, almost nowhere to go. The visitors just wanted to see the places where Vanzetti had lived, Regan said. They would see that Plymouth, a town that honors its forbears, had forgotten the man whom the world regards as a martyr to prejudice and injustice in the land of the free.

For the native-born, English-speaking majority, the anarchist Italian immigrant was never really part of the real town — never part of "us." But Plymouth was clearly part of Vanzetti. He settled in Plymouth in 1913, boarding with the Brinis, and stayed there for four years, the longest period of time he'd spent in one place since coming to America. In 1917 he heeded the advice of the man he called "our master," the anarchist writer and orator Luigi Galleani, and went to Mexico to avoid the draft. There he lived cooperatively with a group of other Italian anarchists (including Sacco), but Mexico did not hold them long. Vanzetti spent some time in the Midwest before drifting back to Plymouth in 1919; he had been away for a year and a half. The Brinis no longer had room for him, so he boarded with Mrs. Mary Fortini on Cherry Street, bought a cart from an Italian immigrant returning to Italy and began to sell fish for a living. He liked working outdoors.

When the immigrant laborer had first arrived in Plymouth in 1913, he got a job as a gardener on the Stone estate at Rocky Point for nearly a year. He then joined Vincenzo Brini at the Plymouth Cordage Co. in the spring of 1914. He loaded coils of rope onto freight cars. When World War I began later that year and orders for rope increased, the company put Vanzetti to work indoors, though by

some twist of ropework logic paid him less. As a teenager Vanzetti had become seriously ill through overwork and he believed that working indoors was bad for his health. He quit the Cordage in January of 1915 and got work as a "pick and shovel" man, first on a breakwater near Plymouth Rock in the employ of the state of Massachusetts and then helping to build a school for the town in the vicinity of the railroad depot. He worked shoveling snow off the tracks for the railroad. He shoveled snow for the town. He cut ice in the winter. He worked on another breakwater.

A "Vanzetti Trail" in Plymouth would include the Stone estate, Plymouth harbor, the railroad tracks from the old Plymouth depot (Citizens Bank at the end of the century) which Vanzetti walked with the Brini children, High Cliff and Castle Hill, and all the old streets of North Plymouth where he pushed his cart selling fish. The trail would make a major stop at the Plymouth Cordage Co. It would stop on Suosso Lane, where Vanzetti stayed up late reading and helped in the garden behind the Brinis' house. It would pause at the site of the Amerigo Vespucci club, which Vanzetti avoided because he did not play cards, but where a fundraising meeting was held for him in August 1927. It would stop at Cordage's Loring Library, to which he escorted the Brini children. He taught them Italian (they spoke a dialect at home), and the children taught him English. The trail would also touch at Jesse's boatyard, where a fisherman painting his boat shot the breeze with Vanzetti on the date the state said he was taking part in a payroll robbery and murder in South Braintree.

The trail would end at the Plymouth courthouse, and the jail.

MEANWHILE ...1920-1930

◆ On Jan. 16, 1920, the 18th Amendment banning the production of alcoholic beverages became the law of the land.

◆ In 1920 Warren Harding was elected president, defeating the Democratic nominee, James M. Cox; Harding pledged to return the country to "normalcy."

◆ Books published in 1920 included *Main Street* by Sinclair Lewis and *This Side of Paradise* by F. Scott Fitzgerald.

◆ 1920: Women granted the right to vote with the ratification of the 19th Amendment.

◆ The 1920 Rose Bowl football game was won by Harvard University, which edged out Oregon, 7-6.

◆ Former President Woodrow Wilson was awarded the 1920 Nobel Peace Prize for his efforts to form a League of Nations. The Senate, however, had already rejected the treaty.

◆ In 1920, there were only 5,000 radio receivers in the country. By 1924 there were 2.5 million.

◆ In the early 1920s, knee-length skirts for women became the standard fashion.

◆ In 1923, President Harding died in office of natural causes and Vice President Calvin Coolidge, former governor of Massachusetts, became president.

Forefathers' Day, 1920

BY JOHN CHAFFEE

The 300th anniversary of the Pilgrim landing was marked in Plymouth by a yearlong series of events highlighted by Forefathers' Day in December 1920 and a tercentenary pageant on the waterfront the following summer.

The overriding theme of the festivities was to commemorate the event that marked the beginning of a small community many considered to be the embryo of a new nation, founded on rudimentary principles of freedom and democracy.

"In appearance weak and persecuted they came, rejected, despised, an insignificant band, in reality strong and independent, a mighty host, of whom the world was not worthy, destined to free mankind," said Massachusetts Gov. Calvin Coolidge, speaking of the Pilgrim settlers on Dec. 21, 1920.

Two years after a world war and during a period of widespread fear of anarchists and communists, the people of Plymouth and to a lesser extent the whole nation reveled in an opportunity to celebrate on that day their origins and to rededicate themselves to a few simple Pilgrim objectives: freedom to worship as they wished and to organize a community on their own terms.

"What an increase, material and spiritual, 300 years has brought that little company is known to all the earth," Coolidge said in his 1920 Forefathers' Day address. "No like body ever cast so great an

FROM *CAPE COD AND ALL THE PILGRIM LAND*

Forefathers' Day, 1920, the day after the Billings canopy over Plymouth Rock had been demolished and the Rock set aside until the completion of a new canopy. Standing in front of the newly exposed Rock are U.S. Sen. Henry Cabot Lodge, at right, with Gov. Calvin Coolidge, left, with his wife, Grace Coolidge, in the middle.

influence on human history," he added.

It was a motif that set the tone and resounded throughout the 300th anniversary festivities.

In 1920, Coolidge spoke at the first of two Forefathers' Day gatherings in the Old Colony Theater adjacent to Town Brook in downtown Plymouth. The site had been chosen because at the time it was the largest meeting hall in town, seating nearly 900 people. The morning exercises featured Coolidge — who at the time was not only the governor but also vice president-elect – and Henry Cabot Lodge, the state's 70-year-old senior U.S. senator who was fresh off his victory in the Senate over President Wilson's proposed League of Nations treaty.

The *Boston Evening Transcript* described the Forefathers' Day scene in Plymouth: "For the occasion Plymouth was en fete. From the country round-about a large number of people had assembled and the streets were decorated for the parade which preceded the exercises in the theater."

The morning exercises were sponsored by the Massachusetts Tercentenary Commission and focused on the need for the nation to maintain the Pilgrim her-

"A pleasing touch was the women ushers in Pilgrim garb."

itage and spirit. Dignitaries from throughout the state and nation, most having arrived at the Plymouth depot by special train, were in attendance. The afternoon's exercises, sponsored by the town's tercentenary commission, were for the people of Plymouth and were more broadly focused on the meaning of the Pilgrim landing to a diverse population. Needless to say, because of the celebrities involved, only the morning exercises garnered national press coverage.

The one celebrity who spoke at both exercises was LeBaron Russell Briggs, Harvard University's Boylston Professor of Rhetoric and Oratory, dean of the faculty of arts and sciences, and president of Radcliffe College. For the occasion, he had composed an anniversary poem, "1620-1920," which, according to the *Old Colony Memorial*, he recited with "much feeling."

In a plea for a return to old Pilgrim values, the poem concluded:

The Pilgrim's faith, the Pilgrim's courage grant us;
Still shines the truth that for the Pilgrim shone.
We are his seed; nor life nor death shall daunt us.
The port is Freedom! Pilgrim heart, sail on!

The featured speaker in the morning was Sen. Lodge who asserted that the Pilgrims laid "the cornerstone of the foundations upon which the great fabric of the United States has been built up." In an hour-long oration, Lodge cited the Mayflower Compact as the essential element in the creation of an orderly society. In signing the compact, "Each and every man of them sacrificed a part of his own liberty that all might be free," he said of the Pilgrims.

"They had a very strong and active sense of public duty," Lodge said, and added: "It is possible that by their example they can on this point teach us something," an obvious reference not only to the Boston police strike the year before but also to outbreaks of lawlessness throughout the world. He turned to Coolidge, who was on the stage nearby, sitting in a historic chair once used by Gov. William Bradford of the Pilgrim colony. "They knew that there could be no organized society unless laws made by the state were obeyed by all, and this mighty principle they planted definitely in the soil of their new country where it has found its latest champion in the successor of Bradford and Winslow, the present governor of Massachusetts," Lodge said.

As described by the *Evening Transcript*, "The little theater, with its tawdry decorations, was ill-suited to the solemnity and dignity of such an occasion, and the draughty stage was evidently uncomfortable for those who had to sit there. Indeed, Sen. Lodge crouched in his overcoat until he had to speak and wore his muffler throughout his oration, while Dean Briggs used his coat for a lap robe. Notwithstanding the incongruity of such a setting, it was the best Plymouth had to offer, and the eminence of the speakers and the distinguished guests drew attention from the surroundings."

The reporter then conceded: "A pleasing touch was the women ushers in Pilgrim garb."

The theatrical highlight of the morning program came as Lodge was citing Daniel Webster's address 100 years earlier on the 200th anniversary of Forefathers' Day. In a much-quoted vision of American continental expansion, Webster in his bicentennial address had prophesized that "from those who shall stand here a hundred years hence the voice of acclamation and gratitude commencing on the Rock of

Massachusetts Gov. Calvin Coolidge as he appeared in an engraving seated on the historic Bradford Chair at the Old Colony Theater, Forefathers' Day 1920.

Plymouth shall be transmitted through millions of sons of the Pilgrims till it lose itself in the murmurs of the Pacific seas."

According to the *OCM*, at the moment Lodge quoted this passage from Webster's address, a telephone bell on the stage rang and Lodge paused. The local manager of the telephone company, Willard Parsons, came on stage, picked up the phone and asked, "Is this the governor of California? Just a moment. I introduce to you Governor Coolidge of Massachusetts."

The candlestick telephone was then passed to the governor who, as the *OCM* put it, "took up the conversation which was fulfilling the prophetic utterances of Webster a century previous, saying, 'Governor Stephens, yes this is Governor Coolidge of Massachusetts. Yes, I am seated in the chair of Governor Bradford at Plymouth. I wish to say that Massachusetts and Plymouth Rock greet California and the Golden Gate, and send the voice which is to be lost in the waves and roar of the Pacific. I'll do so. Goodbye.'"

Lodge then had the audacity to claim that, "It was the merest accident that I read that sentence," just before the telephone rang. It turned out that at the time of the call Gov. Stephens was away on a hunting trip and Coolidge had spoken to his secretary.

The *OCM* reported that "many visitors came by automobile and early trains" to witness the morning exercises. "The business buildings in the center of the town were decorated with the American flags and bunting of the National colors," the paper said, and added: "Private homes also displayed the colors."

School children were dismissed early so they could go to the railroad depot and see the official party arrive. "They did not march but someone

there was arranging them in lines and they had their flags and cheered just as if they were carrying out an official part of the proceedings," the *OCM* said.

"The park and the space before the station were filled with spectators and a line of trolley cars was drawn up on North Park Avenue for the use of the commission and guests," the paper reported. "It was a little after 11 a.m. when the special train of four cars rolled in and the visitors alighted."

I wish to say that Massachusetts and Plymouth Rock greet California and the Golden Gate.

According to the local newspaper's account, Sheriff Earl P. Blake "met them in full uniform and escorted Mrs. Calvin Coolidge to a waiting automobile" before returning for Gov. Coolidge, Sen. Lodge and the others.

Gov. Coolidge was reported to have boarded a "one-man trolley car" and rode away toward the theater. "Others took the trolley cars, but the majority walked, in no special order, along Court and Main streets" to the theater. "There had been a throng waiting for a chance to get in there since early morning, for seats had been reserved for the guests of the commission, and after these were filled the rest were available for the public, but the number of aspirants for admission outnumbered the seating capacity of the playhouse."

After the state commission ceremonies had concluded, the visitors were taken to lunch at the state armory "and after that enjoyed themselves in

rambling about the town," the *OCM* reported. "Gov. Coolidge went unattended and did a bit of shopping in some of the stores, visited the Antiquarian House, where he expresses regret that the building was marked for probable destruction in the preparations for a new town hall, and also saw the relics of the Pilgrims in Pilgrim Hall.

"The party left late in the afternoon on its special train for Boston," the *OCM* said.

Meanwhile, back at the theater, the town's tercentenary celebration began at 2:30 p.m. The *OCM* reported that "the house was filled," presumably by many foreign-born residents who had been recruited to work in local mills. In addition to Dean Briggs, who repeated his poem spanning the years from 1620 to 1920, three speakers focused on the Pilgrim heritage for non-Pilgrims. Boston School Supt. Frank V. Thompson, for example, spoke on "For the Rights Accorded the Immigrant, What May America Justly Expect of Him?" Dr. Ashley D. Leavitt of Brookline talked about "The Day We Commemorate: Its Privileges and Responsibilities; Our Heritage." And Vittorio Orlandini of Boston discussed "The Immigrant's Share in Our Heritage – What Part May He Fairly Expect?" Unfortunately, the *OCM* failed to report the details of these speeches so no excerpts are available.

But for Plymouth residents of whatever origin, the theme of the day had been pronounced by Gov. Coolidge earlier when he said of the Pilgrims: "Measured by standards of men or their time they were the humble of the earth. Measured by later accomplishments they were the mighty."

GURNET LIGHT SINGLED OUT

After more than 150 years as twin beacons at the entrance to the Plymouth Harbor channel, one of the two lighthouses at Gurnet Point was dismantled in early 1924.

Officially known as Plymouth Light Station, the twin towers were originally constructed in 1768 by the Massachusetts Colonial government. During the American Revolution, they attracted unwanted attention from a British frigate that fired on the station in 1778.

When the twin towers accidently burned down in 1801, they were replaced by the federal government with two new lights that were rebuilt again in 1843. The 72-feet high wooden and shingled towers stood 102 feet above mean low water and on a clear night their lights were visible from more than 12 miles away.

When one of the two towers was taken down, the remaining light on the Gurnet promontory became a revolving flashing beacon of greater intensity. At the time, the *Old Colony Memorial* said in an editorial, "While no doubt the new beacon will be more effective as a warning to navigators, it will never possess to us the romance as those lights which have for so many hundreds of nights beamed from their lonely location on the Gurnet.

"We who have lived so near the 'Twin Lights' and who have watched their friendly beams for so many nights will miss them when they are gone."

PILGRIM SOCIETY COLLECTION
Gurnet Point with its twin lighthouses as seen from the end of Plymouth Long Beach.

OLD COLONY CLUB COLLECTION
The Plymouth Light Station at Gurnet Point c. 1915. Accessible by land only by way of Duxbury Beach, Gurnet Point lost one of its two lighthouses in 1924.

Memorial Hall and Hedge House

In 1919, following the death of Mrs. Lydia Hedge Lothrop, the Court Street house in which she had lived was sold to the town for $20,000 so a war memorial auditorium could be built on the site.

Her house was slated to be razed, but to save the early 18th century structure the Plymouth Antiquarian Society was formed and the building was moved to a nearby location and preserved by the society as Hedge House.

In October 1919, town meeting voted both to build a municipal building on the site and to sell the house for $1 to the newly formed Antiquarian Society on the condition that the house be moved when the town was ready to build Memorial Hall. As a result, the town saved the cost of clearing the lot and insured the preservation of a historic building.

The land on which the new memorial building was to be constructed was part of a parcel granted to Francis Eaton, a Mayflower passenger, in 1623. Between then and 1809, the land was owned by a number of Plymouth residents, including one-time Plymouth Colony Gov. Edward Winslow. In 1809, William Hammett purchased the land and built a house there. In 1830 the house was bought and enlarged by Thomas Hedge. The house and land later became the property of his daughter, Lydia Hedge Lothrop whose heirs sold it to the town.

After being acquired by the Antiquarian Society, the house was open to the public on its original site

for four successive summers, 1920-23. It also was open on Forefathers' Day in December 1920, the 300th anniversary of the landing of the Pilgrims, for a succotash supper. Gov. Calvin Coolidge was among those who attended.

Meanwhile, plans to build a war memorial auditorium on the site in time for the 1921 tercentenary

PLYMOUTH PUBLIC LIBRARY CORP. COLLECTION

Hedge House when it was known as Lothrop House at its original Court Street location. The 1809 house was moved by the Antiquarian Society to make room for a Plymouth war veterans memorial building

celebrations were delayed because the original design for a combined memorial hall and new town office building proved too costly. The $300,000 appropriated by town meeting fell far short of the minimum estimated construction cost of $488,423.

So, despite the wishes of many residents, the

plans were revised and limited to the construction of a combined war memorial and municipal auditorium. For the time being, town offices would have to remain in the 1749 courthouse. On March 12, 1924, town meeting voted 513-102 to build what would officially become the Plymouth Memorial Building, but to become more popularly known throughout town as "Memorial Hall."

However, before construction could begin, the Antiquarian Society had to move the Lothrop House. In April 1924, a month after the town meeting vote, the society bought a lot of land adjoining the house for $3,000 and made arrangements to move the house. For another $3,000, a new cellar and foundation was built and teams of horses moved the house in sections more than 400 feet and turned it completely around to face the harbor.

Soon thereafter, construction of the town's memorial building began on the former house site. On Nov. 14, 1924, the *Old Colony Memorial* reported contractors were taking advantage of favorable weather to rush completion of the building: "The foundations are entirely placed up to the portion of the building where the stage is to be located, and on the front portions, the brick facing has been started."

And on a cold December Sunday, Forefathers' Day and 100 years from the day Pilgrim Hall had been dedicated, the cornerstone of the new memorial building was laid.

The Plymouth Memorial Building or Memorial Hall, which was built during the 1920s to honor Plymouth war veterans.

There was a parade that stopped at Plymouth Rock for the firing of three volleys and music by the Pilgrim Band. Veterans from the Civil War, Spanish-American War and World War I participated. In exercises at the armory diagonally across Court Street from the memorial building site, Selectman Chairman William T. Eldridge gave a short address, a prayer was offered by the pastor of the First Church, Unitarian, there was community singing and the benediction was pronounced by the pastor of St. Peter's, the church directly across the street from the new memorial building.

The remaining exercises were held on the building site where George L. Gooding, secretary of the building committee, laid the cornerstone. Enclosed in the cornerstone was a copper box containing a variety of articles pertaining to town affairs, including a large bronze town seal, three volumes of town records, a copy of the first issue of the OCM and a history of the 1921 tercentenary celebration of the Pilgrim landing.

In 1925 the town purchased from the Roman Catholic Archbishop of Boston a strip of land 24 feet wide running from Court Street to Water Street between the memorial building and the St. Peter's Church rectory. This became Memorial Drive, forever a one-way street from Court to Water, under the terms of the purchase.

When it was completed in 1926 the Plymouth Memorial Building included first-floor office and meeting space for veterans of three wars: Civil — Collingwood Post 76, Grand Army of the Republic (GAR); Spanish-American — Emil Pickard Post, United Spanish War Veterans; and World War I — Plymouth Post 40, American Legion. But the highlight of the building was its 1,500-seat multipurpose auditorium with room to seat 800 more on the main floor.

On Patriot's Day 1926 the building was dedicated in ceremonies the *OCM* said were attended by "several thousands." The festivities began with a concert by a 15-piece orchestra conducted by G. Herbert Clarke. Judge Harry B. Davis, chairman of the building committee, made the opening address and Selectman Chairman Eldridge responded. The junior high school chorus sang and after a series of additional speeches the program ended with the singing of the Star Spangled Banner.

That evening, a grand military ball was held in the new hall with dancing until well after midnight.

The next year, 1927, the Antiquarian Society bought a lot on Water Street at the corner of Memorial Drive from the American Woolen Co. The building on the lot, originally a factory and more recently the headquarters of the Plymouth Boys Club, was torn down and the space was used to extend the Lothrop, later Hedge House lawn to Water Street. Meanwhile the boys club moved into the red-brick former GAR building on Middle Street where it remained for the rest of the century.

At the time it was built and for the remainder of the 20th century Plymouth's Memorial Building provided the largest indoor meeting hall in southeastern Massachusetts, a favorite site for a variety of community, social and recreational activities.

BUILDERS AND SAVERS

The founders and incorporators of the Plymouth Antiquarian Society were: Helen E. Millar, president; Anne B. Craig, secretary; Susan D. Barnes, treasurer; Jane R. Burgess, Mary P. Litchfield, Alice D. Hitchcock, Mary M. Boyden and Anne Mullins. The society was incorporated on Oct. 29, 1919.

Members of the town's building committee for the erection of the Plymouth Memorial Building were: Judge Harry B. Davis, chairman; George L. Gooding, secretary; Francis C. Holmes, Carrold D. Howland, LeBaron Barker, Arthur E. Blackmer, Andrew J. Carr, William Anderson, Frank Eastwood and John H. Damon. The building opened to the public on April 19, 1926.

25

Plymouth Trolleys

BY KARIN GOLDSTEIN

A winter day, 1910. As horses strain to pull loaded carts over the snowy street, a small train with a nose plow pushes snow off the track in the middle of the street. Workers with lunch pails line up to ride the trolley that follows to the factory. Groups of giggling school children wait for the trolley to take them to school. Where is this, you might wonder, Boston? No- Plymouth! While little evidence remained at the end of the 20th century, the trolley was a familiar sight on Plymouth streets for 40 years, from 1889 to 1928.

Urban transportation systems blossomed in the 1880s as lines of horse-drawn trams, and later, trolleys, connected towns and factories. This new transport made possible the development of "street-car suburbs" in Boston. By the late 1880s, when Plymouth started thinking of a network of its own, electric-powered trains were the latest technology. Rather than investing money in an antiquated horse system, Plymouth investors decided to risk the new electrical technology. Construction of the Plymouth and Kingston electric railway began in 1889, and service from Jabez Corner in Plymouth to Cobb's Lane in Kingston began June 8, 1889. Plymouth was forward thinking in embracing the new technology. In fact, the Plymouth and Kingston line was the second electric system in Massachusetts (after Salem), and one of the earliest in the nation.

Trolley systems served commuters. An expanded transportation system meant that workers and man-

PILGRIM SOCIETY COLLECTION

Southbound, the trolley Pilgrim is about to make the turn from Main Street into Town Square and Market Street and on to the end of the line at the Pilgrim Hotel overlooking Plymouth Beach c. 1900.

agers no longer had to live within walking distance of mills. In Plymouth, workers from North Plymouth could work in the woolen mills in central Plymouth, and workers from the Town Brook area could ride the three miles to the Plymouth Cordage Co.

Commuting was not the only rationale for the trolley in Plymouth, however. Tourism played a major role in the development of trolley systems in the town. In fact, the most frequent service ran in summer. With the extension of the trolley line from

Hotel Pilgrim on Warren Avenue in 1891, summer visitors could take the train to Plymouth, pick up the trolley at the railroad station, and ride to the hotel. Starting in 1899, summer visitors could change at Hotel Pilgrim to the Plymouth and Sandwich Street Railway and ride to the Manomet post office.

In 1899, several small local railway lines were reorganized into the Brockton and Plymouth Street Railway, with service between the two centers. The new railway was run by the Stone and Webster firm of Boston (Charles Stone liked Plymouth so much that he purchased an estate off Rocky Hill Road). One could travel from Hotel Pilgrim in Chiltonville through Plymouth via Market Street, up Court Street to North Plymouth and into Kingston, along Pembroke Street to Pembroke, then through Hanson and Whitman. The route was similar to what later became Route 27.

Service to Brockton took about two hours and 10 minutes with trains every half hour to an hour, depending on the season. Fare cost 5 cents per zone, with service to Brockton priced at 30 cents one way, 50 cents round trip. Hotel Pilgrim to the Kingston line was one zone. Fares rose in 1908 to 10 cents per zone, but school children rode for half-fare.

The railway consisted of about 25 miles of single track with 19 turnouts for trains to wait for oncoming trolley cars to pass. Electric power came from overhead feeder cable, provided by a generator plant built by Stone and Webster on Water Street near Plymouth Rock. The electric generators were powered by coal-fired boilers. Vincent (Jelly) Baietti remembered his father listening to the wires at the turnout at Knapp Terrace in North Plymouth to tell when the next trolley was coming.

In 1901 the Brockton and Plymouth owned a variety of rolling stock: nine closed cars, 16 open cars, two service cars and three snow plows. The closed cars were painted green with gold lettering, and the open cars were yellow. Open cars were used in summer, and local children looked forward to their arrival. Rolling stock was stored in three car

The trolley made it easier for Plymouth residents to travel, particularly if they didn't own a car or horse and wagon.

barns. The largest, Car Barn #1, was located on the west side of Sandwich Street, just south of Fremont Street. In addition to carrying passengers, the Brockton and Plymouth started a freight express line in 1907, which carried mail as well as packages.

The trolley made it easier for Plymouth residents to travel, particularly if they didn't own a car or horse and wagon. Harold Boyer remembered taking the trolley to band rehearsal at the Plymouth Cordage Co., as he wasn't old enough to drive. Jean Whiting Patenaude recalled her family taking the trolley to visit her uncle in North Plymouth, as they didn't have a car. People also took the trolley for shopping expeditions. Jeanette Morton Holmes took the trolley to Brockton with her mother to pick out her spring coat. Decades later she had fond memories of that coat—"black and white check with a silk lining."

One of the favorite trolley destinations was Mayflower Grove, a park owned by the railway in the Bryantville section of Pembroke. Jeanette

Holmes remembered the special trip to Mayflower Grove with her family at the end of summer. Friends who rode the trolley gave them coupons for rides from strip tickets. The coupons were good for rides, like the tunnel slide, which children rode on an oilcloth cushion, or for the novelty concession. Harold Boyer went once or twice a summer with his family. An avid music fan, he remembered the stage shows and dance bands, including the Ellsmore-Nash Band, which played jazz there in the early 1920s. Occasionally Boyer even performed at Mayflower Grove, filling in for the drummer in Joe Pioppi's Orchestra, playing Irving Berlin tunes.

The trolley was profitable until about 1916, when several factors contributed to its demise over the next dozen years. Escalating labor costs due to World War I were a major factor, as was the increasing number of cars on the road. In 1919 the Brockton and Plymouth went into receivership. It was eventually reorganized in 1922 as the Plymouth and Brockton Street Railway. The railway now purchased its power — the power generating plant had been sold in 1920, and razed for the tercentenary reconstruction project.

Changes in technology spelled the end for the trolley. In 1923 the railway purchased its first bus. Trolleys faced competition from cars and unlicensed automobile jitneys that carried commuters and tourists. By 1925, all service west of Kingston ended, including service to Mayflower Grove. The last trolley ran on June 27, 1928. Some of the cars were sold, others abandoned. The track was finally removed in the 1930s. At the end of the century, all that remained of Plymouth's 40 years of trolley service was part of Car Barn #1.

26

Trial of the Century:

CRIMES, PROSECUTION AND DEFENSE

BY ROBERT KNOX

The years immediately after World War I — 1919 and 1920 — were years of strikes, unemployment, inflation — and armed robberies. Factory workers were paid in cash, not by check or electronic transfer to a bank account. Payroll money was carried from bank to factory by hand and so drew the attention of criminals.

At 7:40 on the morning of Dec. 24, 1919, three men got out of a car on Broad Street in Bridgewater and began shooting at an approaching payroll truck. One of them, a man with a clipped moustache who looked Italian (or like "a Greek," one witness said; or "a Pole," another thought), fired a shotgun at the payroll car and the three men inside. The driver turned sharply to the side of the road, using an oncoming streetcar as a shield, and the bandits abruptly gave up the attempt and drove off. Five months later, Bartolomeo Vanzetti was charged with taking part in the crime.

A successful payroll holdup took place in South Braintree on April 15, 1920. The robbery of the Slater and Morrill shoe factory payroll, in which two men were killed, is the crime for which both Nicola Sacco and Vanzetti were charged, found guilty and ultimately executed. Witnesses testified to seeing two unknown men loitering around their black car in South Braintree Square on the day of the holdup, and even though paymaster Frederick Parmenter commented that there were some "strange people" hanging around that day, he kept to the usual routine. Parmenter and guard Alessandro Berardelli were on foot carrying the $15,776 payroll around

> *Sacco and Vanzetti were radicals, they were foreigners and they were draft dodgers.*

three o'clock that afternoon when they were attacked by two men on Pearl Street, underneath the walls of the shoe factories that lined both sides of Pearl Street in South Braintree Square. The men had waited by a metal fence in front of the Rice and Hutchins factory until the paymaster and his guard passed them, and then began shooting. Witnesses looked up after the first shots. According to those with the best view, a gunman leaned over Berardelli's crouching body after he had already been shot and fired down again at point blank range. Parmenter was shot twice; he died from his wounds the next day. The two bandits escaped with three confederates (or two) in a car that had been waiting for them up the street. Another of the bandits fired a shot at Berardelli's prone form from the car, and they also fired in the direction of passersby as the getaway car raced through the narrow streets of South Braintree.

The connection between the Bridgewater attempted holdup and the Braintree robbery-murder existed at first only in the mind of Bridgewater Police Chief Michael Stewart. After two alien anarchists, Sacco and Vanzetti, had been taken into custody, the state of Massachusetts would buy Stewart's theory, rejecting the view of its own top cop that the Slater and Morrill robbery-murder had been carried out by professional criminals. The route from the Braintree crime to Vanzetti and Nicola Sacco is a circuitous one, hanging on Stewart's suspicion that radicals were responsible for both crimes.

The great majority of eyewitnesses to the two crimes failed to identify Sacco and Vanzetti as participants, but the prosecution got a few tentative identifications and worked hard in the following months to turn them into positive identifications.

Vanzetti was charged with the Bridgewater robbery attempt, partly it seems because of his moustache, and both he and Sacco were charged with the Braintree robbery and murders. Chief Stewart and Norfolk County District Attorney Frederick Katzmann told the press that authorities had found a "gang of anarchists" they had been seeking, and newspapers reported the prosecutors were satisfied "beyond any doubt" that Sacco and Vanzetti had been involved in both crimes. An angry mob surrounded the Brockton courthouse for their arraignment a few days later.

Sacco and Vanzetti were radicals, they were foreigners and they were draft dodgers. "They were exactly the kind of people," historian Arthur Schlesinger said, "that 100 percent Americans felt might be guilty of anything."

But the state's senior police officer, Capt. William Proctor, was not satisfied they had the right men. The suspects' fingerprints failed to match those on the car, and Proctor thought the South Braintree holdup was a professional job. The prosecution replaced him with someone who thought the defendants were guilty — Bridgewater's Chief Stewart. Katzmann took charge of prosecuting both cases.

The first trial in what would become an internationally famous case took place in Plymouth's 1820 courthouse. Vanzetti's trial for allegedly participating in the Bridgewater robbery attempt began on June 23, 1920. The case against him included several eyewitness identifications (as memories improved between initial investigation and courtroom testimony), a shotgun shell found in his pocket when he was arrested, which the state argued

The realization that their word counted for so little was a humiliation for the North Plymouth witnesses.

matched one found at the scene of the crime and the evidence that presiding judge Webster Thayer called "consciousness of guilt." Vanzetti's defense committee hired two well-known local lawyers, J.P. Vahey and J.M. Graham, which his advisers believed would help his case. His defense relied on witnesses who placed Vanzetti in Plymouth on the day of the crime, December 24, 1919.

PILGRIM SOCIETY COLLECTION

The Plymouth Courthouse, where Vanzetti was first tried.

On Christmas Eve in those days, Italians ate eels, regardless of the price. "To eat eels and fish on Christmas Eve, is with the Italian people an ancient tradition, beside, we are very fond of such food," Vanzetti wrote later in a pamphlet entitled *Background of the Plymouth Trial.* He promised to deliver eels to his customers on Christmas Eve: "This had never happened before in the history of the Plymouth colony."

Vanzetti was out early that morning selling fish, assisted by 13-year-old Beltrando Brini. Many Plymoutheans remembered seeing him that day. The names of the defense witnesses who testified in the Plymouth courthouse have a familiar ring, even for those who came to Plymouth much later: Mary Fortini (his Cherry Street landlady), Carol Balboni, John DiCarlo, Rosa Balboni (of South Cherry Street), Enrico Bastoni (the Cherry Street baker), Therese Malaguti (of Cherry Street), Adeladi Bongiovanni, Margherita Fiocchi, Emma Borsari, Esther Christofori (of Suosso Lane, a high school student), and Vincent Longhi of Cherry Street, who testified in English. Beltrando Brini and his mother testified, as did police officer Joseph Schilling. But the inference the jury took from this array of local testimony, and which the prosecution encouraged, was: all the Italians stick together. Katzmann attacked the defense testimony by arguing it was coached. Young Beltrando had learned his story well, he told the witness; how many times had he practiced it?

The realization that their word counted for so little was a humiliation for the North Plymouth witnesses. "That's been the terrible thing for me," Brini told historian Francis Russell years later, recalling his testimony at the Plymouth trial. "I was with him all that morning long, and I couldn't make them believe me."

Vanzetti did not testify in his own behalf because, he claimed, his lawyers convinced him his radical political beliefs would work against him with an "uneducated, conservative" jury. But an unwillingness to take the stand also counts against a defendant, and this decision probably hurt him even more.

The jury reached its verdict quickly, with little discussion and no disagreement. Its native-born American members identified with the prosecution, not with the Italian immigrant defendant and witnesses. Judge Thayer imposed an unusually harsh sentence — 12 to 15 years, for assault with intent to rob and murder. The absence of any similar sentence from that period for the charge of which Vanzetti was convicted suggests the desire to make an example of him. Thayer seemed to be saying this is how crime by political radicals in Massachusetts would be treated.

The case's political dimension was clearly in the air, even though both sides kept it, at least explicitly, out of their courtroom presentations. The *OCM* reported that "two carloads of officers, well armed" attended Vanzetti's sentencing at Plymouth's federalist courthouse, "ready for trouble." According to the paper, people who attended the session were scrutinized and some questioned. "Nearly 100 spectators

gathered in the courtroom, about two-thirds of these apparently of Italian ancestry and a few women being among the group," the paper reported. It's hard to miss the "us and them" tone in this reporting, a tone that grows stronger in the paper's stories on the executions seven years later. Off the bench, Judge Thayer told people that he was not going to be intimidated by the radicals; on the contrary, the presence of well-armed police at the sentencing and the scrutinizing and questioning of spectators suggests that intimidation came from the other direction.

While local authorities may have been wary of trouble at the Plymouth courthouse, Vanzetti's plight did not become a national and international cause until labor union lawyer Sam Moore took over the defense for the Braintree robbery and murder trial. A Californian, Moore had defended International Workers of the World organizers (or "Wobblies," the most radical of America's unions) on the West Coast. His contacts with the labor movement brought publicity, expressions of support and money to the defense. A letter from Moore could mean a rally in Chicago, a donation from a local in the Midwest or the Far West. But Moore's leftist politics and his longhaired Western informality — he could be seen taking his jacket off in public — exacerbated Judge Thayer's distaste for the defendants. Moore began the trial in Dedham courthouse by declaring the defendants could not receive a fair trial in Norfolk County and infuriated the judge, who also had presided at the earlier trial in Plymouth, by objecting to prospective juror after juror.

The trial began May 31, 1921, more than a year after the crime. It was a hot summer and often sweltering inside the Dedham Courthouse.

Even those who believe the defendants (or one of them, Sacco) guilty of the Braintree murders have trouble defending the conduct of the trial. Prosecution eyewitness testimony that appeared damning was in fact weak. Thirty eyewitnesses with a good view of the South Braintree crime did not identify either Sacco or Vanzetti. Several witnesses taken by police to look at pictures of known criminals positively identified the image of a New York gangster who turned out to be inconveniently in prison. A few people who were vague about what they saw when they first spoke to investigators made positive identifications on the witness stand after they were pressured by the prosecution to do so. Of the state's four main witnesses, all had something in their background that made them vulnerable to pressure. One was wanted for bigamy in another state; one was a former prostitute; a third had a drinking problem. The fourth had a reputation for unreliability.

Fourteen witnesses to the Braintree crime took a look at Vanzetti after his arrest in Brockton; 13 said they had never seen him before. Only one, a gatetender at the Pearl Street railroad crossing named Michael Levangie, said Vanzetti was the man driving the getaway car. Levangie originally told investigators that the driver of the car was a stocky, 50-year-old clean-shaven man; by the inquest that description had metamorphosed into a man with a dark brown mustache. His North Plymouth neighbors laughed at the idea that Bart Vanzetti, who could not drive, was at the wheel of the getaway car. Katzmann theorized that the man Levangie had seen was actually sitting in the back seat and had leaned over to the front, causing the gatekeeper to think he was the driver. A number of other witnesses described the driver as a young, light-complexioned man.

Just as in his first trial, Vanzetti's defense called people from Plymouth to place him in the town on the date of the crime, April 15. Vanzetti said he had been selling fish that day; his account of the day includes a great deal of buying, complaining and shooting the breeze. That morning Vanzetti met a traveling salesman named Joseph Rosen. He brought Rosen and the cloth Rosen was trying to sell to Alfonsina Brini. Though living on Cherry Street he was still close to the Brinis, who had moved to Cherry Court. Mrs. Brini had worked at a woolen mill and knew good cloth. Vanzetti sold fish to factory worker Abgel Guidobone (spelled that way on the court records), shot the breeze with fisherman Melvin Corl, and then the two of them spoke with boatbuilder Frank Jesse.

Witnesses corroborated Vanzetti's claims, but the prosecution attacked the witnesses' ability to date these encounters precisely. Rosen confirmed his recollection of the date by citing the rooming house in Whitman where he had spent that night; the rooming house's records confirmed he had rented a room that night. Other witnesses confirmed dates and times with references to important personal events like doctor's appointments or to weekly rituals like eating fish on Friday.

Vanzetti's account of his activities on April 15 shines a light on daily life in North Plymouth in the

> **Vanzetti's defense called people from Plymouth to place him in the town on the date of the crime, April 15.**

1920s. The traveling salesman Rosen arrived by train in the morning and ate breakfast at Ventura's Restaurant on Court Street. Vanzetti brought Rosen and his cloth to Alfonsina Brini, who was at home because she had been laid off from the woolen mill. The sale must have proceeded in a leisurely manner because they heard the midday whistles at the factories blowing when they left the Brinis'. LeFavre Brini testified that Vanzetti had brought fish by earlier that morning before returning with a peddler around noon. Guidobone, a rug-weaver who lived on Suosso Lane, said he bought cod from Vanzetti during the lunch hour. Corl told the court he had been painting his boat in Jesse's boatyard. He said that Vanzetti came by around two and complained to him that the fish business was so bad he was looking for another way to make a living. Frank Jesse said he remembered Vanzetti and Corl talking, but he could not say for certain on what date he had seen them.

Katzmann described Alfonsina Brini as "a stock, convenient and ready witness as well as friend." He attacked LeFavre Brini's ability to place the events she described on April 15 by questioning her ability to remember events on other dates, a stock courtroom technique. "Don't you fix March 18?" Katzmann demanded. "Doesn't that date mean anything to you — March 18, 1920." When the witness replied, "Why should it?" the prosecutor replied, "Is that your answer to me? Do you love your mother, Miss

THE BOSTON GLOBE VIA MERLIN-NET.COM

Bartolomeo Vanzetti and Nicola Sacco in the prisoner's dock at the Dedham courthouse.

Brini?" March 18 was the day her mother was taken to Jordan Hospital.

Guidobone testified he received the codfish from Vanzetti that he had ordered the day before around 12:30 p.m., fixing the date by reference to an appendicitis operation he had on April 19. When he was challenged on how he knew he had bought it that day and not one or two days before, he replied, "I buy fish on Thursday and eat it on Friday." Challenged again, he asked heatedly, "Do you think I keep fish in the house for a week?"

Melvin Corl said he heard Frank Jesse talk with Vanzetti that day about an automobile. He fixed the date by reference to his wife's birthday.

Sacco's alibi was more complicated because he had not worked at his shoe factory on April 15. He had taken a train to Boston to check on his passport at the Italian embassy. Sacco's word for what he did that day was "loafed." Various witnesses testified to seeing him or talking to him on the train to Boston or in the city's North End that day. An officer of the Italian consulate testified that Sacco had brought an

Vanzetti's account of his activities on April 15 shines a light on daily life in North Plymouth in the 1920s.

overly large photograph of his family for use on the passport; he remembered the incident well because the photo was comically oversized for the purpose.

The evidence in the prosecution's case taken most seriously today is the argument that one of the bullets taken from Berardelli's body was fired by the gun in Sacco's possession when he was arrested. Being armed when they were arrested counted

The jury found both defendants guilty of murder.

against the defendants in court, but it was hardly decisive by itself since Americans in the 1920s were no less zealous of their Second Amendment rights than Americans at the end of the century. Even Katzmann acknowledged that many Italian immigrants routinely carried firearms.

Forensics was an infant science in 1920 and ballistics barely existed. The prosecution argued that Sacco was one of two gunmen who did the killing because one of the bullets — known as bullet number III — taken from Berardelli's body could have been fired by Sacco's gun. In 1920 no one believed that a bullet could be successfully traced to a particular gun. The prosecution merely sought to show that the bullet could have been fired from the type and caliber of revolver Sacco carried. Since state police commander Proctor was not convinced this was demonstrable — though he allowed his testimony to be framed by Katzmann in a such a way to imply that he did, a prosecutorial sleight of hand that led to one of the motions for a new trial — the prosecution found a weapons expert, Charles Van Amburgh, who testified more enthusiastically for this theory. In 1961, in the course of writing *Tragedy in Dedham,* Francis Russell persuaded the state to allow new tests to be performed on Sacco's

gun. Given the advanced state of ballistics by then, two experts were able to determine that the bullet marked III — supposedly by the surgeon who removed it from Berardelli's body — was fired by Sacco's gun. All the other bullets, three from Berardelli's body and two from Parmenter's, came from the same, undiscovered gun. This evidence was enough to lead Russell and others to believe that Sacco was guilty.

However, as early as 1923 the defense (then under William G. Thompson, the Brahmin attorney who had replaced Moore) argued that the prosecution substituted the bullet III introduced in evidence for the bullet originally marked number III by the surgeon who performed the autopsy on Berardelli.

This time both defendants took the stand in their defense. To explain what they were doing in Bridgewater on the night of their arrest, Vanzetti (who testified first) related that the four anarchists were planning to collect radical literature and store it somewhere because they were afraid of persecution for their political beliefs. For the prosecution, this was open season on the defendant's politics, particularly their draft dodging. After Sacco testified, Katzmann attacked his statement that he had come to America because he wanted to live in a free country. "Did you love this country in the month of May 1917?" the prosecutor demanded. Sacco struggled to explain why he believed the war was wrong, but this was not an explanation that won points with the jury.

Sacco later told Thompson why they were armed that night: "We were at war with the government." This sounds like truth, but it was hardly an argument that would resonate with an American jury.

The jury found both defendants guilty of murder.

After the trial was over, the defense made a series of motions for appeal. Disposing of these would eventually take six years. According to Massachusetts law at that time, the trial judge himself had to review each motion before a higher court could review it. While the defendants languished in jail, the case's profile continued to grow in America and overseas. Moore called on the labor movement and its liberal upper-class sympathizers to support Sacco and Vanzetti. Socialist, Communist and labor movements took up the cause overseas. In the fall of 1921 the first mass demonstrations took place in European cities.

Vanzetti learned more of the greater American society and met more non-immigrant Americans in his first years in prison than he had in his previous 13 years in the country. In Charlestown jail (where he had been first sent to serve time for his robbery conviction in the Plymouth trial), Vanzetti read, studied English, worked on various prison jobs, received visitors and wrote letters.

In December 1923 he writes a letter to Plymouth, addressed to "My Dear Brinis," seeking to reassure them of his determination "to win" his struggle with the law. "So my dears, be of good cheer and strong heart — I love the courageous — those who know to banish the black and sorrowful thought. To know my friends and my loved ones brave — is the sweetest to my soul. Give my heart regards to all my friends and their family — to the Plymouth folks..."

The last and perhaps most important of the defense motions based on new evidence was prompted by the confession to the Braintree crime by Celestino Madeiros, a member of the notorious Joe Morelli gang of Providence, R.I. Already convicted of killing a cashier in a bank robbery in Wrentham in 1924, Madeiros said he was in the bandit car during the South Braintree holdup but refused to name the others. The prosecution argued he had nothing to lose and was merely trying to seek help for himself from the Sacco-Vanzetti

> ...in all my life I have never stolen, and I have never killed and I have never spilled blood.

defense fund. Books have been written about Madeiros and the possibility of the Morelli gang committing the crime; some historians have found the Morelli connection credible, and others have concluded there are too many holes in Madeiros's account of the crime. Madeiros would go to the electric chair for the Wrentham crime the same night that Sacco and Vanzetti were executed.

On Oct. 23, 1926, Judge Thayer rejected the Madeiros defense motion. In January 1927 William G. Thompson (the lawyer Vanzetti believed would have saved him if they had had him in court) argued before the Massachusetts Supreme Court in Boston that his clients were entitled to a new trial because of an abuse of judicial discretion in Judge Thayer's denial of the Madeiros motion. Harvard Law School Prof. Felix Frankfurter's devastating attack on Thayer's ruling on the Madeiros motion and the prosecution's case generally was published in the *Atlantic Monthly* in March, bringing doubts about the fairness of the trial to a national audience of middle-class readers. But in April 1927, with the eyes of the country and the world on its verdict, the Massachusetts Supreme Court ruled on narrow legal grounds that the state was not required to grant the motion for a new trial.

Sacco and Vanzetti were brought to the Dedham Courthouse to be sentenced on April 9; police with rifles surrounded the court. Asked if he had anything to say before being sentenced, Sacco replied that his English was not good enough to express what he wanted to say and that therefore he would not speak for long. He did however say: "I never know, never heard, even read in history anything so cruel as this court... I know the sentence will be between two classes, the oppressed class and the rich class, and there will always be collision between one and the other. We fraternize the people with the books, the literature. You persecute the people, tyrannize them and kill them. We try the education of people always. You try to put a path between us and some other nationality that hates each other. That is why I am here today on this bench, for having been of the oppressed class. Well, you are the oppressor..."

Vanzetti, as Sacco had promised he would, spoke longer. The irony of his imprisonment, that only behind bars had his native gift for language and study been given the conditions it needed to flourish, is apparent in his speech to the court. He was now articulate in a language he had struggled with in 1920.

"What I say is that I am innocent, not only of the Braintree crime, but also of the Bridgewater crime. That I am not only innocent of these two crimes, but in all my life I have never stolen, and I have never killed and I have never spilled blood.

That is what I want to say. And that is not all. Not only am I innocent of these two crimes... but I have struggled all my life, since I began to reason, to eliminate crime from the earth...

"Now I should say that I am not only innocent of all these things, not only have I never committed a real crime in my life — though some sins but not crimes — not only have I struggled all my life to eliminate crimes, the crimes that the official law and the moral law condemns, but also the crimes that the moral law and the official law sanction and sanctify — the exploitation and the oppression of the man by the man, and if there is a reason why I am here as a guilty and, if there is a reason why you in a few minutes can doom me, it is this reason and none else...

"This is what I say: I would not wish to a dog or to a snake, to the most low and misfortunate creature of the earth — I would not wish to any of them what I have had to suffer for things that I am not guilty of. I am suffering because I am a radical and indeed I am a radical; I have suffered because I am an Italian, and indeed I am an Italian; I have suffered more for my family and for my beloved than for myself; but I am so convinced to be right that you can only kill me once but if you could execute me two times, and if I could be reborn two other times, I would live again to do what I have already done.

"I have finished. Thank you."

Judge Thayer then pronounced sentence of death, while Vanzetti sought futilely to interrupt him, having remembered something he'd forgotten to say — to praise his fellow defendant Sacco.

MEANWHILE ...1920-1930

◆ More autos were built in the U.S. in 1923 than had been produced in the first 15 years of the century.

◆ Jazz, a uniquely American form of music, became both popular and respectable. The 1920s came to be known as the "jazz age."

◆ In 1924, President Coolidge won a four-year term of his own by defeating the Democratic nominee, John W. Davis.

◆ A new Ford Model T auto without a self-starter sold for $290 in 1924.

◆ Magazines first published in the 1920s included *Reader's Digest*, *Time* and *The New Yorker*.

◆ An estimated 40,000 white-robed Ku Klux Klan members held a massive rally in Washington, D.C. in 1925, marching down Pennsylvania Avenue and raising their arms in a fascist-like salute.

◆ In 1926 Henry Ford introduced the 40-hour workweek, a move that shocked other industry leaders.

◆ Popular songs during the 1920s included "April Showers," "Bye Bye Blackbird," "Makin' Whoopee," "Silver Moon" and "Button Up Your Overcoat."

◆ Airmail service between Boston and New York City began in 1926.

◆ A revolution in book selling and publishing began in 1926 with the organization of the Book-of-the-Month Club.

◆ In 1926 Edgar Bergen & dummy Charlie McCarthy debuted in vaudeville.

◆ In May 1927 Charles A. Lindbergh completed the first non-stop solo flight across the Atlantic, a feat that attracted worldwide attention.

◆ 1927: Babe Ruth set a record with a 60-home-run season. The record held for 34 years.

◆ In the 1928 presidential election, Gov. Alfred E. Smith of New York, a Catholic who favored repeal of Prohibition, was defeated by the Republican candidate, Herbert Hoover.

◆ 1928: Mickey Mouse, created by Walt Disney, made his debut in the film cartoon "Steamboat Willie."

◆ An economic boom that began in 1922 burst in 1929 when the stock market crashed and a great Depression began.

FROM POWDERHOUSE TO PORTICO: 1920-21 TERCENTENARY EVENTS

Although many years of advance planning took place behind-the-scenes, public activities and events linked to Plymouth's tercentenary lasted nearly 14 months — from early October 1920 to late November the following year. While Forefathers' Day 1920 and Plymouth Day 1921 garnered most of the public attention and newspaper headlines, a series of key events kept the 300th anniversary of the Pilgrim landing ever present in local minds. These included:

▼ *Waterfront renovations* — certainly the most visible, dramatic and lasting change to the town as a result of the tercentenary. Under the aegis of the state tercentenary commission, a large portion of the Plymouth waterfront, from the bottom of North Street to the mouth of Town Brook, was transformed from a collection of wharfs, warehouses and shops to a broad open space that was at first labeled Pageant Field and later Pilgrim Memorial State Park. No fewer than six wharfs and their adjacent buildings were torn down to make room for the grand pageant, *The Pilgrim Spirit*, which was performed a dozen times during July and August 1921.

▼ *Powderhouse memorial dedicated.* On Oct. 12, 1920, the Massachusetts Society Sons of the American Revolution dedicated a brick replica of the old powderhouse at the northwest end of Burial Hill as its contribution to the tercentenary. It was the first of many memorials to be dedicated in conjunction with the 300th anniversary of the Pilgrim landing.

▼ *Plymouth Rock moved.* In December 1920 the canopy over Plymouth Rock was demolished. To make room for construction of a new portico, the Rock was moved a few feet away by a steam-powered crane. At the same time, the bones of those Pilgrims who had died the first winter were taken from the roof of the old canopy and prepared for reburial in a sarcophagus on Cole's Hill.

▼ *Mayflower departure commemorated.* On April 15, 1921, exercises commemorating the 300th anniversary of the day the original Mayflower set sail from the Plymouth settlement for its return to England were held in the Old Colony Theater.

▼ *Harlow House opened.* The William Harlow House, built in 1677, was first opened to the public in conjunction with the tercentenary. One of the few buildings remaining that existed during the lifetime of any of those who came over on the *Mayflower*, the house was framed with oak timbers taken from the fort the Pilgrims built on Burial Hill.

▼ *Pilgrim Progress re-enacted.* As part of the tercentenary observances during the summer of 1921, there were frequent costumed reenactments of the Pilgrim procession from Plymouth Rock up Leyden Street to the fort and meetinghouse at the top of Burial Hill.

▼ *Indian village displayed at Morton Park.* During the summer of 1921, a group of Passamaquoddy Indians from Maine, under contract, were camped at Little Pond in Morton Park. Their display of Native American culture turned out to be what the *Old Colony Memorial* termed "one of the most popular attractions of the tercentenary celebration."

▼ *Massasoit unveiled.* On Sept. 5, 1921 the larger-than-life bronze statute of Massasoit, the Native American friend and ally of the Pilgrims, was unveiled on Cole's Hill. A gift of the Improved Order of Red Men and the Daughters of Pocahontas, the ceremony attracted a large crowd, many of whom also attended a sunset service on Burial Hill, a band concert at Pageant Field and a fireworks display over the harbor to mark the official end of tercentenary activities.

▼ *Pilgrim Sarcophagus dedicated.* On Sept. 8, 1921, the Pilgrim Sarcophagus, a memorial to the Mayflower Pilgrims, was dedicated on Cole's Hill. Erected by the General Society of Mayflower Descendants, the memorial holds the Pilgrim bones that were preserved for many years in the old canopy over Plymouth Rock.

▼ *New Plymouth Rock portico dedicated.* While a northeaster raged outside, the new Plymouth Rock portico was dedicated on Nov. 29, 1921, in ceremonies at the First Church. A gift of the National Society of the Colonial Dames of America, the new portico had remained unfinished while tercentenary activities took place earlier that year. However, during the summer Plymouth Rock had been restored to its proper resting place within the foundation of the new portico.

Pilgrim Tercentenary 1921

BY JOHN CHAFFEE

On Aug. 1, 1921, the president of the United States came to Plymouth to mark the tercentenary (300th anniversary) of the Pilgrim landing. For Warren Gamaliel Harding in his sixth month in office, it was a festive opportunity to promote the theme of his election campaign and administration: that the country return to "normalcy" in the wake of a war waged by Americans to make the world "safe for democracy."

For the people of Plymouth, Aug. 1 was the single-day highlight of a year devoted to paying homage to those hardy few who landed near Town Brook 300 years earlier and established a modest settlement that ultimately led to a great nation.

It was Plymouth Day in Plymouth—a day laced with ceremonies, a huge parade, a presidential speech and a waterfront pageant unlike any before or since. In his history of tercentenary events, *Old Colony Memorial* publisher Frederick Bittinger reported the weather "could not have been improved if made to order."

The theme of the day – Plymouth as America's hometown — was embodied in the baton of the parade's chief marshal, Sherman Whipple. As reported in the *Boston Evening Transcript*, "Three pieces of wood composed (the baton), one end being of wood from the Howland House, Sandwich Street, erected 1667; the center piece of elm from the Town Tree, set out in 1783 in Town Square and long used for a bulletin board, until it was blown down in a storm, Dec. 26, 1885; while the

PLYMOUTH PUBLIC LIBRARY CORP. COLLECTION

A jubilant crowd in downtown Plymouth cheers as President Harding's car turns from Main Street on to Leyden Street. Note the secret service agent in the white hat near the back of the president's car and the photographer looking down into his camera at right.

> ## It was "a striking marine panorama... with the battleships ahead and the Mayflower following."

other end was a piece of oak taken from one of the timbers of the old fort which stood on Fort (now Burial) Hill, an extension of the original fort of 1621-22. A piece of Plymouth Rock was set in one end and in the other a bit of stone from the National Monument to the Forefathers."

The evening before the president's arrival, the British cruiser *Cambrian* anchored off Saquish Beach, followed soon after by three U.S. Navy battleships: the *Delaware*, *North Dakota* and *Pennsylvania*. The ships exchanged salutes and Bittinger reported "the trio made a pretty sight at night with their lights, lying outside of and southward of the Gurnet." On land, he said, "the town was dressed in flags from end to end…"

Early the next morning the three battleships steamed south to the mouth of the Cape Cod Canal where they met the presidential yacht *Mayflower*, escorted by six destroyers. The yacht and destroyers had spent the night anchored in Buzzards Bay. After assembling into a mini-fleet, the flotilla made

A 1920 drawing from a tercentenary guidebook showing the Plymouth waterfront cleared of wharfs and buildings with Plymouth Rock under a new canopy.

its way north toward Plymouth Harbor, steaming past the Manomet Coast Guard Station and then was seen off Rocky Point. Bittinger reported it was "a striking marine panorama… with the battleships ahead and the *Mayflower* following with three of the smaller craft on each side."

The battleships dropped anchor off Gurnet Point while the *Mayflower* continued up the shipping channel to an anchorage off the end of Plymouth Long Beach. According to Bittinger, a subchaser was used to bring the presidential party ashore.

As President Harding set foot on State Pier, the local Army National Guard unit fired a 21-gun salute and thousands of spectators assembled along the waterfront cheered. The presidential party was greeted by the selectmen and members of the Plymouth Tercentenary Committee.

Before moving on to the parade, the president paused to take part in the first formal ceremony of the day — the presentation of medals for their proficiency in English to 30 New Bedford school pupils, the children of foreign-born parents and winners of a competition sponsored by the *New Bedford Standard*.

Escorted by a troop of mounted cavalry and a 125-piece Shriners band, the presidential party motored up North Street past saluting Marines and British sailors to Shirley Square, then north on Court Street to Holmes Field in North Plymouth where the parade was forming.

As described by Bittinger, the presidential party included President and Mrs. Harding, Vice President and Mrs. Calvin Coolidge, Gov. and Mrs. Channing Cox, Sen. Henry Cabot Lodge, the governor of Rhode Island, the commanders of the battleships, foreign dignitaries and various officials.

"The grand parade was perhaps the finest in every way ever seen in this part of the world," Bittinger said. "There was a tremendous crowd in town," he added, including "thousands of automobiles." The parade route was down Court and Main streets to Market and Pleasant streets to South Street, down a section of South Street to Sandwich Street, north on Sandwich Street to Water Street and past the reviewing stand at Pageant Field — the waterfront area below Leyden Street and at the base of Cole's Hill that had been cleared of wharfs, stores and warehouses to form a tercentenary stage. At the corner of Main and Leyden streets the automobiles of the presidential party, with cavalry escort, left the parade and went down Leyden Street to the reviewing stand.

The parade, in five divisions, began with marching units from the Army, Navy and Marines, followed by veterans from three conflicts – the Civil War, Spanish-American War and the recently concluded World War I. Then came the floats, first from a variety of civic, religious and fraternal organizations, followed by floats from 32 communities in Plymouth, Barnstable and Dukes counties that commemorated some early history of each town. The fifth division featured floats representing industrial Plymouth: George Mabbett & Sons Co., Standish Worsted Co., Puritan Mills, Plymouth Cordage Co., Plymouth Electric Light Co., Plymouth Gas Light Co., Deacon Brothers, Sinclair Refining Co., Armour & Co., S.S. Pierce Co., Atherton Furniture Co., Louis Knife & Son and the Modern Baking Co.

The float of George Mabbett & Sons Co., a woolen manufacturing company on the downtown waterfront, won second prize in the commercial division of the tercentenary parade.

Prize-winning floats included those of the town of Marshfield; the Portuguese Society, Sao Gabriel, Plymouth; and the Plymouth Cordage Co.

On the reviewing stand, President Harding sat on a chair once occupied by Gov. William Bradford of the Plymouth Colony – the same chair that had been used by then-Gov. Coolidge on the previous Forefathers' Day. After the parade the presidential party went to an informal lunch at the Samoset House.

That afternoon, following a band concert, the president was the featured speaker at Pageant Field ceremonies. In introducing him, Gov. Cox said, "While the Pilgrims were men of remarkable vision, we may well doubt if any of them ever dreamed that from the seed of their planting, here in Plymouth, in the humble beginnings of the colony, great commonwealths would grow and would expand into a nation of imperial proportions."

The president, too, paid tribute to the Pilgrims. At the same time, he also proved to be an articulate advocate for his partisan cause: "Just as the Pilgrim fathers had a practical mind for material things amid effective pursuit of their higher ideals, so must we with our inheritance," he said, and added: "God never intended an achievement without great effort."

President Harding then warned: "Just as these fathers drew together toward ample community authority to make the nation and still preserve the freedom of those who compose it, so must we guard against the supreme centralization of power at home

OLD COLONY CLUB COLLECTION

President Harding, Vice President Coolidge, Sen. Lodge, Gov. Cox and other dignitaries assembled on the tercentenary parade reviewing stand on the waterfront below Cole's Hill.

and the superstate to the world."

Others who spoke more briefly at the ceremonies included representatives from the Netherlands and Great Britain, Vice President Coolidge and Sen. Lodge.

After a formal dinner for the president and 250 guests at the Hotel Pilgrim, the visiting dignitaries and a crowd estimated at more than 10,000 gathered on Cole's Hill and at Pageant Field to witness a special performance of Harvard University professor George P. Baker's tercentenary pageant, *The Pilgrim Spirit*. Harding viewed the performance from the front seat of a centrally located elevated box.

The pageant, which had been performed five times in July and would be acted and sung on six

additional occasions in August, had a cast of 1,300 drawn from residents of Plymouth, Kingston, Duxbury and Marshfield. Many in the cast were descendants of the early settlers they portrayed, but many others were foreign-born newcomers to the area. In addition, there was a 300-voice chorus and a huge orchestra. Bittinger said, "Probably this pageant was the greatest event of that sort ever attempted with non-professional actors anywhere in this country." The German historian Udo Hebel called the pageant "one of the most elaborate and prestigious attempts to stage American history and use historical pageantry as a 'public ritual of communal self-discovery.'"

The pageant opened with a voice from Plymouth Rock: "I, the rock of Plymouth, speak to you, Americans." There followed a series of historical scenes involving the rock in its "primordial ooze," many of them predating the landing of the Pilgrims, including Norsemen and Capt. John Smith of the Virginia Colony. And then the Pilgrim story unfolded with an emphasis on how it formed the embryo of a great nation. Indeed, in one scene Gov. William Bradford of the Plymouth Colony was joined by George Washington and Abraham Lincoln, each of whom spoke a few lines.

The staging made elaborate use of electric lighting and on the night of Aug. 1 the battleships off Gurnet Point added a searchlight drill that Bittinger described as "an illuminated dance of the beams, which laced in with each other, whirled aloft or sprayed out like the stream of a tremendous fountain."

The pageant ended with a parade of flags, first of the allied nations in the recent Great War, followed by those of the (then) 48 states of the nation that had been founded by Pilgrims. The voice from the rock proclaims, "The path of the *Mayflower* must forever be kept free."

After the procession of allied flags, the chorus began to sing the words of a poem by a very young Robert Frost, commissioned especially for the pageant:

When landing weary from the narrow deck,
You stumbled up the rugged beach and fell,
Here still afraid of God, though safe from wreck,
You spoke a vow that was a prayer as well....

Then, linking the *Mayflower* to all those who followed:

No ship at all that under sail or steam
Have gathered races to us more and more

But, Pilgrim-manned, the Mayflower in a dream
Has been their anxious convoy to the shore...

As 48 women bearing the state flags and accompanied by Pilgrims appeared, the chorus concluded the singing of the Frost poem:

Come in a Second Coming to the West,
Coming in a Second Coming to the land
Where once you left the print of feet impressed
As deep in rock as others have in sand.
Come seeing fresh again from wind and wave.
Say for us we have held the meaning fast;
We are good keepers of the gift you gave,
Confirm us keepers of it to the last.

As the last line was sung, Pageant Field was darkened until there was light only on the *Mayflower* in the harbor. The voice from the rock concluded the pageant with words from Abraham Lincoln: "With malice toward none and charity for all it is for us to resolve that this nation under God shall have a new birth of freedom."

When the pageant ended on Aug. 1, the national,

state and colonial flags converged in front of the president's box and everyone stood while the orchestra played *The Star-Spangled Banner*.

In his final report as executive secretary of the Plymouth Tercentenary Committee, M. J. Duryea recalled the excitement of the August day the president came to town: "None of us who spent that wonderful day in Plymouth will ever forget it. Nature joined in our day of commemoration and brought, as her contribution to the program, the most perfect weather...It was a great day, a big day, a wonderful day. For years to come memory will bring to our ears the crashing music of that magnificent Shriner band and to our eyes the vision of the president, vice president, governors, foreign representatives, soldiers, sailors, beautiful floats, majestic battleships, swift and graceful destroyers, great throngs of happy people and all the other things that made Plymouth's own day of celebration one to be long remembered."

Circuit camera panoramic view of President Harding addressing the tercentenary crowd that gathered on Cole's Hill at the right and on grandstands erected on newly cleared waterfront land at the left.

29

First Grade at the Alden Street School

BY ALBA THOMPSON

In 1924, Rose, Jennie and I went off to first grade together. I walked up Lothrop Street from Mill Village, met Rose in front of her handsome family home across the street from the Episcopal Church, and we then proceeded a short distance up Court Street to the Quartz grocery store, later the dental office of Dr. Phillip Schwartz.

Just beyond the Quartz store was a dirt path skirting a damp, bumpy field. That path led to the one-room Alden Street School where dignified Miss Keene taught a classroom of children.

Jennie approached the Alden Street School from the west. Her family lived at the outermost limits of Alden Street, in a wooded area known as "Stump Town." At the time, her home was at the farthest west edge of Plymouth's development.

First grade was high adventure for most children since, at that time, there were no public kindergartens in Plymouth. Only a few fortunate children had had the benefit of the private kindergartens that welcomed those families with tuition money. As a result, first grade became a magical beginning called "school," a rich experience of new friendships, tight discipline, group cooperation and the wonder of having a desk. Mine was up against the big windows overlooking the always-wet field stretching towards Court Street. In the spring, that meadow was filled with buttercups and puddles of water.

PILGRIM SOCIETY COLLECTION

A young Helen Ward posts a letter at a downtown streetside mailbox c. 1931.

The school day began by singing:

"Good morning to you, good morning to you.
We're all in our places with sunshiny faces.
Oh, this is the way to start a new day."

A prayer and the Pledge of Allegiance followed the song.

At the front and center of what seemed like a large high-ceiling room was a tall black stove. It was round, perhaps 18 inches in diameter, with a small door in the front. A tiny mica window seemed always to be lit by the inner coal fire. It radiated a large circle of warmth, a cozy ambience for a ring of small chairs where we read on cold days.

Sometimes those chairs were draped with a pair of drying pants or underwear if some excited child had wet himself. Jennie remembered that Freddie had one of those accidents. Rose remembered that Winifred had one too. I only remembered a vague ammoniac odor and that on rainy days the chairs held a full complement of drying coats and sweaters. Damp wool smells were mixed with coal stove smells.

Jennie said Miss Keene made hot cocoa on the tall stove for us after we had walked through snowy streets in the cold, cold winter.

Behind the one-room school was an outhouse, with a girls' side and a boys' side. Each side had a long plank with three holes - no running water, of course. I recall losing a mitten down one of those odious holes, and my hero, John D., crawled underneath the outhouse to retrieve it! No wonder John remained my secret hero throughout the first grade even though he had "stayed back" and was already Peck's Bad Boy. Dire forecasts of what could happen to "bad" kids like John colored our days, and we shivered inwardly at our own danger if we became discipline problems.

By third grade, held in the Cold Spring School — a two-room schoolhouse with a second and a third grade (later the home of the Christian Science Church on Court Street, opposite Nelson Street) — John had become a hunter of small wild creatures. Miss Douglas, the third grade teacher, once had John bury his outer clothing in the earth outside the classroom after he had met up with an angry skunk. I presume that was to absorb the awful stink, but none of that bothered his classmates who had a well-concealed admiration for his daring. I am sad to relate that John lived up to his teachers' expectations of disaster. Early in his teens he had a fatal accident when he climbed an electric light pole that carried high-tension wires.

Early in our school careers we all learned how to behave. We sat in solemn rows, with hands folded on our desks, listening to our teachers. Our desks, open in the front, were always in order with books neatly stacked within, and we saved all paper work, cutting each used page into quarters whose reverse side was used again as "scratch" paper. We raised our hands and waited patiently to be called on to answer a question.

Miss MacDonald, the school nurse, came in periodically to demonstrate how to brush our teeth properly. She also inspected our heads for "nits" of lice, which could spread with high speed from one child to another. I recall one occasion when my alarmed mother found me infected and washed my hair in kerosene. I presume that was the end of the episode, but I still recall the vague shame I felt and the sharp prickling of my scalp as the kerosene

> *We learned by absorption, like receptive sponges. We were eager to please, and happy within a system that severely defined right and wrong.*

seemed to burn its way through my black hair.

We went to school "neat," with proper shoes newly purchased, always with "growing" room, just before the September opening of school. I recall that we hated those black rubbers that fit over our shoes to protect them on rainy days. We also hated our snowshoes, made of a black canvas-like material that reached up to our knees and had four buckles. The movies of the 1920s taught us that "flappers," those Clara Bow girls with pouting lips, left their snowshoes unbuckled, so we tramped stylishly as best we could, with those buckles clashing. When we could get away with it, we left our rubbers and our snowshoes hidden outside under our house porches and went joyously, if damply, unprotected to school. This was quite an act of defiance since there were never "no school" days because of inclement weather

or heavy snow. And there were no buses. However, there is no recollection of suffering, only the wonderful crunch of walking in the snow by the side of the road where the piled-up snow reached above our waists. Either it snowed more heavily in those days or we were so small it seemed to be deeper than it is today.

We learned by absorption, like receptive sponges. We were eager to please, and happy within a system that severely defined right and wrong. Maybe all first graders love their teachers. Certainly we did, and our parents never questioned either the system or Miss Keene. She had enormous respect. She was never wrong.

The school day ended with another song:
"Let us put our books away.
Study time is over.
Gaily tripping, gaily skipping,
Soon we'll be at rest."

Jennie Mazzilli Sears, Rose Sherman Geller, Alba Martinelli Thompson, all in their early 80s at the turn of a new century, looked back on those days at the Alden Street School, long since demolished. It was a marvelous educational beginning, now overlaid by a sweet nostalgia. All we remember clearly is a great mixture of odors, Maypole dances on the wet field, wooden desks and an awesome teacher. Thank you, Miss Keene! Do you know we turned out quite well and that we always vote?

Written by Alba Thompson with the help of Rose Geller and Jennie Sears

30

Temperance and Rumrunning

BY KARIN GOLDSTEIN

In December 1927, Plymouth police arrested a man in Town Square. He had two bottles of alcohol hidden in his clothing and was apparently waiting for a customer. Upon searching the area, police found more booze hidden under the side steps of the Church of the Pilgrimage. He was charged with "keeping and exposing liquor for illegal sale" and fined $100. It was during the Prohibition era — that "noble experiment" in American history that began in 1920 and ended in 1933 — when the manufacture, sale or transportation of alcoholic beverages was not only illegal but unconstitutional as well.

Prohibition often calls to mind scenes of rowdy speakeasies and bathtub gin, of flappers and police raids. In small town Plymouth, there certainly was bootlegging and moonshine. Prohibition in Plymouth was not known for famous raids or swinging nightlife, but rather for revealing the cultural divide among its approximately 13,000 residents. Prohibition highlighted the differences between old-stock Yankees, many of who supported temperance, and the more recent immigrants from southern Europe, who enjoyed alcoholic beverages as part of their traditional culture.

The temperance movement had a long history in Plymouth. The local Temperance Society was founded in 1827 by leading businessmen of the community who saw drunkenness as a threat to productivity. Women reformers saw it as a threat to

the family. The Society promoted temperance through lectures. The anti-liquor atmosphere spread through Plymouth. The proprietor of one store even advertised in the *Old Colony Memorial* his refusal to sell liquor, "that giant foe to human happiness." Temperance was an important women's cause throughout the 19th and early 20th centuries. Preventing drunkenness was considered a way to protect family values. Indeed, there was a chapter of

> *The temperance movement had a long history in Plymouth.*

the Women's Christian Temperance Union (WCTU) in Plymouth both during and after Prohibition, which met the first and third Thursdays of each month at members' houses.

Temperance groups throughout the nation finally succeeded in curbing liquor production and sales with the adoption of the 18th Amendment in 1919. Later that year, Congress overrode President Wilson's veto and passed the Volstead Act to enforce the new constitutional provision. The new law, which went into effect January 1920, made it illegal to manufacture, sell or transport alcoholic beverages.

While the law did not prevent the private consumption of liquor, the amendment ultimately proved unpopular and was finally repealed with the enactment of the 21st Amendment in 1933.

Many long-time Plymouth residents were raised in the heyday of the temperance movement. One such resident, who grew up downtown in the 1930s, remembers her parents as teetotalers. When a liquor store opened near their house after the repeal of Prohibition, her mother would cross the street to avoid walking past the liquor outlet. Jeanette Morton Holmes' parents were teetotalers as well. The only liquor in their house was a little bottle of rum in the bathroom medicine closet, kept for emergencies but never used. Harold Boyer, who attended the Zion Lutheran Church as a youth and First Parish after he married, remembered sermons supporting Prohibition at both churches.

Not all Yankees were dry, however. While Brooks Barnes remembered some of her relatives as teetotalers, others enjoyed an occasional drink. Her mother, Mercy Hatch, who spent summers on Ship Pond in Vallerville, remembered the rumrunners coming into the harbor at night. Some of the lobster fishermen used their boats at night for transporting liquor. Apparently her grandfather got involved at times, "because he wanted some of what they brought!" Her uncle and grandfather also made homemade wine from grape juice. The Hornblower family of Boston summered in

Prohibition—everyone made their own." Most families made small amounts of wine and beer for their own consumption. Jelly remembered his older brother Elio making home brew in a large stoneware cask. German neighbors taught him the recipe, which called for 10 pounds of crushed malt, a pound of hops, three cakes of yeast, and 5 to 10 pounds of sugar. When the beer had brewed for a week or so, they poured it into glass bottles and sealed them with a bottle-capping tool.

Families made their own wine from grapes imported from California in late summer or early fall, when grapes ripened. Mitchell Toabe, who grew up in North Plymouth, remembered his father making wine in the basement of their store in a 50-gallon cask. Other families used even larger casks, up to 150 gallons, to make enough for the year. People crushed the grapes in a bowl or ground them. Local fruit, such as wild cherries, was soaked in wine or pure alcohol to make cordials.

Jelly Baietti, who worked at Knife's store on Court Street in North Plymouth, remembered how people bought flavor extracts to flavor both cakes and cordials. A one-ounce bottle sold for 15 cents

JELLY BAIETTI COLLECTION

A stoneware cask and bottle-capping tool used by the Baietti Family of North Plymouth for brewing beer.

Chiltonville, where they kept a well-stocked wine cellar for entertaining. According to local legend, Ralph Hornblower, Sr. stocked up on liquor before Prohibition went into effect. One winter, local rumrunners discovered the contents of his summer home cellar, and cleaned it out in a matter of months.

The attitude toward liquor was different in immigrant North Plymouth. Alcoholic beverages were part of the culture—Italians drank wine, Germans had beer, and Portuguese had their cordials. Vincent (Jelly) Baietti, who grew up in North Plymouth, recalled that "we never had

around 1930, he said. A woman who grew up in North Plymouth recalled, "We'd buy extract, rum or whisky, from Boston or from Cappannari's [store], mix it with the alcohol in an aluminum tin, and split it with water, add a little bit of sugar, [and] cork it."

Where did people get alcohol? Occasionally a resident might sell some home brew to make extra money. Guests could find alcohol at various clubs, like the Amerigo Vespucci Club in North Plymouth or the Cold Spring Club at the foot of Lothrop Street. During the 1920s, Harold Boyer played in an orchestra for theaters, clubs and dance halls; he remembered people bringing their own flasks to dances. Indeed, Mitchell Toabe used to stop at a local house on his way to dances to buy a quart of Italian red wine for 50 cents. He remembered that he used to stash the wine underneath the seat of his Model T! People also found liquor at the Hotel Pilgrim or the Plymouth Rock Hotel, depending on "who you knew and what you knew."

Pure alcohol, which came from places like Belgium and Cuba, had to be smuggled into town. Rumrunners brought liquor from as far away as Canada by boat. The boats would anchor 10-12 miles off the coast by night, where they were met by small fishing boats that ferried the alcohol into port. Liquor bottles were frequently wrapped in burlap sacks padded with straw for easier handling.

Older residents remembered favorite landing points: near Ship Pond in Vallerville, Ellisville Harbor, Atwood's Lumber yard (later the yacht club), the foot of Bradford Street in central Plymouth, the foot of Robbins Road in North Plymouth, the boatyard on Landing Road in Kingston, the Bay Farm in Duxbury. With so many possible landing points, the Coast Guard found it impossible to patrol them all. At the waterfront, trucks met the fishing boats to carry the liquor to inland towns. Ruth Dale Griswold remembered stories of gangsters armed with machine guns coming from Boston in big cars to oversee the loading of bootleg liquor at Ship Pond.

Some of the bootleg was sold locally. A woman who grew up in North Plymouth remembered her father buying alcohol from a rumrunner. They'd arrange a price and a time to meet. The rumrunner would bring the alcohol and be waiting at the specified time. "He knew people who brought it in—they got it from a bigger boat. Everybody knew the boats were coming... We never mentioned names," she said.

Jelly Baietti remembered getting into trouble as a boy for playing with flashlights on a North Plymouth-Kingston hill near where rumrunners apparently signaled their boats, and he and his friends were messing up the signals!

Rumrunning was a lucrative trade, if one didn't get caught. Young men strong enough to lift cases of liquor could get a job unloading the boats for $5 a night, recalled Mitchell Toabe, who thinks his older brother might have taken advantage of the opportunity on occasion. As a girl, Nita Fiocchi Scagliarini recalled a hairdresser who lived in North Plymouth and wore a fur coat. On one occasion, the woman's hand was wrapped from an injury. The woman told Nita that she had a "bad boo-boo." Nita told her mother, who responded, "Hah, I know what happened there!" That night Nita's parents discussed the matter: "She got shot last night, you know she was on the boat!" Apparently the hairdresser made enough money from rumrunning to afford fur coats.

Another man used the proceeds of years of rumrunning to open a lumber business.

Rumrunning required skill — knowing how to handle a boat, the tides, landing places and the ability to judge when it was dark enough to transport the liquor safely. Some boats ran aground on the many sandbars in Plymouth's harbor. In August 1924, the Coast Guard found a boat with its name and license number erased, stranded on a sandbar between Gurnet Point and Saquish Beach. They seized 2,695 gallons of Belgian alcohol, worth an estimated $10,000. In May 1925, the Coast Guard seized the *Pegg II* off Billingsgate Shoal. The 50-foot speedboat had eluded capture for more than a year. She was carrying $80,000 worth of fine liquor wrapped in burlap sacks.

In the early morning of Aug. 20, 1924, local police and prohibition officers captured three boats, arrested 14 men and seized 10,000 gallons of alcohol in cans and wooden cases worth an estimated $25,000-$30,000.

According to the *OCM*, "A watch had been maintained for some weeks on Plymouth shores in connection with supposed operations of liquor smugglers." On the night of Aug. 19, a "liquor squad went to the shore north of the railroad station near the building formerly used for a clam cannery, hid themselves and waited with patience." Shortly after 2 a.m. Wednesday, four motorboats headed in toward a little pier in back of the former cannery building.

"As the boats made the shore, the officers rushed forth, fired several automatic pistols over the heads of the boat crews and most of the men gave up," the *OCM* reported. "Some of the men jumped overboard, either from fear of being shot or in an

attempt to escape from the officers... Some attempts to hide in the cannery building were made, but all the lawbreakers were found later, and with them a further haul of 2,000 gallons of cased alcohol which was stored in the structure."

According to the newspaper account of the incident, one boat escaped in the darkness but was later found by the Coast Guard in the inner harbor near the Stephens Field playground. Another of the four boats slipped its mooring line at the pier, drifted slowly away and when ordered to stop, the crew started the engine and roared away in the dark as shots were fired over their heads. That boat made a "clean getaway" with an estimated 2,600 gallons of Cuban alcohol aboard. Of the 14 men arrested, eight gave Plymouth addresses.

Many Plymoutheans greeted the repeal of Prohibition in 1933 with pleasure. Bootleggers went out of business, and the price of liquor decreased so that the average person could afford it. Lawmakers were also in favor of the repeal, as it allowed federal, state and local governments to benefit from liquor taxes.

However, repealing the 18th Amendment didn't solve all of the problems associated with Prohibition overnight. Cheap liquor of dubious quality appeared for sale. In the Dec. 22, 1933 edition of the *OCM*, editor Paul Bittinger recommended the establishment of government-run liquor stores to control quality and price, with profits to be used for a national temperance effort.

By 1936, there were five liquor stores in town. Temperance was still alive and well, however. The WCTU chapter continued to meet regularly.

SUMMER PEOPLE

BY JOAN H. BARTLETT

EEL RIVER FARM

Louise Fry Meyer married a grandson of Henry Hornblower and remembers life at Eel River Farm (later to become Plimoth Plantation).

"My grandfather's farm, The Forges, was near Henry Hornblower's Eel River Farm. They were friends all through the years and they were both very spiritual and very spirited individuals. The Hornblowers lived on Beacon Hill in Boston and came to Eel River Farm for the summers. I used to go over to Eel River Farm with my mother before I was married to visit Eleanor Hornblower. She'd take us out on the porch and show us the arrowheads the boys had collected. My mother used to write plays about fairies and silver bells. We'd put these plays on in Mrs. Hornblower's garden for the ladies and then we'd have a tea party afterward.

"There used to be a bridge over the Eel River to the beach. We could go down from the house and walk across Warren Avenue to the bathhouse. On the left was a tennis court surrounded by a wire fence covered with pink rambler roses. You could change your clothes in the bathhouse after playing tennis and put on your bathing suit and go to the public beach.

"In 1929 Mr. Hornblower gave the land for the Eel River Beach Club. He also wanted to give some land to make a golf club. My uncle, who was a lawyer, told him he would have to sell it so that it would be legal. The land was sold for a dollar and the Plymouth Country Club was formed.

"In the early years, my grandfather brought his horses from Brookline to Plymouth. He and my mother and her sister and some friends rode the horses down. When they arrived in Plymouth after the long ride, they would go to the Pilgrim Hotel for a meal. There were hitching posts for the horses. After dinner at the Pilgrim Hotel they rode home to The Forges and the horses were there for the summer. That was one big day. They'd start at about 5 o'clock in the morning and ride all the way in one day, spring and fall."

CYNTHIA BUTTNER FISCHER FAMILY COLLECTION

The Eel River Beach Club on Warren Avenue and Sherman Whipple Withington diving into the pool in 1936.

Trial of the Century:
LAST DAYS

By Robert Knox

In 1927, after Sacco and Vanzetti had been sentenced to die, protests from foreign dignitaries came to President Calvin Coolidge. Others wrote letters or sent petitions protesting the sentence to Massachusetts Gov. Alvan Tufts Fuller. The British novelist H.G. Wells attacked the persecution of Sacco and Vanzetti in the *London Sunday Express*. Graduating seniors in colleges throughout New England signed petitions, including three-quarters of the graduating class of Harvard Law School. Opposition to execution and demands for a new trial came from well-known authors, businessmen, and politicians, including Norman Thomas, Jane Addams, Alfred Landon, Sen. Robert LaFollette, John Dewey, and H.L. Mencken. The defense committee brought a rolled petition to the State House containing almost 500,000 names.

Vanzetti petitioned the governor for clemency, but Sacco refused to have anything further to do with the courts or government of Massachusetts and began a hunger strike. With world attention now on the governor, Fuller acceded to a plea from the Episcopal bishop of Massachusetts, William Lawrence, and set up an

advisory commission to review the fairness of the trial before weighing a pardon or a commutation of the death sentence. Even before this decision, Fuller did his own investigation, calling attorneys and wit-

THE BOSTON GLOBE VIA MERLIN-NET.COM
Boston police arrest Sacco-Vanzetti supporters, Aug. 10, 1927. Author Katherine Anne Porter is fourth from the left.

nesses in the case to see him. Beltrando Brini went to see him. On June 1 Fuller named a three-man advisory committee headed by Harvard President Abbott Lawrence Lowell. A Brahmin throwback,

Lowell proved an unfortunate choice to consider the fairness of a criminal case brought against immigrant radicals. In *Tragedy in Dedham*, his 1962 study of the case, Francis Russell wrote of the Harvard president: "To Lowell the mass newcomers - the Famine Irish and the later Italians and Jews - were an intrusion on the Athens of America that Boston might have been. Dismayed at the appearance among his undergraduates of increasing numbers of Polish-born Jewish day students, he at one time planned to limit their admission to Harvard to a small fixed quota."

Fuller granted a stay of execution until Aug. 10 to allow his advisory committee time to consider the case. The prisoners were transferred to the Cherry Hill section of Charlestown Jail, where the death row prisoners waited. The proceedings of the Lowell committee were the farce that followed the tragedy. The committee devoted its energy to trying to break down the defense case, such as the testimony of an Italian witness who placed Sacco in the North End on April 15. The witness confirmed the date by reference to a banquet he had attended the day before. The Lowell committee was convinced the banquet was on another date, but an Italian journalist brought an account of the banquet published in an Italian newspaper proving the witness correct about the date. The committee was forced to concede the point, but had already convinced themselves of the defendants' guilt.

On July 27 the Lowell committee reported to Gov. Fuller that the defendants had received a fair trial, though making some criticism of Judge Thayer. On Aug. 3, waiting until 11:25 p.m. so that morning newspapers could carry no reaction to his statement in the next day's editions, Fuller announced his rejection of clemency. Newspaper headlines summed up the statement in two words: "They die."

International reaction was strong. In Paris pro-

Internationally, tension built over the date of the execution.

testers marched with linked hands behind Luigia Vanzetti, who carried a banner reading: "Parisian People, save my brother and Sacco. Thanks." Rallies were held on Boston Common. When defense committee member Mary Donovan held a banner reading "Did you see what I did to those anarchist bastards? - Judge Thayer," police Supt. Michael Crowley closed down the rally. Edward James, nephew to William and Henry, was arrested. Pickets appeared before the State House, entering forbidden turf a few at a time, and were arrested, including a few famous names — John Dos Passos, Dorothy Parker, Edna St. Vincent Millay — but most of those arrested were foreign-born workers. In New York, 100,000 walked out in a general strike, but response to a similar call in Boston was much weaker. Machine guns were set up on the top of the prison wall in Charlestown.

Defense committee lawyers approached every judge they could find to file "exceptions" to the legal process. U. S. Supreme Court Justice Oliver Wendell Holmes said the federal courts did not have jurisdiction in the case. He told defense lawyers who found him at his summer home, "If I listened to you any more I would do it. I must not do it."

Still, to give lawyers time to have their final exceptions heard, Fuller decided — on Aug. 10, the date set for execution — to grant a 12-day reprieve. The reprieve meant that Vanzetti would live to see his sister, who had been making her way from Italy at a pre-jet age pace. A statement signed by prominent attorneys and intellectuals asked the U.S. attorney general to intervene.

But the Lowell report had settled doubts for middle-of-the-road Massachusetts opinion. "Outside opposition and criticism had long since contracted the mood of the Massachusetts community beyond reason," Russell wrote. When a member of the jury's house in Milton was bombed on Aug. 15, opposition turned to hatred of the defendants and their supporters.

Internationally, tension built over the date of the execution. Protests spilled into violence in the capitals of Europe, Berlin, Amsterdam, Athens, Copenhagen, Bucharest, Stockholm, and Prague. The United States government received pleas from Madame Curie, the grandson of Lafayette, Alfred Dreyfus and the president of Czechoslovakia, among many, many others. *New York Times* headlines in August of 1927 included: "World Stir over Decision"; "500,000 Called for Sacco Strike Here"; "Mobilize for March on Prison in Boston"; "British Urge Mercy for Doomed Men"; "Europe on Edge: Expected Reprieve"; "City Crowds Silent on News of Death"; "Paris Mobs Loot Shops."

Vanzetti's sister arrived in Boston and announced that she had come to guide her brother back to the religion he had fallen from, so that he could meet his maker. On Sunday, Aug. 21, with no permits issued by the city and no meetings allowed at Boston Common, about 20,000 people showed up anyway. A march began, was tolerated by the police for a while and then broken up.

On death row Sacco wrote a goodbye letter to his son, Dante. "...But always remember, Dante, in the play of happiness, don't you use all for yourself only, but down yourself just one step, at your side and help the weak ones that cry for help, help the prosecuted and the victim, because that are your better friends; they are the comrades that fight and fall as your father and Bartolo fought and fell yesterday for the conquest of the joy of freedom for all and the poor workers. In this struggle of life you will find more love and you will be loved."

Vanzetti wrote to Dante too: "...I tell you that for and of all I know of your father, he is not a criminal, but one of the bravest men I ever knew...."

Hours before the execution, which took place just after midnight on Aug. 23, defense attorney Thompson spoke to his clients on death row. When he sought reassurance of their innocence, Thompson reported that Vanzetti "said to me quietly and calm-

Vanzetti's final words were: "I now wish to forgive some people for what they are doing to me."

ly and with a sincerity which I could not doubt, that I need have no worry about this matter; that both he and Sacco were absolutely innocent of the South Braintree crime...and that in reality he had been convicted on evidence that would not have convicted him if he had not been an anarchist; so that he was in a very real sense dying for his cause."

Sacco then thanked Thompson for his efforts. "It was magnanimous in him," Thompson wrote, "not to refer in detail to our previous difference of opinion because the root of it all lay in his conviction, often expressed to me, that all efforts on his behalf, either in court or with public authorities, would be useless because no capitalistic society could afford to accord him justice. I had taken the contrary view; but at this last interview he did not suggest that the result justified his view and not mine."

Before he died in the electric chair, Sacco called out, "Long live anarchy!"

Vanzetti's final words were: "I now wish to forgive some people for what they are doing to me." All accounts of the execution make reference to the tears of the warden as Vanzetti was put to death.

The funeral was held at Langone's Funeral Home

"Monday night passed very quietly in this town...

in the North End of Boston. One hundred thousand people came to view the bodies. The funeral procession, beginning with about 5,000 mourners, marched from the North End through the center of town to the Forest Hills Crematory. Russell called it "the most spectacular funeral the city had ever seen."

But a reader didn't get much sense of the world attention focused on the case from the Plymouth newspaper, even in the climactic month of August

1927. They might have been rioting in Paris and marching on Beacon Hill, but Yankee-run Plymouth knew how to put the matter in its place, and that place wasn't a very large one. While Gov. Fuller's initial decision not to delay the executions drew a storm of protest elsewhere, Main Street Plymouth shrugged. In a front-page story on Aug. 5, the *Old Colony Memorial* reported that the announcement "caused little that could be construed as excitement here." The paper continued, "In some quarters, the opinion was expressed that with due regard to the statutes of Massachusetts and his thorough examination of the Braintree affair, the chief executive of this Commonwealth could not have done otherwise than he did and his decision having the indorsement [sic] of the associates he had called in was regarded as fitting." Seventy years later, one can't help wonder by whom, exactly, "the opinion was expressed." The newspaper's editor, Paul Bittinger, was a businessman whose peers were other significant businessmen in town; at times he was also a selectman. The story went on to say that Vanzetti was not well-liked by his fellows, reporting, without named sources or quotes, that "residents who claim to know are quoted as saying that

THE BOSTON GLOBE VIA MERLIN-NET.COM
The Sacco-Vanzetti funeral procession from the top of Boston's Trinity Church, Aug. 29, 1927.

Vanzetti was not held in high regard by his countrymen, of whom there are many living in that part of town."

But in truth many local people did care deeply about the case, and Vanzetti clearly had his supporters, especially in North Plymouth. The same Aug. 5 issue of the *OCM* in a separate story reported that Sacco and Vanzetti supporters held a gathering that drew between 300 and 400, "many of them being friends and former neighbors of Bartolomeo Vanzetti," to the Amerigo Vespucci Hall on Suosso Lane. Beltrando Brini chaired the meeting. Speakers included a number of supporters who were prominent in the last act of the long cause celebre:

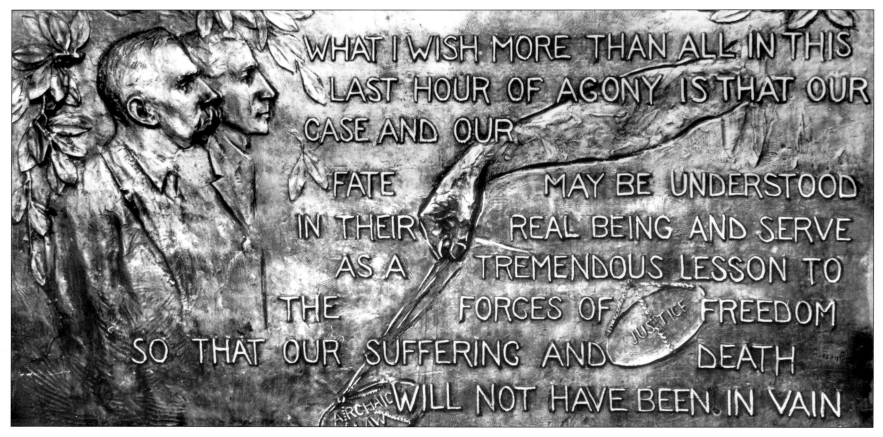

WHAT I WISH MORE THAN ALL IN THIS LAST HOUR OF AGONY IS THAT OUR CASE AND OUR FATE MAY BE UNDERSTOOD IN THEIR REAL BEING AND SERVE AS A TREMENDOUS LESSON TO THE FORCES OF FREEDOM SO THAT OUR SUFFERING AND DEATH WILL NOT HAVE BEEN IN VAIN

Sacco-Vanzetti memorial plaque, with some of Vanzetti's final thoughts, in the Boston Public Library.

Edward Holton James, the eccentric nephew of famous American intellectuals William and Henry James; the indefatigable labor lawyer Michael Musmanno; and one "Miss Mary Donovan," the emotional, suspicious, iron-willed and indefatigable recording secretary of the defense committee, who devoted years of her life to the cause. Two speakers spoke in Italian and were interrupted at times by applause. A collection was taken to support the

defense fund.

And while Gov. Fuller's decision to execute may have aroused "No stir" in Plymouth (according to the Aug. 5 headline), the next week's paper headlined its story: "Nervous Tension Exists in Plymouth over Sacco-Vanzetti case." While there were no demonstrations in connection with the case, the paper reported, "there seems to be an undercurrent among some of the residents akin to nervousness

and a desire to have the case closed in some manner if possible." The desire to have it over and done with appears to be the Plymouth establishment's main response to the legal and political drama that engaged millions.

The same issue carried another story, also on the front page, titled "Property under Guard in Ply." This story repeated that while no demonstrations had taken place, precautions were being taken to guard public buildings and that some "prominent private citizens" were granted permits to carry arms. The paper further reported that police found two people passing out leaflets, one in North Plymouth and the other near the Puritan Mill on Court Street. The story then rehearsed the argument of the "handbill," which urged all supporters of Sacco and Vanzetti to come to Boston for demonstrations before the Aug. 10 execution date. But as for depicting the degree of "nervous tension" and the attitude of local authorities toward the case, the smoking gun comes in the very last sentence of this story: "Distribution of papers was checked by the police, and a considerable number of copies which had not been passed out were seized." When it came to protesting the execution of Sacco and Vanzetti, free speech was abridged in Plymouth.

Making no mention of reaction elsewhere, the Aug. 26 issue of the *OCM* headlined its story "All Quiet Here Night Vanzetti Was Executed." "There was plenty of interest in the last attempts of his [Vanzetti's] counsel to secure a reprieve," the paper reported, but when those efforts failed, "Monday night passed very quietly in this town... Owners of radio sets listened closely for the news flashes, both regular and special, and there were many who remained at their sets until the last word at 12:30 a.m. Tuesday announced the electrocution..." the paper stated. The final sentence is again the telling one: "It seemed to be a general feeling after the details were given in the Boston morning papers, of

Luigia Vanzetti

YANKEE DOUBTS

Although it was not popular within Boston's Yankee establishment to plead for justice for Sacco and Vanzetti, there was one notable exception. On Oct.26, 1926, *The Boston Herald*, a bastion of Brahmin opinion, broke ranks and called for a new trial.

In an editorial, the Herald reversed its original position, which upheld the convictions, and while rejecting the defendants' "half-baked views," called for a new trial "on the basis of new evidence not yet examined in open court."

There was no new trial and Judge Thayer sentenced Sacco and Vanzetti to die in the electric chair.

But in the spring of 1927, the Herald was awarded journalism's highest honor, a Pulitzer Prize for its "great courage to reverse itself when it had reason to believe it was mistaken."

relief that the whole case was now a closed matter."

The local epilogue came in a brief story on the bottom of the front page (the only news page in the 1920s) of the Sept. 2, 1927 edition. "Miss Vanzetti in Plymouth," the headline reads. "Luigia Vanzetti, sister of the late Bartolomeo Vanzetti, once of Plymouth, is visiting friends here, and at present is the guest of Mr. and Mrs. Vincent Brini, 5 Cherry St., where she is recuperating from the strain of recent events, which occupied worldwide attention." Once the outcome of the case was a "closed matter," the reference to the world's interest made its way into the paper for the first time. "Miss Vanzetti also plans to spend some time with other friends in Plymouth," the story reported.

But the "general feeling" the *OCM* reported on Aug. 26 was premature, and the case is still not a closed matter, though it has been

largely forgotten in the town where Vanzetti lived. Books continued to be written about their case long after the execution of Sacco and Vanzetti, arguing different sides of the question of guilt, providing the historical context and evaluating its meaning.

At age 93 and unable to see or hear well, Beltrando Brini replied to an end-of-the-century request for an interview with written responses to a few questions and a copy of a video documentary on the case made in 1998. In this video (*Greatest Trials of All Time: Sacco and Vanzetti*) Brini sums up his opinion of Bartolomeo Vanzetti: "He was an extremely kind man, who was conscious of the inequalities of society and wanted to improve them."

Adapted from Trial of the Century, *unpublished manuscript, 2001.*

CORDAGE FROM COURT STREET

"There was a two-story brick building, seeming to extend forever along the bay-front; built in the fashion of a fortress, with a steel fence in front, and a pond which had been turned into a moat in medieval style. High up in the blue sky floated an American flag, to let you know that this was not a Rhine castle of the middle ages, but a center of industry in the land of the Pilgrim's pride. ...

"...The windows of the long factory were open, and (an observer) heard the roar of spinning machinery, and saw the figures of men and women moving about. Suddenly a siren boomed; and as if by magic, the various buildings began to belch human figures. Apparently they had been lined up just inside the doors, like runners at the start of a race; they behaved as if the building were on fire, or full of poison gas. More and more dense grew the throngs of escapers, until the roadway was gray and blue with the shirts of men and the multi-colored dresses of girls. For the most part they were foreigners, Italians, Portuguese and other dark peoples. They were small and stunted, the older ones bent with toil, walking mechanically, looking neither to right nor to left. The younger ones chatted in twos and threes..."

From the documentary novel, Boston, *By Upton Sinclair, 1928*

Main entrance of the Plymouth Cordage Co. as seen from Court Street. The signature tower and smoke stacks remained a visible landmark for sailors at the end of the 20th century.

Oak Street School in the 1930s

BY MARIE FEHLOW

The Oak Street School was first the seed and then the root with which my educational growth was established. In 1930 it sat nicely in a quiet residential neighborhood, a dark brown shingled two-room schoolhouse that housed four grades, first and second in one room, third and fourth in the other. The playground stretched in an L-shape along the south side and back of the building, bordered by a stone wall just the right height for sitting with a best friend at recess.

The wall also served to retain the sloping hillside behind. One of my classmates, Amos McGinnis, lived in a house perched up on that hill. I thought Amos was so lucky, having only to dash down to school along a winding walk with an iron pipe railing and then back up, quick as a wink, to return home.

With my pudgy little legs I walked to and from the Oak Street School four miles a day – a mile each way twice a day because we went home for lunch and then back to school for an afternoon session.

There was no kindergarten then, but I was only 5 years old when I started at Oak Street, not the required 6. I had passed a test for early entrance. As a result, all through my early school years when I overheard someone say, "But she's so

EVELYN HATHAWAY COLLECTION

The Oak Street School, a Colonial Revival style two-room schoolhouse, opened in 1902 and continued to serve the town as a school throughout the 20th century. In this 1966 photo, Sabrina Desmaine, left, and Angie Hathaway Spencer are about 8 years old.

young," there always followed the proud pronouncement: "She passed THE TEST." For many years I felt very special.

My sister Sylvia, 16 years older than I, had become responsible for me after I was born so my mother could return to her fulltime job at the Puritan Mill downtown. Sylvia remembered walking me to school with the required Turkish towel on which to sit so I could take THE TEST.

Clementine Ortolani was my first and second grade teacher. She was tall and angular and wore her hair pulled back in a shiny black bun. When I think of her I immediately recall her sharp elbows, always red and chapped-looking. Occasionally when I was called to her desk for a conference she would put her arm around me and ask if her brother Frank had been by recently to call on Sylvia. As young as I was, I was aware that Frank was not destined for Sylvia if Miss Ortolani had anything to say about it, and I became increasingly uncomfortable encircled in those sharp, red elbows.

Having passed THE TEST I had no trouble even at that tender age moving rapidly through each grade. It was not so much intelligence as maturity, due to being the baby in a household of much older siblings. And so I passed easily to the "big kids" classroom where the bump on the second finger of a pupil's writing hand became stained with ink, a badge of accomplishment first and second graders could only dream of.

Mrs. Randall, my third and fourth grade teacher, ruled with a much sterner demeanor than Miss Red Elbows. At that time, married teachers were virtually unknown. Being single was a requisite for a woman to be employed as a teacher. But Mrs. Randall lived close by the school on Oak Street and had a husband. There seemed to be something mildly suspect about her influence with the school committee. Valid or not, her authoritative sternness was acknowledged as somehow linked to her special status. One didn't try Mrs. Randall's patience.

Everyone walked to and from school, and all of the pupils went home at noon for lunch since the school had no cafeteria. For those of us who lived at the far edge of the school's attendance area – about one mile – the allotted time to leave, eat and return was just barely enough, especially if you hopped, skipped and jumped over the cracks in the sidewalk and stopped to stick propeller-like maple seeds on the bridge of your nose.

One of my traveling companions to and from school was Johnny Paty, who lived only a half-mile from school. I would often meet Johnny just as the Puritan Mill whistle blew at 1 p.m., the back-to-work signal for the mill workers after their mid-day break. It was a 15-minute warning for us to get back to school for the afternoon session before the clang of the school bell. If you didn't make it, you were in big trouble, especially if your teacher was Mrs. Randall.

It was rainy and misty one mid-day when Johnny and I connected returning to school after lunch. I always seemed to be late on rainy days and still am. Maybe it takes more time to put on your rubbers, struggle into a raincoat and fumble with an umbrella. Johnny and I knew we were in trouble that day

when we returned to school to note the empty playground, the strange quietness, and the closed doors. Had we missed the warning whistle splashing through too many mud puddles? We always entered the school through the big, heavy back door. Only grownups used the front door. But the back door was locked, or so it seemed. When we tried to turn the unbudging knob, my heart began to beat faster and I lost all reason and coping skills at the prospect of facing a fierce Mrs. Randall. I told Johnny that my father had told me that if I ever found the school door locked I was to come straight home. I made a hasty retreat and left Johnny to face the music.

But I couldn't face my father when I arrived home. We had a screened-in grape arbor that kept creatures away from the grapes and helped shelter our old beagle hound. I parked my umbrella against the doghouse and crawled in with doggy where I spent a cozy, warm afternoon watching the drip, drip of raindrops off the overhang of the doghouse doorway. As the afternoon wore on, I got better and better at hitting the rain barrel with spit-out Concord grape skins. Even without a watch I managed to exit and brush myself off at about the same time I would normally arrive home in late afternoon.

Alas, I was found out. The next day Papa confronted me with the remnants of a much chewed-on umbrella, the handiwork of a dumb dog that couldn't be trusted, not to mention John Paty who ratted on me at school.

Sometimes my big brother Bruno, who drove an enormous truck for the A.K. Finney Construction Co., timed his noon break to coincide with mine. I would find him noisily revving his truck engine in

front of the school as we dashed out. "Get in," he would say unceremoniously. Embarrassed by his outrageous presence, I would resist, too short to even get a leg up on the high running board. He would lean over, reach down and scoop me up with one big muscular arm. Off we would go in a thunderous departure. Little did I notice that my fellow classmates, especially the boys, watched with awestruck envy.

But it was I who envied the other kids whose mothers came to observe classes in session. I wished it could have been my mother, too, but I knew she could never come, for her life was ruled by those Puritan Mill whistles. The ceremonial Mom's Chair was placed up front of the class, close to the teacher's desk. I would steal glances at the visiting mom to see how she was dressed – her coat, hat, shoes, gloves and always a dangling purse. A mom's visit was always good for a few days of teacher "pet-ness" for some lucky pupil.

At the end of the century, the Oak Street School was still there, one of the few remaining as-is, as-was buildings that connect us to those early beginnings, growing up in Plymouth, an anchor to one's past. I remember the dark, oiled floors, the portraits of George Washington and Abraham Lincoln staring gravely down on us, the screwed-to-the-floor desks in rows.

Best of all was the long awaited day when the ink bottles were dropped into the wells on the desk tops and we began to write with pens with sharp nibs and our fingers gradually became ink-stained.

Oak Street, like life, was taking one mile at a time, avoiding cracks in the sidewalk, listening for whistles and knocking on doors even if they seemed locked.

35

Plymouth During the Depression

THE EARLY YEARS

BY KARIN GOLDSTEIN

Many people think of the Depression as shanty-towns, breadlines and sidewalks full of the possessions of evicted residents. Such scenes, however, did not represent all of America. Massachusetts fared slightly better than many states. The rural, small-town quality of Plymouth helped soften the blow in this seaside community. While New Deal programs provided some assistance, it was primarily community ties that really helped Plymoutheans get through the Depression

On the eve of the Depression in 1930, Plymouth was a town of about 13,000 people, employed in a variety of industries. Tourism was an important summer business. Most of the immigrants in North Plymouth and downtown, as well as some Yankees, worked for the Plymouth Cordage Co. or cloth mills like Standish Worsted, Puritan Mills, or Mabbett's Mills. Up to 1925, when immigration restrictions went into effect, immigrants from Italy, Portugal and Portuguese territories, particularly the Azores and Cape Verde islands had swelled Plymouth's population, which had increased from about 7,000 in 1890 to 13,000 by 1920. Central Plymouth in 1930 had the establishments typical of any small town at that time: insurance agencies, dry goods stores, doctors, lawyers, and other small businesses. South of town,

many residents supported themselves by farming, especially raising chickens and cranberries. Cape Verdean immigrants worked on cranberry bogs, which were generally owned by Yankees.

Plymouth's economy was healthy. In December 1929 the Plymouth Cordage Co. reported an 11 percent profit and declared extra dividends. That same month, the Plymouth National Bank opened a

It was primarily community ties that really helped Plymoutheans get through the Depression

new building on Main Street. Perhaps the best indication of Plymouth's economic health in the 1920s was the modest amount of aid to the poor mentioned in town reports.

According to a welfare board report, in 1928 the town provided assistance to 289 persons living independently (that is, not in the infirmary or at the poor farm). "Occasionally we get a call from some of the younger improvident, people who living up to the weekly wage as fast, or faster, than it comes, find that with the cessation of work, and with no

credit... that hunger is right at their own door..." That year, the town Board of Public Welfare spent $28,779.40 for poor relief. Within five years, that figure would be seen as a drop in the bucket, as the number of poor the town would be called upon to help increased tenfold.

The stock market crash of 1929 had little direct effect on most Plymoutheans, whether Yankee or immigrant. In 1930 the *Old Colony Memorial* expressed optimism. "Ever since the stock market crash last fall, many conflicting opinions have been expressed. Encouraging reports have been forthcoming... so it appears that the temporary depression may soon be ended."

Long-time residents agreed that the immediate impact of the Depression was slight. "The crash didn't affect us. We were too poor to have anything invested in the stock market," recalled Doris Gerard Woolson.

Investing in the stock market was not a common experience for immigrants in North Plymouth. Those with extra money to invest, such as community leader Louis Knife (Luigi Cortelli), invested locally, lending money to homeowners and businessmen. While few residents invested in the stock market, the factories that employed a great many local residents did, as did businesses that bought their products.

Two waitresses stand at the counter of Gambini's Luncheonette on Court Street at Shirley Square c. 1930s.

However, by 1931 the town began to feel the effects of unemployment. According to the 1931 town report, the welfare board had a difficult time keeping up with the needs of local families: "The citizen who is still enjoying full-time work or is not dependent on his weekly salary is little aware of the hardships in many homes in our town. Never in the history of the local Welfare Board has there been such a demand for aid as in the past year…"

Town government was not alone in trying to help those newly unemployed. The *OCM* urged residents to find jobs for those out of work, and offered "free advertising space in the Positions Wanted columns" for those without jobs. The newspaper also offered a barter service. The chamber of commerce formed an employment bureau, printing in the local newspaper registration blanks for persons out of work and for those who might provide a job. Based on the suggestion of Martin Collingwood, president of the chamber, the community coordinated a program to secure unused land for garden plots for people without jobs. The American Legion coordinated a "Create-a-Job Campaign" to encourage homeowners to create temporary jobs, ranging from painting to washing windows. The campaign received 691 pledges, valued at more than $200,000.

Local charitable organizations helped with direct aid as well. The Plymouth Fragment Society, a women's charitable organization formed in 1820, provided anonymous aid to families in need. In 1932 the society helped 127 families, providing assistance ranging from shoes and rubbers to fuel. The American Red Cross distributed food, cloth and clothing, both old and new, to those in need.

Local businesses strove for an optimistic note to promote consumer confidence. They advertised in a "Believe in Plymouth" page of the newspaper and held various holiday and special-event sales to encourage business. Newspaper editorials repeatedly urged citizens to shop locally to increase local prosperity: "This country is again experiencing what is really a "buyers' strike… thrift is commendable… too much hoarding is equally detrimental," said the *OCM* .

One kind of local business — movie theaters — actually expanded during the early years of the Depression. In the fall of 1930, the Old Colony Theater downtown was demolished and rebuilt to become "not only a real colonial-type playhouse, but one of the future showplaces of this historic town." The Plymouth Theater in North Plymouth was remodeled, to feature a new canopy marquee and lobby. To encourage business, manager Bill Resnick announced reduced prices in November 1931: children paid 10 cents for all shows, while adults paid 25 cents for matinees and 50 cents for shows after 7:30 p.m.

As the Depression deepened, unemployment grew worse. By the end of 1932, one of the town's factories, Puritan Mills, temporarily closed. Work in the mills was sporadic. Doris Gerard Woolson remembers that when work at the mill was slack,

By 1931 the town began to feel the effects of unemployment.

her father would travel to other towns looking for work. "He was a wonderful provider," she recalled. Plymouth Cordage Co. cut workers back to a 35-hour week. In October 1932, the Cordage reduced wages about 10 percent to cut the competitive price of their product. The workweek was later increased to 40 hours, however, to help make up for lower wages. Rope sales were suffering, and that year the company reported a $232,000 loss, its first of the decade. The company was obliged to cut positions. By February 1933, the Cordage again cut back to a 35-hour week, and reduced the wages for salaried employees. As management had a long history of paternalism, cuts were carefully considered: "We have spent a great deal of time on problems of personnel to determine considerate and fair means of reducing our force to meet the necessities of the business. Every effort has been made to…distribute the work which we have to give some employment to the greatest possible number of employees…"

The Bongiovanni family of North Plymouth was one of many affected by Cordage cuts. While Ramo Bongiovanni's father lost his job at the rope factory, his sister was kept on as an employee. "They tried to keep at least one member of the family working," he said. Keeping one family member working was crucial, as many workers lived in Cordage-owned employee housing.

Seasonal laborers also suffered, as they were less likely to be hired during hard times. Working in the cranberry bogs and fishing, seasonal occupations to which people had turned in the past, were not adequate. In 1931, the welfare board had to help those who "have always found work enough to provide for their families and never dreamed that they would ever ask the town for aid… these people, their savings used up… are forced in ever-increasing numbers to seek assistance." That year, the town's park, highway, health, school and water departments hired unemployed men for a variety of manual tasks, including clearing parks and campgrounds.

By 1932, foreclosures had mushroomed. While

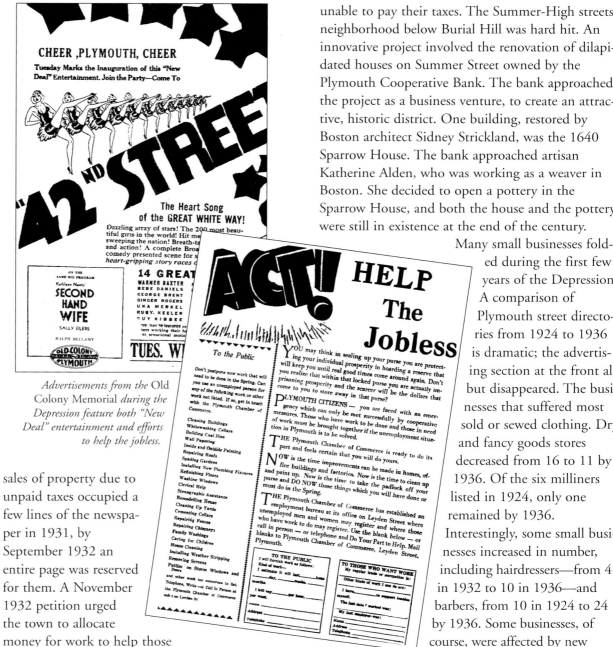

Advertisements from the Old Colony Memorial *during the Depression feature both "New Deal" entertainment and efforts to help the jobless.*

sales of property due to unpaid taxes occupied a few lines of the newspaper in 1931, by September 1932 an entire page was reserved for them. A November 1932 petition urged the town to allocate money for work to help those

unable to pay their taxes. The Summer-High streets neighborhood below Burial Hill was hard hit. An innovative project involved the renovation of dilapidated houses on Summer Street owned by the Plymouth Cooperative Bank. The bank approached the project as a business venture, to create an attractive, historic district. One building, restored by Boston architect Sidney Strickland, was the 1640 Sparrow House. The bank approached artisan Katherine Alden, who was working as a weaver in Boston. She decided to open a pottery in the Sparrow House, and both the house and the pottery were still in existence at the end of the century.

Many small businesses folded during the first few years of the Depression. A comparison of Plymouth street directories from 1924 to 1936 is dramatic; the advertising section at the front all but disappeared. The businesses that suffered most sold or sewed clothing. Dry and fancy goods stores decreased from 16 to 11 by 1936. Of the six milliners listed in 1924, only one remained by 1936.

Interestingly, some small businesses increased in number, including hairdressers—from 4 in 1932 to 10 in 1936—and barbers, from 10 in 1924 to 24 by 1936. Some businesses, of course, were affected by new technology. As more and more people bought cars, for example, there were fewer hay and feed stores and more filling stations.

The effects of unemployment were evident in other areas of town life. With the lack of work came an unwelcome increase in leisure time. Many spent it reading. The library reported a 160 percent increase in the number of books checked out, as well as a greater number of patrons.

The Depression and New Deal combined to spur a dramatic increase in the number of high school students. With few jobs available, students stayed in school longer. In a better economy, students 16 and under might have applied for certificates to leave school and go to work. The number of work certificates issued to minors by the school department dropped markedly (about 50 percent for 14- to 16-year-olds, and about 20 percent for those 16 and over). The lack of jobs, coupled with a New Deal incentive against hiring those under 16, meant that the local high school on Lincoln Street was subject to unprecedented crowding. Students attended in shifts: morning and afternoon. School administrators were concerned about the learning capacity of additional students, and urged the town government to consider alternative tracks offering practical skills, as "college preparatory studies is not democratic and is decidedly against American traditions of equality... This condition must be provided for." One of the students who might otherwise have dropped out of

CYNTHIA BUTTNER FISCHER FAMILY COLLECTION

Gasoline pumps at the Bradford Store at Jabez Corner in the Wellingsley section of Plymouth c. 1930s. Such facilities were known as "filling stations."

school to work under other circumstances was Ramo Bongiovanni, who stressed how good his high

As more people bought cars there were more filling stations.

school education was, and how well it prepared him for life.

To provide money for relief for the unemployed,

both the county and the town were obliged to cut their budgets. In April 1932, the town cut the salaries of local employees who were making more than $1,000 per year, including teachers, by 10 percent. But while town costs were decreasing, so too were tax valuations. In July 1932, the tax valuation for the Plymouth Cordage Co. was cut $1,000,000, and Mabbett's Mills assessed value was reduced by $100,000.

In 1933 Franklin Delano Roosevelt was inaugurated president and the New Deal began. Instead of Herbert Hoover's reliance on self-sufficiency, Roosevelt brought government intervention to help solve the economic crisis. Plymouth County had historically favored the GOP. While large towns and cities like Plymouth and Brockton had pockets of industrial workers who voted Democratic, the rest of the county was rural and conservative. In 1932, there were six tickets for Plymouth voters to choose from: Republican, Democratic, Prohibitionist, Communist, Socialist Labor and Socialist. In spite of bad weather, the national election that November drew the highest number of Plymouth voters to date – 4,406. Despite the sour economy, 2,546 or 58 percent voted for Hoover, while only 1,767 (40 percent) favored Roosevelt.

To conservative Yankees in central Plymouth, Roosevelt was "that Man in the White House." Helen Belcher's father was a dyed-in-the-wool Republican. He thought Roosevelt would bring the country to disaster with his new programs. Jean Whiting Patenaude remembered that talk of FDR used to "send her father into orbit." "He couldn't stand him. Roosevelt was the cause of all that was wrong in the country," she said. Jean later voted for FDR, but didn't tell her family. Harold Boyer also remembered not being crazy about Roosevelt at the time, but being extremely appreciative of Social Security payments later! Grocer Guy Cooper, who was the proprietor of a store at Jabez Corner, when interviewed by a newspaper about voting, quipped, "I tried that once. I voted against Roosevelt. It didn't work, so I didn't do it again."

One of Roosevelt's first acts upon taking office was to declare a bank holiday. While many banks across the country had failed, Plymouth's banks remained solvent throughout the Depression. While there were mergers (Old Colony Trust with Plymouth National Bank in November 1934), no bank in Plymouth failed. Imagine the disgust of conservative Yankee bankers and industrialists who found that they could not meet their payrolls due to the bank holiday! Several local industries, including Edes Manufacturing, the Cordage, Mabbett's Mills and others, were obliged to issue a total of $20,000 of scrip in $1, $2, $5 and $10 denominations in lieu of real money. The scrip was redeemable for cash three days after the end of the bank holiday. Fortunately, most local businesses, with the notable exception of the A&P market, accepted the scrip. Jelly Baietti, who worked for Knife's store in North Plymouth, remembered accepting the scrip. The first of Roosevelt's "alphabet soup" acts to affect Plymouth was the Emergency Relief Act, which granted money to each state to distribute through either direct relief or work relief. Over the next sev-

eral years, the ERA funded a wide variety of relief activities, ranging from road construction to sewing projects. Short-term New Deal employment projects were first funded through the Civil Works Administration and later through the Works Progress Administration.

Meeting the needs of hundreds of unemployed families required filling out numerous new government forms, a challenge for Plymouth's small welfare department. The town's archives on the ERA contain numerous letters from the Boston ERA office, urging the town to complete various forms. To apply for aid, a member of the family applied to the welfare board at the Town House at Town Square. Not only did Plymouth not have a social worker, it did not have adequate facilities for private meetings with clients. In some instances, the welfare board was so understaffed that the police were asked to assist in investigating claims.

In 1933, the new Civilian Conservation Corps created the first of two forestry camps with 200 men each in the Myles Standish State Forest in Plymouth and Carver. The first spring 25 young men from Plymouth were accepted and 30 World War I veterans were added that summer. The following year, 30 Plymouth youths from welfare families enrolled, and, according to the *OCM*, "the $25 of their monthly wage, pledged to their family has been a great help in relieving" the welfare board. A Plymouth resident who visited the 102nd CCC Camp, described for the newspaper young men living in neat rows of tents, rising at 6 a.m. and at work by 8 a.m. The military style existence included Saturday inspections by officers. The men created roads and trails, and spread creosote to combat gypsy moths.

Despite Roosevelt's creative work programs, hardships continued. By the end of 1933, the town welfare board reported that "unemployment has increased to such a volume that the increase in welfare and soldier's relief greatly exceeded our estimates." That year the town spent $130,000 on relief, helping more than 439 families, and running $40,000 over budget. The welfare board helped even more people in 1934 – 2,400 — the most during any year of the Depression.

One new government program that provided job funding was the Civil Works Administration. According to the 1933 town report, "Too much cannot be said in regard to CWA. The relief this brought to the town cannot be estimated by any individual." In 1933, almost 400 people were employed in CWA projects, including 160 in water works, as well as eight women heads of households. Unemployed men and women, as well as those on welfare or soldiers' relief, were given jobs like painting schools and shingling the roofs of public buildings.

Painter Harold Boyer was involved in several civic improvement projects. In 1934 the town approached him with a proposition to rent his painting equipment (staging, brushes, ladders, drop cloths, etc.) for relief projects. In turn, he was appointed supervisor of painting crews made up of men on relief for PWA (and later, WPA) projects. Boyer, who quit his job as a musician in 1929 to get married and open a paint business, said he remembered hard times during the first few years of the Depression, but CWA and PWA projects helped his family survive.

SUMMER PEOPLE

BY JOAN H. BARTLETT

MANOMET AND MANTERS POINT

Jean and Marie Blessington spent their childhood years in two different summer colonies, Manomet and Manters Point, before they settled into their Manters Point house year-round. They first came to Plymouth in 1936.

"We used to rent a house in Manomet and we stayed in that same house for 20 or so years. We thought of it as our own and had our own rooms. We all knew each other in Manomet, which is why we went there in the first place. And if we didn't know our neighbors before, we knew them after we got there.

"When we first went to Manomet, there was nothing but cornfields all the way to Ellisville. We bought our supplies at the general store, which was in the living room of a small house nearby. A little wicket in the hallway of this house was the Manomet Post Office.

"We'd go to the beach every day. There was a nice community of young people and we did everything together. We had a record collection of Viennese waltzes and Glen Miller. We danced and we played card games, the adults and the kids together.

"We met some year-round people but mostly other summer people. We learned later there was a Long Pond group and a Boot Pond group and a beach club group and never the twain shall meet. I was at a party recently where someone from Boot Pond was introduced to someone from Long Pond. The person who introduced them thought surely they would have known each other, but they hadn't previously met.

"When the owners decided to move back to the

CYNTHIA BUTTNER FISCHER FAMILY COLLECTION
A family enjoys fresh watermelon at the beach c. 1930s.

house we were renting in Manomet, we started going to Manters Point. Most of the houses on Manters Point were built in the 1890's. They were all summer houses. The houses were part of family compounds and were rented out when family was not using them.

"A streetcar used to come down Warren Avenue and stop at Franklin House, the hotel at the entrance to Manters Point. Later, when the hotel went out of business, it was cut up and became two houses on Manters Point. One of these houses still has numbers on the rooms.

"Sometimes we went to the Pilgrim Hotel for entertainment. It was a big, square, white summer hotel farther down Warren Avenue patronized by wealthy New Yorkers. They'd dress for dinner. One night we were going out on a double date and decided to go to the Pilgrim. We walked in wearing beach-type clothes. The band, which had been playing sophisticated New York tunes, suddenly switched and started playing, 'The Wearing of the Green.' They thought we were Irish.

"At high tide you used to be able to walk all the way out to the end of the beach on the ocean side of the rocks. We'd pack a picnic and go — burning ourselves to a crisp. You used to climb up over a sand dune to get to the beach. The dunes were covered with beach roses. By 4:30 in the afternoon, you could have your supper in the shadow of the dunes in front of the Beach Club because they were so high."

Two Theaters and a Reel Runner

BY PHILIP FORMAN

During the first half of the 20th century two movie theaters provided much of Plymouth's entertainment. The 720-seat Old Colony Theater on Main Street Extension (later the Landmark Building) in downtown Plymouth and the smaller Plymouth Theater on Court Street in North Plymouth (later the site of The Cleanist) offered both children and adults inexpensive cinema programs daily. The programs always combined a double feature, a cartoon, a comedy short, a newsreel, a 20-minute chapter of an ongoing serial and a preview of coming attractions.

The program package changed three times weekly with the major features of the week playing Tuesday, Wednesday and Thursday. Tuesday was the big movie night in Plymouth, with the top feature film of the week opening that night. Another combination of films was offered every Friday and Saturday and a third set on Sunday and Monday. Children's matinees were popular on Saturdays, Sundays and holidays.

Prior to the advent of talkies in 1927, organ or piano music accompanied silent films and the entertainment package included vaudeville acts such as Coates and Soule (comedy talking and singing) and Harry Latoy (comedy juggler with his dancing hats). Both the Plymouth and Old Colony theaters had stages suitable for vaudeville as well as a big square screen for the movies.

Before the 1930s Plymouth also had a few short-lived nickelodeon theaters, including the Pastime in

ROCKLAND TRUST CO. COLLECTION

The Plymouth Theater on Court Street in North Plymouth c. 1930.

the *Old Colony Memorial* building on Middle Street, and the Park or Princess, both located downtown. But for most of the first half of the century the Plymouth Theater, built in 1909, and the Old Colony Theater, which opened in 1914, dominated the movie-going scene.

Because the two theaters were owned by the same man — Charles Moning — they showed the same movies at staggered show times each day. The reels were shuttled from one theater to another by a "reel runner," most often by Manuel "Barney" Pimental, the fourth oldest of 10 children of a North Plymouth family with roots in the Azores.

"It cost 6 cents to get in," recalled Leo Ceccarelli, referring to the early years of the Plymouth Theater. He also remembered that slides were used for advertisements between films, and that the toilets at the Plymouth theater were "upstairs, with the staircase on the outside."

"The acoustics were better [at the Plymouth] than at the Old Colony Theater," recalled Manny Valente when he was interviewed at the end of the century.

"Tuesday night was the big movie night, it was usually a couples night," Valente said. "Friday night was the night most people in North Plymouth grocery shopped, paid bills and so forth," he added.

"We didn't have much to do then," Valente pointed out, recalling a time with few radios or cars and no television. "It was a great time to go to the movies," he said, adding: "The majority walked to the theater."

On Thursdays during the 1930s, Valente and four or five friends would bundle and mail the movie news flyers for the following week, which earned them a free pass to one of the shows.

"Believe me," he recalled, "people looked forward to getting that program."

Valente said that by the late 1930s ticket prices at both theaters were 35 cents for adults and 10 cents for children.

Charlie Moning, the Plymouth native who rose from poverty to own the two theaters and a great deal of other real estate in town, often made it easy for youngsters to see the movies.

Once the show was about to begin, "Charlie purposely turned his back so the kids could sneak in and save their dime," recalled Rose Sherman Geller at the end of the 20th century.

Richard "Mousey" Pimental remembered that his brother Barney, the "reel runner," had to hustle. Barney was allocated only 15-20 minutes to get two to four 35-mm film reels from the upstairs projection booth at the Plymouth Theater down to the street and drive the 1.75 miles along what was then Route 3 to the Old Colony and back. It was a cycle he would repeat up to 12 times daily. "There were no traffic lights then and you could count the number of cars on the road on one hand," Pimental said. For nearly 20 years that was how his brother Barney made his living and raised a family.

Kenneth Peck, grandson of the builder of the Plymouth Theater, was an usher there before going into the Navy during World War II. Upon his return, he became a doorman and then assistant manager.

"Uniforms were worn," Peck recalled. "As a doorman, it was in the classic style, with a jacket and cap and a bow tie... The doorman collected the tickets and an usher showed people to a seat. It was a courtesy, but most people sat where they wanted

to anyway."

In his 1999 memoir, *Stroll Through North Plymouth*, 1920s-1940s, Jerry Rezendes remembered that the Plymouth Theater "was affectionately known as the 'garlic temple,' so-called because the tenants that lived in the same building used a great deal of garlic and the strong smell would find its way into the theater."

From an old news flyer, Rezendes cited the movie schedule for the week beginning May 7, 1939: on Sunday and Monday the main feature was "The Story of Alexander Graham Bell," starring Don Ameche, Loretta Young and Henry Fonda. On Tuesday, Wednesday and Thursday, the main feature was "Dark Victory," starring Bette Davis. The Friday and Saturday feature was "The Return of the Cisco Kid," starring Warner Baxter. The Saturday matinee featured Chapter 7 of "The Lone Ranger Rides Again."

But perhaps the biggest drama of the period was provided not by any movie but by the death of the man who owned the theaters.

Early one November morning in 1938, Charlie Moning was in his second-floor Main Street real

PIMENTAL FAMILY COLLECTION

Manuel "Barney" Pimental, who shuttled film reels from one Plymouth theater to another.

estate office. Alone and seated at his desk, he leaned over in his chair, placed a bucket or basin on the floor below, took out a freshly sharpened straight razor and slashed his throat from ear to ear, dying a very bloody death at the age of 69.

A fastidious and debonair man-about-town, a ladies man who never married, a man who began working as a downtown barber and went on to become a successful businessman and two-term selectman, Moning's death puzzled his friends and business associates.

In a front-page story reporting the suicide, the *Old Colony Memorial* wrote that Moning "took his own life for reasons one shall never know and for reasons no other one than he had a right to know."

But the two theaters, then being operated by the Interstate Theater chain under terms of a 1930 lease, continued to provide Plymouth with motion picture entertainment until the Plymouth closed in 1954 and the Old Colony in 1971.

And when his services were no longer needed as a reel runner, Barney Pimental continued to drive around town. He became a school bus driver.

38

Memories of Plymouth

Excerpted from
"Time Lines: Memories of Plymouth,"
a supplement to the *Old Colony Memorial,*
Dec. 10, 2001.

BY MAGGIE MILLS

My first home at 48 Court St. remains a special place in my memories for our eight-room apartment was located on one of the loveliest main streets in New England.

This is how historians and poets for years described Court Street, Plymouth's first public way. Established from a cart path used by the Pilgrims, it ran from Shirley Square to Cold Spring in the middle of the 19th century, then later to the Plymouth/Kingston town boundary.

It was on Court Street that the town's first environmentalist, Andrew L. Russell, planted elm trees on both sides of the street in 1830.

Though many of the trees were cut down to make way for the coming of the street railway in the 1890s, there were still a few elms left in the 1920s. The one I remember well was a huge elm with its roots pushing through the black bituminous pavement in front of 48 Court St., where Papa had his barbershop on the second floor. Our rented apartment was next door off the hall.

Below the barbershop on the street level was a store where Jacob Cohen sold all kinds of pots and kettles, crockery, and glassware, rain gear, and work clothes for the woolen mills, tack factories and cordage company workers.

Our apartment on the second floor, rented from Jacob and Harry Cohen, contained a kitchen, living room, and two bedrooms. As our family grew, Papa also rented the third floor, using two of the four bedrooms for his children and the remaining two for renters.

BACK TO SCHOOL

When school re-opens every year in September, my mind often goes back to the six years I spent at the Cornish and Burton schools on North Russell Street, the site of the old Plymouth Police Station.

It saddened me when the Plymouth School Committee closed the school buildings in 1963 following 123 years of continuous education in the Cornish, which was the older of the two buildings. The Cornish was built in 1840 and the Burton School across the yard was built in 1896.

Of the seven children in the Ketchen family, I believe it was my brother Billy and sister Miriam and I who liked school the best. It was both the teaching we received and all the extracurricular activities, especially the daily exercises and special seasonal highlights like Halloween, Christmas, Easter and, best of all, the May Pole dance in May.

For daily exercise in good weather, our physical education instructor, Miss Beatrice Garvin, had several classes at one time on the schoolyard abut-

PILGRIM SOCIETY COLLECTION

WILLIAM FORNACIARI COLLECTION

The Cornish and Burton schools on Russell Street, later the site of the Plymouth Police Headquarters. The Cornish School at the left was built in 1840 while the Burton School across the yard was built in 1896.

ting Burial Hill. We'd bend and stretch, squat and kick, all in rhythm to her loud commands. I can't remember anyone in the class disliking Miss Garvin, especially me.

The month of May never comes that I don't think of the May Pole dance Miss Garvin set up in the yard area between the Cornish and Burton schools, which is now a parking area. The big boys in the sixth grade would shimmy up to the top of the May Pole to attach pastel color ribbons, which dropped to the ground. Then, following Miss Garvin's instructions, and with music coming from a portable gramophone, 20 or 30 boys and girls would have the time of their lives skipping around the pole, at the same time twisting the pastel streamers. We loved that activity, especially when our parents were invited to look on.

I can't say I remember my very first day of school other than I was glad the Keough twins, Richard and Bobby, were in my first floor classroom, which faced Burial Hill.

Since my birthday fell on Jan. 26, and the twins' birthday fell on Feb. 22, and we lived in the same neighborhood, it was only natural that we walked to school together. The Ketchens lived at 48 Court St. and the Keoughs lived on the easterly side of Court Street, near the Methodist church, now the Beth Jacob Community Center.

Each morning I'd walk to Court House green to wait for Mrs. Keough to bring her twins across the street so we could walk together up North Russell Street. We made the trip to and from school together twice a day as we went home for lunch.

My third grade teacher, Helen Holmes, actually was my Sunday school teacher and I already loved her before I passed into her room. Reading became such a joy with Miss Holmes. She also taught me how to write, not print, my name in ink so I could take books out from the Plymouth Public Library. The head librarian, Minnie E. Burke Figmic, had a rule that children could have a library card only

She certainly was stern with her pupils, but we learned well.

when they could write their name in ink.

When I reached the fourth grade in the Burton School, I learned a good lesson. You shouldn't listen to other people's stories, good or bad, about what to expect from a teacher. When I was assigned to Terese Rogan's fourth grade I was somewhat apprehensive. I had heard that she was extremely religious since she faithfully attended Mass in St. Peter's Church before school.

I remember well her walking past our house every morning, her arms filled with lilacs in the spring for the church altar. She was always dressed in a coal black dress, coat, and hat, with a large black bag hanging from her arm. Never in all the years I knew her did she wear any color but black.

She certainly was stern with her pupils, but we learned well. But there was something more than that. We learned that she cared if her pupils went to school in rags, had holes in their shoes, or lacked pennies for milk in the 1920s.

To this day I remember the time she called me into the hall closet to tell me I was to do an errand for her. She reached out to a brass hook on the wall from which hung her black pocketbook. Upon opening it, she pulled out an envelope containing two dollars. I'll never forget her command, for that's exactly what it was. I was to escort one of the boys in the class to Eddie Hand's shoe store, which was next to Cooper's Drug Store in Town Square.

Miss Rogan said, "You're to take this envelope to Mr. Hand and tell him to fit (the boy) to a pair of shoes, nice ones, mind you. And you must never tell anyone," she added. So off we went, my classmate and I, over Burial Hill, all the while I'm thinking, what a kind person Miss Rogan really is.

It was in Anne Wilson's fifth grade class that I discovered teachers do have romance in their lives. That was when Miss Wilson's boyfriend, the band-leader Bunny Loring, would sneak up the fire escape to our second floor classroom to see my teacher.

Miss Wilson would step outside on the iron platform where they would exchange words. He then would give her a quick peck on the cheek, and turn to leave, his shoes making a clattering noise as they hit the iron steps leading down to the play-ground. She'd return to the room, her cheeks some-what pink, and pick up the lesson book to continue teaching where she had left off when interrupted by Bunny.

I also remember the exquisite miniature enameled animal pins he gave her as gifts from his father's jewelry store where he worked part-time when he was not playing with his band. She'd wear a different animal pin every day on her stylish dress, which she bought from Sadow's Dress Shop on Court Street.

HARBOR PLUNGE

While growing up at 48 Court St. in the 1920s and '30s, we children were permitted to play in a neighborhood that stretched from Shirley Square in downtown Plymouth, south to the magnificent Samoset House across from South Park Avenue. Our playmates mostly lived on Howland Street and Howland Court with a few others on Clyfton and Chilton streets. They were Italians, Irish, Greeks, French, and Jews, with a few Yanks.

There was no class distinction in the neighborhood except when the mistress of the Hedge House

There was no class distinction in the neighborhood

at the corner of Court and North Russell streets entertained her grandchildren, nieces and nephews. We had no warm feelings for these children, for they and their grandmother's gardener would rout us when we climbed over the weathered fence from our own backyard at 48 Court St. to snitch forbidden fruit: the juicy pears, deep red cherries and tart apples from the well-tended Hedge garden.

At the time, the Hedge garden extended northerly from the back of the mansion, now the Compass Bank, behind the stores and houses along Court Street to a sand pit which abutted the block at 52 Court St., owned by John Collas and Nick Collas.

We children looked forward to summers, for we were permitted to remain outdoors until 8 and sometimes 9 p.m. If we took our time to horse around on our way home, officer Lincoln Wixon would meet us near Johnny King's variety store at the corner of Court and Howland streets to warn us that Papa was on the lookout and that we better get

in the house before we got caught.

This happened almost every night after we did the supper dishes. Billy, myself and sometimes our younger sister Rob would head for Howland Court where the Zucchelli, Keenan, Stringer, Locatelli, Cingolani and Venturi children gathered to compete in challenging games until the sun went down.

Sitting on the front steps of the weathered shingled houses, originally built for fishermen, were the mothers of the Zucchellis and Keenans, and the old maids in the Stringer family who would yell that if we didn't cut out the screaming and hollering, we'd be banished from the court. Of course, they really didn't mean it. They were just annoyed because our yells were drowning out their gossiping.

Even rain or heavy fog creeping in from Plymouth harbor did not faze us, for in the court at the rear of the Old Colony Laundry was a very old barn with pigeons flying in and out of the gaping holes in the roof. We'd take shelter in the barn to play hide and seek or even "ghosts." The flickering light from the candles we had smuggled out of our home made the barn an eerie place.

I must have been 5 or 6 at the time for I could count the curfew bells rung by the sexton in the Unitarian Church. Papa told us over and over that when we heard the bells it was time to come home, and there was no maybe about it.

We also had wonderful times during the daylight hours, for all of us would go down to the waterfront to play on the sandy beach at the foot of Brewster Street.

Very few in our gang, including me, could swim. Despite this handicap, we had great fun playing on the State Pier abutting our beach. Better still, we were panhandling from tourists who came from

Boston on the Old Colony or the Nantasket steamboat line to tour the town, eat a shore meal at Haire's restaurant across the street, or buy imported souvenirs from the shops on Water Street.

Bored by the boys rattling on about the history of Plymouth Rock, some of the tourists would break away to stroll up North Street to A.S. Burbank's shop opposite Moore's department store, which later became Buttner's.

At Burbank's the tourists would buy blue Pilgrim plates, cups and saucers imported from England, cheap pewter showing scenes of historic sites in town and postcards and calendars with the Pilgrim theme.

TO MARKET

When my family, the Ketchens, lived at 48 Russell St., our neighborhood grocery store was Clough's Market at 84 Summer St.

I was a sophomore in Plymouth High School when Mama made me do the food shopping. Every day after school, she would hand me a list of items to buy to feed the six kids and two adults in our household.

Because Mama was a saver, a habit I picked up from her, she always told me to look for specials, especially on canned goods, which Mr. Clough Sr. promoted.

For example, four cans of Campbell's tomato soup sold for 25 cents. Add a can of water to each can and Mama had enough to give us a second helping. With this, we had soda crackers (six packages for 25 cents) or graham crackers (two one pound packages for 27 cents.)

I got these prices from the ads Mr. Clough ran

weekly in the *Old Colony Memorial*.

If Papa had a good day in his barbershop, then he'd hand Mama her daily $2 stipend to buy the groceries the next day.

Every morning, she'd tell our Whiting milkman to leave three quarts of whole milk on the back steps of our big white painted house at the corner of Russell Street and Bartlett Lane. Later, we lived at 39 High St.

Each quart of milk cost 12 cents. Lodi's farm, much farther up on Summer Street, sold their bottled milk for 10 cents a quart, I believe.

Luckily, we had an enormous wooden icebox in our back hallway, which held a big block of ice to keep the milk from going sour and the meats fresh, not that we had much meat.

During the summer, the iceman, who hauled loads of ice from the plant on Hedges Road in North Plymouth, was a very popular man with the children in our neighborhood. After he chopped a sizeable block of ice, which he carried in a canvas bag into our house, we children would rush to the rear of his old truck to gather up ice chips in our sweaty hands to wet our tongues, parched from racing around with our friends.

Once in a while, during the extremely hot summer days, Mama would break down to open her purse so I could run down to Clough's market to purchase six bottles of Coca Cola for 25 cents or a bottle of Zarex which she stretched out to take care of her children for two days.

One of the things Mama liked best about Mr. Clough were his weekend specials, which he sold

Ellis Brewster at the wheel of his car in Town Square with students in the back seat c. 1913. The Town House is at the left.

Fridays and Saturdays. These were very popular dinner specials. The boiled dinner included three pounds of fancy brisket corned beef, three pounds of potatoes, a turnip and one new cabbage, all for $1.

Or if Mama didn't want to smell up the house on a Sunday, then she'd have me buy a 3 1/2 pound fowl, three pounds of potatoes, a can of cranberry sauce and a can of best peas or corn for $1.43.

Ice Age

I still remember the iceman coming up the backyard steps of the stoop to my parents' second-floor apartment at 48 Court St.

In later years when we lived on High Street, Orrin Sherman and his son, Carleton, would come to the neighborhood in their old truck, painted white, which replaced the horse and wagon they earlier used to deliver ice in the summer.

Carleton's widow, Ida, told me her father-in-law, Orrin, cut ice on four different ponds, one in Carver and three in Plymouth, among them Russell Mills Pond in Chiltonville.

What I liked best was when our iceman chipped blocks of ice in the truck to fit into our icebox.

While he was in the house, sliding the ice block into the icebox, we kids would be out on Spring Lane. We'd boost one of our gang up into Sherman's wagon to scoop out slivers of ice by hand into our paws. When we saw Mr. Sherman come out of the house, we'd run like hares up the granite steps on the south side of Burial Hill to hide behind the big monument in memory of Thomas Cushing.

I think Papa bought our old icebox from Sears, Roebuck or Harry Cohen, who used to sell secondhand appliances from his neat little shop on Market Street.

I remember well the first refrigerator Papa got for Mama later, when we were living at 39 High St. I know the refrigerator was secondhand because it was scratched and had small dents. Mama insisted it go in the back entry of the High Street house, which opened up on Spring Lane.

Papa had also just replaced our black oil stove with a brand new cream and green trimmed enamel range with oil burners.

Believe it or not, Mama was never happy with the new stove, for Papa had it delivered as a surprise without consulting her about the color.

39

Plymouth During the Depression

THE LATER YEARS

BY KARIN GOLDSTEIN

By 1935, confidence in the New Deal was beginning to wane. In August the Emergency Relief Act had run out of funding for Plymouth and many residents were jobless while they waited for new projects to be approved. Unemployment reached 1,736 (1,367 men and 369 women) by August, dropping to 1,360, or 24.8 percent of the employable population by October.

Even the *Old Colony Memorial*, usually supportive of New Deal relief programs, expressed a need for better solutions. An editorial on Aug. 8, 1935 forecast a landslide Republican victory in Rhode Island as "the beginning of the end," claiming that "the American people are becoming fed up with broken promises . . .(and) huge deficits." It was feared that ERA projects would "create a permanent pauper class . . . unwilling to go back to private industry for work." To that end, the *OCM* editorial encouraged federal help in reopening local industries such as the Plymouth Foundry to create gainful employment. The town had high

HELEN BELCHER COLLECTION

Looking south down Main Street from Shirley Square, early 1940s. Note the downtown post office building at the far end of the street.

hopes for a government loan to reopen Standish Mills with funds matched by local subscribers, but the project fell through in December.

Some of Roosevelt's early programs were beginning to run their course. One of the two Civilian Conservation Corps camps in the Plymouth area, the 103rd, was ordered to leave Myles Standish State Forest for another location once projects were com-

pleted. During the preceding months, annoyance with occasional CCC hooliganism and drunkenness on town visits had diminished. The "undesirables" left, and Plymoutheans became fond of those remaining. The newspaper carried occasional paragraphs on CCC vaudeville shows and human-interest stories.

The 102nd CCC Camp spent four and one-half years at Myles Standish State Forest. Townspeople were fond of "the boys" in spite of the fact that by 1937 most of them were from cities like Brockton and Fall River, rather than Plymouth. Townspeople were invited to open houses to see their progress and share a meal. "We can never repay you," said Selectman James White at the camp's fourth birthday. That year, 75,000 people visited Myles Standish State Forest and used the roads and camps built by the Civilian Conservation Corps. Camping was a fast-growing industry in Plymouth. By November, the 102nd was the only CCC unit on the South Shore, including Cape Cod and the islands. The camp disbanded in December, to the sorrow of the town.

Federal relief funding gradually shifted from manual labor typified by the Civil Works Administration, to public works projects. The Public Works Administration, founded as part of the National Industrial Recovery Act in 1933, was responsible for the construction of causeways, bridges, dams, and most of the schools built in that era. Plymouth had three major public works proposals: a new high school, a new sewage system, and the development of waterfront facilities. In October of 1935, the federal government offered a grant of $138,150 to construct a new high school, to be matched by $189,850 from the town. Groundbreaking on Lincoln Street across from the existing high school began in December. The school committee had been urging construction of a larger school for years to relieve overcrowding, exacerbated by the bad economy. The project was funded through the PWA and employed local laborers and carpenters, both working and on relief. When completed, it featured an auditorium so students didn't have to stand for assemblies, as well as a modern chemistry lab.

Roosevelt responded to the need for new solu-

MARY MARVELLI BAIETTI COLLECTION
An early 1930s Marvelli family photo.

tions with the "second New Deal," to win back the support of the American people. His efforts appear to have been successful, as the 1936 election brought an unprecedented 91 percent of Plymouth's registered voters to the polls. While Alfred Landon, the Republican candidate for president, received 50 percent of the Plymouth vote, Roosevelt had a respectable 44 percent.

One of the most important parts of the second New Deal was the Works Progress Administration, created as part of the Emergency Relief Appropriation Act in April 1935. The WPA was to have a significant impact on work life in Plymouth over the next several years.

Plymouth's first WPA effort — a sewing project — began in October 1935. The project initially funded 45 women for six hours of work, five days a week. The women sewed clothes for WPA, ERA and welfare families in rooms above the old jail. There had been a smaller scale sewing project in 1934, funded by the ERA, which employed 15 women. The WPA sewing project continued until 1941. At its peak in 1936, it employed 46 local women, mostly married. The women worked four days a week from 8:30 a.m. to 4:30 p.m. In 1937, they were producing 375 garments per week, mostly

durable work clothes, but occasionally a graduation or communion dress. The clothes were distributed through a warehouse on Alden Street. One drawback of the WPA and other federal relief efforts cited by recent historians is the reinforcement of traditional gender roles. In other words, only one married partner was employed, typically the husband. The women employed in the Plymouth sewing project were considered heads of household.

Lydia Marvelli was one of the seamstresses for the WPA Sewing Project. She was considered a head of household because her husband, Robert, a master weaver for Puritan Mills, lost an arm in a hunting accident in 1924. Their daughter, Mary Marvelli Baietti, remembered that for her father, losing his arm was like losing his masculinity. "Nobody hired handicapped people then for any length of time," Mary recalled. Lydia raised her three children, took care of the grandparents, sewed for the WPA during the day and for the well-to-do Knife family at night. Robert gardened, looked after the chickens, and cooked. Like many immigrant families in North Plymouth, the Marvellis had tremendous pride and refused to accept clothing from the sewing project, even though they were entitled to it. Mary remembered, "My mother tried not to dress us in things that came from the WPA — that's why she made clothes left over from the Knife (Cortelli) family. She'd rip apart clothes from the Knifes and make us dresses or skirts so we wouldn't be singled out from the other children in school."

With the establishment of the WPA, the ERA came to an end. It closed in Plymouth in December of 1935. WPA jobs were sporadic, subject to funding. Some WPA jobs were short-term in nature, such as snow removal. After a January snowstorm,

350 men were employed for three days to clear streets and sidewalks. The stereotype of WPA workers leaning on their shovels was present in Plymouth. One Plymouth resident, who grew up on North Street, recalled hearing remarks about snow shovelers "slacking off." Years later, she remembered that the men would lift the snow up several feet onto the back of a truck, without the benefit of a hydraulic lift. Then they would stop for a while and lean on their shovels. "I think they were resting," she said. "Snow shoveling is heavy work."

The WPA sponsored several significant public works projects. One of the most enduring was the improvement of Plymouth's waterfront. Workers created a 40-foot fill at the Water Street beach, formerly occupied by wharves prior to 1921. A 12-foot retaining wall was built to separate the beach from the sidewalk and parking spaces above. As more and more Americans purchased cars, parking spaces were needed for tourists. Another lasting WPA project was the construction of Taylor Avenue in Manomet, connecting Manomet Point with White Horse Beach. The crew filled the marshy ground and built 3,100 feet of dirt road. Many other streets were repaved and had curbs added under the auspices of the WPA. Ramo Bongiovanni worked for the WPA, constructing curbs on the state highway, then Route 3, in Manomet in 1938. "You couldn't *buy* a job when we graduated," he recalled.

Not everyone was eligible for a WPA job. According to the *OCM*, only about 275 men and 55 women were employed in May of 1936. The town picked up some of those not eligible, as in the case of a man employed in seasonal odd jobs who applied to the town for work to pay two years of back taxes. "It's the first time in my life that I've ever sought the help of you gentlemen . . . I've enough money to get by on food and clothing but I would like some work to get money for the taxes," one man wrote to the newspaper that year. Workers employed by the welfare department earned less money than federally employed workers did. Pay for the WPA was 50 cents per hour, but only 25 cents per hour for welfare workers.

Another program established by the second New Deal was the National Youth Administration, designed to help young people in high school and college as well as non-students. In Plymouth, NYA funding was used to employ 17 youths to lead recreation activities ranging from baseball to dancing. Another recreation program, run by the WPA, organized checker and horseshoe tournaments. The NYA joined with the WPA recreation project again in 1937 to offer a range of programs from baseball to tennis to pottery. One of the projects for the 27 employed youths was to work with the parks department on the upkeep of Stephens Field. The NYA also employed young men to help shelve books at the library.

As a schoolgirl, Nellie Youngman Barboza was employed by a federal program, probably the NYA. Her family's financial situation was tight, as her father was seasonally employed as a fisherman. When someone suggested that her mother apply for aid, Mrs. Youngman vehemently refused. "My mother would rather *eat crumbs* than apply for aid." Working for pay was a different story. Nellie stayed after school to wash the blackboards and help the teacher. She brought her pay home to her mother. "This is for the coal," her mother would say.

Plymouth didn't just depend on the government for unemployment relief and benefits for its citizens.

Groups like the firemen and policemen held fundraisers to help the jobless. Businessmen also helped, through efforts like the continuation of the rest and nutrition classes at Hedge School. North Plymouth merchants gave funds to provide milk for undernourished children in their community when the five-year-old program was threatened. In May 1935, North Plymouth entrepreneur Louis Knife (Luigi Cortelli) donated a field for a children's playground.

Local charities like the Fragment Society continued to help those in need. In 1936, the women's organization assisted 95 families and 16 individuals with clothing, shoes, bedding, furniture and medical care. The Fragment Society was very discreet about offering assistance. Helen Belcher remembered riding with her mother, a Fragment Society member, to people's houses to bring donations. Helen, then a young girl, had to stay in the car in order to protect the privacy of the client.

Even those who worked for the WPA helped their neighbors. During the Red Cross fund drive shortly after the 1938 hurricane, 20 of the women who participated in the WPA sewing project donated their own time to sew Red Cross banners to hang on Court Street. The women couldn't afford the money to join the Red Cross, so they helped in their own way.

Local merchants, particularly grocers, helped their neighbors by extending credit. "The grocers carried us all through the Depression," remembered Jean Patenaude. The family shopped at George Mayer's market on Sandwich Street. Her father paid every week, and if he couldn't pay the whole bill, Mr. Mayer put it on his account. Painter Harold Boyer recalled his gratitude to grocer Guy Cooper.

In the early 1930s, when Boyer's business was just starting, Cooper extended credit during the winter season when work was scarce. Boyer paid him more during the summer when he worked. Jelly Baietti remembered how Knife's and other stores accepted credit. "They let people live like human beings," he said.

Landlords also accepted late payment during those times. Richmond Talbot Sr. remembered his father renting a house on Mayflower Street to a man who worked in the Mayflower Worsted Mills in Kingston. As millwork was often sporadic, the tenant often couldn't pay the rent, but would catch up when there was work. "We had to carry him," Talbot recalled. "People were a lot more responsible about paying back then. If someone said that he'd pay two dollars, he'd have the money when you came for it."

While many people were able to keep their houses through hard times, some families weren't as fortunate. Enzo Monti remembered some neighbors in North Plymouth who lost their house. The father was a carpenter and didn't have enough work to pay the mortgage. Louis Knife ended up owning their house and renting it back to them. Coeli Tarantino Bongiovanni's family also lost their house. Her father, an immigrant shoemaker, died in 1935 of a heart attack, and the family found it difficult to make ends meet. They paid rent to the bank for a time; it was Calli's job to deliver the $20 rent money each month. When the bank found a buyer for the house, the family moved into an apartment on Washington Street. Her husband Ramo's family was able to hold on to their house. "Ramo's mother was set on a house — she saved money. If they had to eat polenta and chicken broth, fine," she recalled.

Sometimes the banks would accept reduced payments on the interest. Marie Martinelli Fehlow, a child during the Depression, later found out that her family had been paying only the interest on the mortgage during those lean years.

While there were pockets of wealth, Plymouth was an average community. Yankees were generally thrifty and conservative by nature. Although her father had a good job, Helen Belcher remembered her mother as a frugal housewife. "She just tightened up during the Depression," said Helen.

"We didn't have much," said Jean Patenaude, but neither did anyone else." Many of the immigrants in North Plymouth who had arrived to start new lives in the previous three decades were used to scrimping. "We didn't know we were poor," remembered Enzo Monti. "Everyone else was in the same boat."

Many people fed their families by hunting and gardening, a long-time habit that helped carry people through hard times. Doris Gerard Woolson's father took care of a huge garden, and frequently hunted for rabbits in the woods off what later became Route 44. The Talbots on Mayflower Street kept a garden, and Richmond Talbot Sr. remembered having a cellar full of preserves. Most of the residents of North Plymouth had gardens, and many kept chickens. Blueberry picking was a popular way to make extra money during the late summer. Blueberries grew in the woods near where Seven Hills Road exists today, as well as at Braunecker's Farm in North Plymouth, where the Plymouth Industrial Park was built later in the century. Jelly Baietti remembered picking cranberries in the Phillips bogs near Forest Avenue and in Smelt Pond in Kingston. He and other children would pick after the scoopers had left, receiving 10 cents for a six-

quart bucket, and $5.00 for 50 buckets. Nita Fiocchi Scagliarini remembered getting up at 7:00 a.m. during blueberry season to pick berries with her family. The money they earned went to pay the taxes.

During the Depression, new clothes were few and far between. Enzo Monti recalled that he got a new outfit every Easter. That became his Sunday clothes, and what used to be his Sunday clothes became school clothes. Old school clothes became play clothes. Jean Blessington remembered a schoolmate making do with shoes that couldn't be resoled anymore by stuffing the soles with cardboard. Other families made their own clothes, including underwear made from flour sacks, trimmed with Hamburg lace.

While thrift was part of the Plymouth character before the Depression, hard times did affect lifestyle, as seen in population statistics. In contrast to the overcrowded school system of the early 1930s, the number of students in the lower grades dropped dramatically, and schools actually had empty classrooms by 1937. Town reports show that the birthrate had been dropping gradually since 1915, with a nadir from 1930-1934. It is not surprising that this period marked the depth of the Depression. The marriage rate also dipped slightly, between 10 and 20 percent during the early and middle 1930s.

The economy in Plymouth began to rally in late 1936. In 1937, town workers' salaries were restored to their 1932 levels, when those earning more than $1,000 had suffered a pay cut of 10 percent. Since 1929, the major industries had decreased wages about 30 percent. Some of that drop was made up in 1935, and the rest by November of 1936, when

Mabbett's Mills, Puritan Mills, Mayflower Worsted, and later, the Plymouth Cordage Co., raised wages 10 percent or more. While the rope industry fluctuated, particularly due to droughts in the Midwest that resulted in fewer orders for binder twine, 1937 was a good year for the Cordage. A Supreme Court decision reduced competition from prison-made rope, which had undercut prices for the past several years. While the defunct Standish Mills was demolished in 1937, new industry was attracted to the town. In November a curtain factory moved into the Plymouth Mills facility on Town Brook.

The slight improvement in local industry was not enough to employ all those who needed jobs. The programs of the second New Deal continued in Plymouth through 1940, decreasing slightly in number each year. In 1938 the town hosted 27 WPA projects (some listed twice in the town report, probably due to funding). Projects expanded that year to include repair to hurricane damage, particularly in the parks department. New projects included a survey of cemeteries and work in the Manomet cemetery. The sewing project, clam seeding and curbing installation continued. In 1939 the town hosted 26 projects, including a new tourist information booth. By 1940, things were improving. The welfare department actually had money left over at the end of the year. The number of WPA projects dropped to 17.

As involvement in the war in Europe drew near and the Depression seemed to be ending, Roosevelt's

1936 TOWN REPORT

The new Plymouth High School, built during the Depression with WPA help c. 1936.

popularity in Plymouth grew. In 1940, 6,094 of 6,998 (87 percent) of eligible Plymouth voters participated in the presidential election. Wendell Willkie, the Republican challenger, received 3,002 votes, 49.3 percent of the votes cast, while Roosevelt got 2,969 votes or 48.7 percent. Roosevelt lost the town by only 33 votes, the closest a Democrat had come to carrying Plymouth since Woodrow Wilson ran second to Theodore Roosevelt and both out-

> ## *As for the rest of the country, the onset of America's involvement in World War II helped to end the decade-long economic depression.*

polled the incumbent Republican president, William Howard Taft, in 1912.

Jean Blessington, whose family summered in Manomet, remembered making "Win for Willkie" badges out of folded dollar bills. She demonstrated, folding the bill in quarters to form a "w", and then accordion pleating the folded bill in the other direction. When opened, the bill formed a flat "w" which could be pinned to one's lapel.

Residents of industrial, immigrant North Plymouth, however, worshipped Roosevelt. "There was no one like FDR," remembered Nellie Youngman Barboza, "he was like a god." "Anyone who ran against FDR was like the Antichrist," mused Enzo Monti. "In high school I saw one of my classmates kiss a picture of Wendell Willkie on the cover of Life magazine. I thought, 'She'll go straight to hell!'" "He was like God," concurred Ramo Bongiovanni. "Many people had a framed picture of Roosevelt on their wall."

As for the rest of the country, the onset of America's involvement in World War II helped to end the decade-long economic depression. By 1941, the town's welfare department was running a job-finding program with industries involved with defense work. WPA funding decreased, and only nine projects operated in Plymouth that year. In 1942, the welfare department's function shifted to providing information to people whose lifestyles were changed by war rationing. That year there were only three WPA projects in Plymouth: nutrition, recreation and household aids. Even the long-running sewing project had ended. The WPA faded out in 1943.

"Plymouth had stabilized by the early 1940s," said Richmond Talbot Sr., who at that time returned to Plymouth to join his father in the insurance business. To Enzo Monti, the Depression ended when mothers went back to work.

Many of the thrifty habits learned during the Depression era were hard to let go. Even at the end of the century, Jean Blessington and many of her contemporaries took special care of their nice clothes, remembering the days when new outfits were rare. To Jelly Baietti, growing up in the Depression meant not throwing anything away; he continued to have a hard time disposing of anything potentially useful.

While some people had sad memories of poverty and insecurity, others fondly remembered the feeling of close-knit community. "I have no bad memories from those times," mused Jelly Baietti.

The legacy of the Depression was more than just thrifty habits. Many products of Depression-era projects still existed at the end of the century. The Sparrow House pottery continued as a museum and ceramic studio. Hundreds of children each year used the 1936 high school building, which later became part of the Nathaniel Morton School. Thousands of visitors enjoyed the fruits of 1930s public works projects like Myles Standish State Forest, Nelson Street Park, and the stone wall along Plymouth's waterfront.

Plymouth survived the Depression, thanks to town and federal government projects, and neighbors helping each other.

MEANWHILE ...1930-1940

◆ According to the U.S. Census, the population of the U.S. in 1930 was 122,775,046.

◆ Immigration of foreign laborers was prohibited by the State Department in 1930, a move that reflected concern about unemployment throughout the country.

◆ *All Quiet on the Western Front* won the Academy Award for best picture of 1929-30.

◆ In 1930, a forest fire in Plymouth spread from White Island Pond toward the Long Pond summer colony, then south to Little Herring Pond. An estimated 24,000 acres burned in 48 hours.

◆ Arthur Fiedler founded the Boston Pops Orchestra in 1930.

◆ The Star-Spangled Banner was officially adopted as the national anthem in 1931.

◆ By 1932, unemployment in the U.S. reached 13 million; more than 1,300 banks throughout the country had closed.

◆ In 1932, first class postage rates rose to three cents an ounce.

◆ 1932: Congress approves the Norris-LaGuardia Act, acknowledging labor's right to organize.

◆ During the summer of 1932, the "Bonus Army" of unemployed veterans of WWI camped out in Washington, D.C., seeking cash payments for their bonus certificates. The Senate refused payment and federal troops were used to drive them out.

◆ In the 1932 presidential election, Franklin Delano Roosevelt was elected in a Democratic landslide, defeating the incumbent Republican, Herbert Hoover.

◆ By 1933, the average life expectancy in the U.S. was 59, a gain of 10 years since 1900.

◆ Prohibition ended on Dec. 5, 1933 when Utah became the 36th state to ratify the 21st Amendment.

◆ In 1933, the first drive-in movie theatre opened in Camden, NJ.

◆ In 1934, Henry Ford restored the $5.00-a-day minimum wage to 47,000 of his 70,000 workers.

◆ The federal Social Security program began in 1935.

◆ Notable stage plays during the 1930s included *Ah, Wilderness!* by Eugene O'Neill, *Our Town* by Thornton Wilder and *Abe Lincoln in Illinois* by Robert E. Sherwood.

◆ On June 22, 1935, the Bourne and Sagamore Bridges opened to traffic across the Cape Cod Canal. The vertical lift railroad bridge opened Dec. 29.

◆ President Roosevelt carried all but two states in the 1936 presidential election, defeating Republican opponent Alf Landon in the largest presidential vote cast to date.

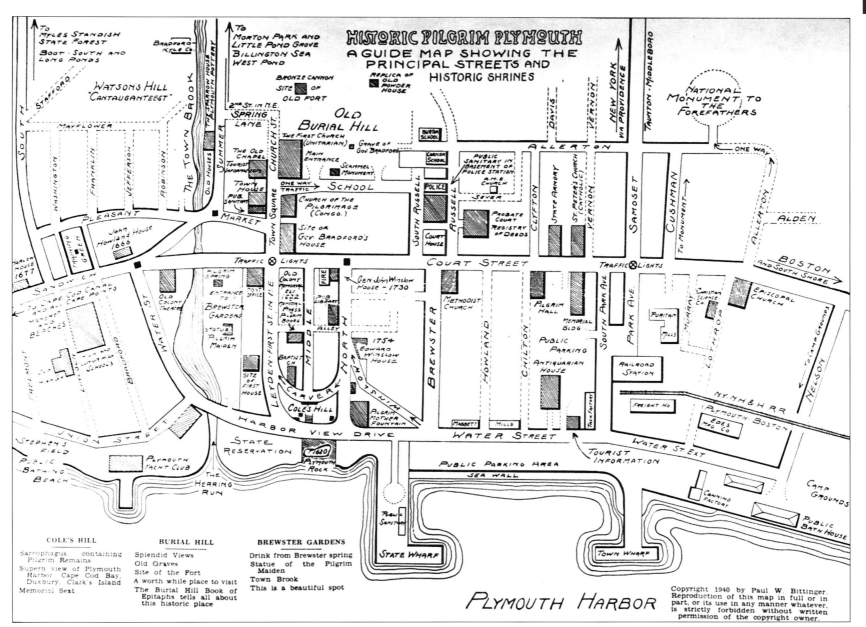

40

HISTORIC PILGRIM PLYMOUTH
A GUIDE MAP SHOWING THE PRINCIPAL STREETS AND HISTORIC SHRINES

COLE'S HILL

Sarcophagus, containing
Pilgrim Remains

Superb view of Plymouth
Harbor Cape Cod Bay,
Duxbury, Clark's Island

Memorial Seat

BURIAL HILL

Splendid Views
Old Graves
Site of the Fort
A worth while place to visit
The Burial Hill Book of
Epitaphs tells all about
this historic place

BREWSTER GARDENS

Drink from Brewster spring
Statue of the Pilgrim
Maiden
Town Brook
This is a beautiful spot

Copyright 1940 by Paul W. Bittinger.
Reproduction of this map in full or in
part, or its use in any manner whatever,
is strictly forbidden without written
permission of the copyright owner.

PLYMOUTH HARBOR

A 1940 map of downtown Plymouth by Old Colony Memorial *publisher Paul Bittinger features "historic shrines."*
Note the references to "public sanitary" facilities at both the police station and Town House.

SUMMER PEOPLE

BY JOAN H. BARTLETT

PLYMOUTH BEACH

The Aimone family spent summers on Plymouth Beach. Two daughters, Linda Donovan and Rose Marie Murphy, recalled those years. They later became year-round residents, as did one brother and many of their children. Another brother remained a summer resident.

"We rented the very last cottage on the beach. We first came for a week or so in the early 1940's. In those days there was a wharf at the end of the beach. Manuel Costa Sr., who had a fishing boat, ferried us to our cottage and back. He also dropped off ice, milk, bread and other supplies each day. The only person who drove on the beach was the curator of the bird sanctuary; otherwise you walked or went by boat. We used to call him The Birdman. He'd come out and check the dunes. There were just four or five cottages on the beach and a few duck blinds. In 1942, after about two years of renting, my parents bought the next to the last cottage.

"It was wartime. There was a little hut on the beach where the Coast Guard kept a patrol. The coastguardsmen walked to the end of the beach and back with a Doberman. We had to keep the wooden shutters on both sides of the house shut after we put on the lights at night. My parents had to have a pass with a picture ID with them at all times. Bug Light was manned by the Coast Guard. The sailors rowed a large boat into Plymouth for their day off and we would wave to them. One night we had a northeast storm and they couldn't get back to Bug Light. We watched them try. My mother thought they were going to drown. They beached the boat and spent the night at our house. That was quite a thrill.

"We lived in Franklin, where my father had his business. He would drive to Plymouth each evening and be brought to the beach by boat and return the same way the next morning. We would be ferried back and forth to the harbor each Sunday as well, because my mother and father insisted that we get to church. Some Sundays we walked down the beach, holding our Mary Jane shoes, crossed Manters Point and were picked up by a bus that went down Warren Avenue to take people to church.

"The dunes seemed enormous. We used to play king of the mountain. We never tired of playing and running on the rocks. We had the ocean on one side and the harbor on the other. There was nobody out there and there were no cars. Some days we would spend all day planning a theatrical which we'd perform for our parents in the evening at about 6 o'clock on the broken down, disintegrating wharf.

"In the early morning you could see the whole fishing fleet heading out and at 4 in the afternoon heading back in. We made friends with the fishermen. My brother John at 7 years old caught his first striped bass. We fished for flounder off the marker — the black marker. At low tides we'd anchor to it. We dug clams. Lobsters were a dime a dozen. We used to climb out and sit on the roof of the porch and sunbathe.

"We went to dances at the yacht club rowing across the harbor together. Linda's job was to sit in the bow with a spotlight; Rose Marie's was to row. We had to leave the yacht club at a certain time or Father would flash a signal from the cottage and our friends would tell us to hurry and go home."

> "In the early morning you could see the whole fishing fleet heading out and at 4 in the afternoon heading back in."

I Remember...

PERSONAL MEMORIES OF 20TH CENTURY PLYMOUTH

At the end of the 20th century many Plymouth residents who were then in their 70s or 80s shared their memories of what the town was like when they were growing up. Some of the most vivid recollections were of North Plymouth:

You should have seen the groups of people walking home from a day's work at the Plymouth Cordage Co. They'd all be singing Italian folk songs from the old country. Many cellars were used to make and store wine and put up vegetables and fruit. North Plymouth was loaded with apple and pear trees. We also had grapevines everywhere. Some

> ### *Everyone in the neighborhood was your friend.*

WILLIAM FORNACIARI COLLECTION

A postcard view of Court Street in North Plymouth c. 1900. The German Lutheran Church is at the right while the Plymouth Cordage Co. Loring Reading Room is on the hill at the left.

nights after work a man would come by with a wheelbarrow full of crabs. We'd all sit on the curb, up and down both sides of the street and eat them. They were two for a nickel.

We were all poor but we never thought about it because we were happy having fun, working hard and always had plenty of food to eat. Everyone in

the neighborhood was your friend. Doors were never locked. People would gather on their porches and visit with each other while singing and eating. It seems that everything we did was done around food, lots of food.

— Arthur Ragazzini

Maria Rosa Marcella, my courageous mother, had left a small town in Portugal, near the northern Spanish border, in search of her dream of becoming a schoolteacher. In Plymouth she met my father, Francisco Maria Janeiro, also from the same area of Portugal, and they were married in 1920 at St. Mary's Church in North Plymouth.

Harris Hall, which housed the Plymouth Cordage Co. restaurant where a worker could get a complete dinner for 25 cents and where the company sponsored vaudeville shows and an annual Christmas program.

Thus began their lives as part of the story of the Plymouth Cordage Co. My sister Aurora was born in 1922 and I was born in 1929. Our home was a typical Cordage "block," No. 5 Ropewalk Court — an eight-family apartment building with another, No. 6 Ropewalk Court, just down the hill. The families were Portuguese, Italian, German and French, with names like Gallo, Soares, Ferreira, Valeriani, Makier, Jesse and Gascoyne. Our lives centered around the Hedge School, the Loring Reading Room, Cordage Auditorium for socials, Cordage Men's Club for bowling and St. Mary's Church.

— Mary Alice Janeiro Post

As I look back, I think of the hope, courage and faith that it must have taken for a Catholic German family of 14 to leave a tiny village in Bavaria,

Germany, and come to the United States. My grandfather, August Brenner, arrived here in 1899, along with his parents, Henry and Anna Wurzburger Brenner, and two brothers. He became a naturalized U.S. citizen in 1905 when he married Mary "Annie" Bassler. Her parents, John and Mary Braunecker Bassler, had a large farm just over the Kingston line.

I remember as a little girl my grandmother used to sit at the kitchen table and make wonderful German pastries. My grandfather would sit in the rocker near the kitchen stove and play his accordion and harmonica. While playing German polkas he'd tap his foot to the music and have a big smile on his face.

My father worked in the Cordage with his brothers and at one time he had the opportunity to

learn the painting trade. My mother and he agreed that he would have to take the cut in pay, from $21 per week to $16 per week, but Mom and Dad knew this was an opportunity to learn a trade and then go into business for themselves, so around 1938 they made this choice.

Mom and Dad opened up a retail store in 1945 in North Plymouth, selling paint, wallpaper and artist supplies. It was called "Brenner's Paint Shop" and it was very successful.

— Jane Brenner Weston

I was born in Italy in 1913 and came over here when I was very young. I lived in North Plymouth all my life. There were 12 children in our family — eight sisters and four brothers. One of my sisters died of whooping cough in 1923.

In the old days you used to call the grocer and they would deliver your groceries. I used to deliver

In the old days you used to call the grocer and they would deliver your groceries.

bread. We'd go up Cherry Street and up Smith's Lane. That used to be farmland. The bread cost 10 cents a loaf. The French bread and what we used to call the "Portagee" bread, the round loaves, were 7 cents a loaf. I used to walk — I was 10, 11, 12 years old.

My father had a horse and team. You know who used to borrow my father's team? Vanzetti (of Sacco-Vanzetti fame). He used to deliver eels on Saturday

The Knapp School on Court Street in North Plymouth c. 1900.

morning. He delivered eels and fish. My violin teacher was with Vanzetti that morning delivering clams. He was a star witness – Beltrando Brini.

— Primo Bastoni

I was born at 417 Court St. in the middle of a block that was owned by the Plymouth Cordage Co., which my father rented, of course, because he worked for the company. That was Aug. 2, 1903. The nurse attending my mother was from the Cordage.

I started school at the Spooner Street School, which has been torn down. It was at the corner of Seaview and Spooner streets. It was a single-room, two-class schoolhouse for first and second grades. For the third grade I went to the new Hedge School, which had been built the year before. I went from there to the Knapp School for fifth, sixth, seventh and eighth grades. We walked to school, of course, because we didn't have a bus.

Then I took the trolley to the Morton School on Lincoln Street for ninth grade and then four years to the high school across the street where the town offices are now. I graduated from Plymouth High School in 1922. There were only 59 in our class.

My father told me I could go to school as long as I behaved myself. If I didn't behave myself and got kicked out or anything like that I was done and I was going to go to work. So I tried to behave myself. In those days you didn't sass the teacher back, and if you did he had a nice strap that was about an inch wide and he took you out in the dressing room and used the strap on you.

—Willard Dittmar

I graduated from Plymouth High School in 1935. It was the middle of the Depression and you couldn't buy a job. A year after I graduated I got a job at Gambini's [luncheonette] – on Main Street, next to Puritan Clothing. I made ice cream and worked in the kitchen for 25 cents an hour, which was the going rate. Then I worked for the WPA off and on for about $12 a week. I worked in Manomet with carpenters and cement makers, making curbing. In 1939 I got a job at the Plymouth Cordage Co. I handed over the pay to my mother and she was able to pay off the mortgage on our North Plymouth house.

My mother was Adelaide Scagliarini. My father was Pasquale Bongiovanni, known as El Bianc ("Blondie") because he was fair for an Italian. They were from northern Italy – Bologna. My father was a socialist from Italy…there were lots of socialists. Mr. Vanzetti was blamed for the armed car robbery and murder. My mother was a witness – she said he was selling fish in North Plymouth that Friday afternoon. She went to court. It was a horrible experience – immigrants couldn't speak English. The attorneys just tore them apart. Sure there was discussion about socialism in the Italian clubs, but I was too young…

Skating on Store Pond opposite the Plymouth Cordage Co. in North Plymouth c. 1930s.

Roosevelt was God. Many houses had framed pictures of him. He was well liked. In '36 he ran against Alf Landon and won in a landslide. It was a wonderful thing – he kept our social programs going, he started it all.

— Ramo Bongiovanni

Everyone in North Plymouth was poor. Many people didn't have phones. My mother made my underthings from flour bags – she'd doctor them up with Hamburg lace and stuff. I used to envy girls from town, from Warren Avenue. They had nicer clothes. There was always sort of a feud between North Plymouth and town – the town team and the Cordage team. In high school it would be, "Oh, she comes from North Plymouth." They'd say, "Well, you can take the people out of North Plymouth, but you can never take North Plymouth out of the people."

— Anita Fiocchi Scagliarini

Other old-time residents remembered other parts of town:

I grew up in the Bradford-Union-Water Street neighborhood downtown. What I remember most were the families – the Francolossi family who lived at the corner of Water and Sandwich streets. Next to them on Water Street was the Frumento family, who lived in a beautiful home with a lovely garden. Next down the street was the Marconi Club where the elder Italian men would gather and play cards or bocce and have a few glasses of their homemade wine. Then there was Cappannari Bros., a neighborhood convenience store. Other families in the neighborhood included Sullivan, Romano, Barbieri, Lombardi, Govoni, Mello, Ellis, Jesse, Burgess, Pina, Schneider, Ruggiero, DiSalvatori, Glassman, Taddia and Zavalcofsky.

As you can see, we were a rather mixed group of people and nationalities, but also a close-knit one.

I especially remember many of the families

Water Street looking north from the foot of Winslow and Brewster streets c. 1910. The mill, with company housing beyond, was bought by George P. Mabbett & Sons in 1907. This shows the waterfront before the WPA Depression-era project provided a new seawall and park.

having their little gardens, which furnished most of their vegetables during the summer months and were canned for winter use. During the months of September and October we had our own Napa Valley with the wine barrels being made ready for the new wine and then later when you walked along certain streets you could smell the odor of the fermentation.

— Pat Farina

I was born in 1918 of immigrant parents, the youngest of 12. We lived on a small farm on South Street. We had kerosene lamps, wood stoves and an outhouse. Growing up on South Street, a mile long, was an education in itself...There

The Training Green, with landscaping designed by the Frederick Law Olmstead architectural firm in the 1890s. In the center is a soldiers and sailors Civil War monument topped with an American eagle.

134

A trolley travels south down Warren Avenue c. 1910.

A bus stopped at Jabez Corner c. 1944. Note the Wellingsley School in the background and the gas pumps of the Bradford Store at the left.

were immigrants of all nationalities living on the street. It was called the League of Nations. There were Portuguese, Cape Verde Islanders, Italians, Jews, Scottish and French, Irish and English. Anyone whose parents or grandparents were born in America was called a "Swamp Yankee."

I don't remember ever having any racial troubles, as we were taught to respect our elders and our neighbors of different colors and nationalities. I didn't know what racial trouble was until I was in the Army and on maneuvers in the South.

We all walked the mile to school in rain, snow or sunshine. We would also walk downtown to the movies, Boys Club, shopping, to church on Sundays or just to hang out with friends. On Sundays we'd sit on the Training Green eating McCarthy's 10-cent ice cream and watching the cars come and go from the Cape, as that was then the main road through Plymouth.

In school we were taught respect for others and ourselves. We had to abide by a dress code, even if our clothes were old or had patches. The teachers and police had five special words for us if we got out of line or were fresh: "I will tell your parents." That was enough for us to shake in our boots.

— Allen Cappella

As soon as we arrived in Plymouth to live in my grandmother's house at 68 Warren Ave., I was enrolled in the second grade at the Wellingsley School at Jabez Corner, about a half-mile away. It was a one-room frame schoolhouse with one row each for grades 1-3, and an outhouse in back. The teacher, Miss Muriel Bradford, was competent, and I did learn the basics. School was from 9 a.m. to noon, an hour for lunch (I rode my bike home and back) and then 1-3 p.m. Lots of kids in those days went to similar schools to learn the three R's and

actually I think I got a pretty good education in that school. You couldn't beat the pupil-teacher ratio!

In 1936 I was 8 years old and in the third grade. I had no real knowledge of the world outside Plymouth, as of course there was no television and I didn't even have a radio. That fall I learned there was to be an election. President Roosevelt, of whom I was vaguely aware, was running for re-election, much to the disgust of my parents. As staunch Republicans they hated him, referring to him as "that man in the White House." His opponent in the election was the nondescript Republican governor of Kansas, Alfred M. Landon. Of course I knew nothing about politics, but that fall I learned the art of self-preservation. One day I set off to school innocently wearing a Landon button on my shirt. Most of my schoolmates came from poor or middle-class families who thought Roosevelt was God. That afternoon I was beaten up by some kids who didn't like anyone wearing a Landon button. The next day I bought a Roosevelt button from some kid and wore it boldly at school, but not at home.

— Arnold A. Blackmur

When my father died of tuberculosis in 1931 the family went on welfare. We received $8 weekly in food stamps and with my sister's $6 weekly salary as a bookkeeper we somehow managed to survive.

I graduated from Plymouth High School in 1939 and to supplement my sister's salary I went to work on the WPA. That was the Works Progress Administration that was enacted into law under President Roosevelt to put men back to work during the Depression years of the 1930s.

I reported to work in September 1939 and was one of a crew of about 40 men who were laying sewer pipe along the Plymouth shoreline. Most of the men were in their 30s, 40s and a few in their 50s. There were only three others in my age group. During the very cold winter of 1939-40 the owner of the Plymouth Lumber Co. gave the WPA crew permission to eat lunch in the warmth of the company garage. I did various jobs such as digging the trenches, helping the masons and hauling by hand the many planks from a finished location to the next work site.

The WPA government check was $48 per month. I worked for one year on that WPA project and then in September 1940 I went to work at the

CYNTHIA BUTTNER FISCHER FAMILY COLLECTION

The Wellingsley School c. 1937. Note the girls' door at the left and the boys' door on the right.

Plymouth Cordage Co. for $18 a week. At first there was the shameful embarrassment of a high school graduate going to work on the WPA digging sewer trenches. But from those wonderful "old men"

The WPA government check was $48 per month.

I worked alongside on the WPA I learned the lessons of life that entail lost jobs, comradeship, hope and the will to look forward and not back.

— Jerry L. Rezendes

The Plymouth depot was a typical country railroad station…great big room with a potbelly stove inside. On your left as you went in was Chester who sold newspapers, chewing gum and candy bars. He had the typical little round wooden bowl – about 12 inches in diameter – in which you put your two pennies for a newspaper or a penny for a stick of gum. And on the right-hand side we also had the Railway Express freight terminal. It was great fun to go down and see the steam trains come in and to smell the hot oil. It was just something that got into your system.

We lived in South Plymouth – Warren Avenue – because once you got up to Bramhall's Corner there was this vast wasteland of terra incognito. Once you got to the country club or up to the top of South Street, about a mile or so from the downtown post office, you were out of town. Growing up in the south end of town you were sort of cut off from the center of town as far as social interaction was concerned. It was rural. Most of the houses between Jabez Corner and Cliff Street have been constructed in my lifetime. We went to the Wellingsley School, which was at Jabez Corner. It was a one-room schoolhouse with five or six rows of seats and one teacher. The boys' entrance was on the right; the girls' entrance was on the left.

— William S. Franks

43

The Homefront 1941-1945

BY BOBBI CLARK

On the first Sunday afternoon in December 1941, gray clouds drifted across the sky above Plymouth Bay. The air had an icy edge to it.

At the Old Colony theater, "Blues in the Night," starring Priscilla Lane was the feature film, and in the auditorium of the five-year-old high school on Lincoln Street, later the Nathaniel Morton School, the Plymouth Philharmonic Orchestra was in concert under the direction of Edgar Beauregarde. Harold Boyer, a percussionist was playing the kettledrums that day, although at other times he played the xylophone.

During intermission, as the audience lazily stretched, talked with neighbors or searched for refreshments, Boyer remembered that Beauregarde confided to the musicians gathered around him, that he'd heard the Japanese had attacked Pearl Harbor. Since the news could not be confirmed, he told orchestra members they would continue the concert, and no announcement would be made until the end of the program. After the final movement of his baton had sliced the air, and harmonious notes of the various instruments stilled to a hush, Beauregarde told the audience about the alleged attack, advising everyone to go home and stay close to their radios for a possible address by President Roosevelt. But the country had to wait until the next day to hear the president's speech to a joint session of Congress:

"Yesterday, Dec. 7, 1941 – a date which will live

MARGIE BURGESS COLLECTION

The Clausson home on Sandwich Street as it appeared during World War II.

in infamy – the United States of America was suddenly and deliberately attacked by naval and air forces of the empire of Japan…

"The attack yesterday on the Hawaiian Islands has caused severe damage to American naval and military forces. I regret to tell that a great many American lives have been lost…"

The president went on to ask the Congress for a declaration of war against Japan, which was quickly forthcoming.

That same morning, Plymouth High School

Principal Edgar Mongan called the entire student body to an assembly in the auditorium only recently vacated by the philharmonic orchestra. As students walked down the aisles to their seats, some noticed the drums of the high school band arranged neatly on the floor immediately below stage; Marie Martinelli Fehlow was one of them.

In a serious and solid baritone, Principal Mongan talked of the assault on our country by the Japanese. His address was something that Marie never forgot: "I remember Mr. Mongan announcing that war had been declared," she recalled nearly 60 years later. "As he spoke his voice reverberated off the drums. This had a profound effect on me. We were 16, 17 years old, sitting silently listening to this—it brought it home to us."

The war was soon to be brought home in many ways—right to the very doorsteps of the high school.

John Russell, also a member of the student body that day, remembered soldiers on the school playground. "All the girls at school were ga-ga over them. They put dummy shells into a howitzer—they were just doing drills. They'd pull a lanyard and the dummy shells would come out onto the ground. I probably spent more time looking out the window than I did studying."

Studying became a challenge for many of the Class of 1942. Charlie Stasinos joined the Coast Guard auxiliary. "They got us a yacht that was converted for patrols and we stood watches. The boat was docked at the state pier. We were afraid of U-boats and espionage. The strange part is that because of a very severe winter, we got frozen in and couldn't go anyplace. All we did was keep a log and sit there; we couldn't do anything. I would stand all night watches on the boat, do my homework when I had time, then go to school."

After school Charlie and a few other boys worked at the Plymouth Boat Yard, later Plymouth Marine. They took the place of men who'd gone to work at the Fore River shipyard in Quincy. Their job was to build boxes to put on the roofs of houses and factories in case of an incendiary bomb attack. The boxes were filled with sand and covered with canvas to keep the sand dry, so it could be used to put out the flames of a fire caused by a bomb attack.

Threat of a German attack became an immediate concern. Elide Benati Butters, Class of 1944, lived near the ocean on Shaw Court, off of Nelson Street, which she said had become a very scary thing. "There was fear, fear of enemy ships. So there were blackouts and patrols on the waterfront everywhere."

Blackouts soon eliminated streetlights, dark shades masked interior lights in every house in Plymouth. Elide said civil defense officials recommended "that you not go out in the evening unless you absolutely had to, especially in cars."

> *Blackouts soon eliminated streetlights, dark shades masked interior lights in every house in Plymouth.*

All car owners were required to tape their headlights and gas was rationed. John Russell said, "You were allowed only a sort of peephole on each headlight. That was because German U-boats were out patrolling in Cape Cod Bay."

John did some patrolling himself. "I remember vividly driving with the headlights taped up. One night during the war, a buddy of mine from high school and I were driving along Warren Avenue. I won't tell you his name—don't think he'd appreciate it. It was a stunning car, a convertible V-8 Ford; it had a rumble seat. He had a knob on the dashboard and when it was pulled out, the exhaust bypassed the muffler, which produced a loud explosion. He had another trick. When he was driving along and passing someone, he'd turn the ignition off and

quickly back on, so that raw gas would go into the muffler, down the hot tailpipe. It would explode just like a cannon going off. This night we passed a car and he did that and made a huge sound—bam-bam-bam! We sped off to Bert's, which was then a one-story affair famous for blue-plate clambake. The car we passed had followed us into the parking lot. It was the police chief and he took my friend's license. That's how I got to drive him around all that summer."

And if John and his friend had happened to turn on the car radio in their drives around town, they might have heard either Glenn Miller's band, or the Andrew Sisters' rendition of "Don't Sit Under the Apple-Tree With Anyone Else But Me," or Kaye Kaiser's College of Musical Knowledge advising, "Praise The Lord And Pass The Ammunition,"—two songs that were high on the charts in the summer of 1942.

That summer Manny Valente expected an important piece of mail. "I was 21 years old, on a ladder painting my house and the mailman walks up Hamilton Street waving a letter in his hand and calling to me: 'Here it is.' It was greetings from President Roosevelt that told me to report to the draft board. The draftees were told to meet in front of the Registry of Deeds at 6 a.m. There was a band there of about 10-15 men, and while we lined up on the steps for a picture, they played patriotic songs. Then we marched to the New Haven Railroad depot (later replaced by a bank building) near the Puritan Mill."

One of the mill workers at Puritan was Elisa Martinelli, Marie's mother. "Many women who had been stay-at-home wives and moms were entering the work force then—Rosie the riveters. My mother always worked, but then she worked longer and more hours at the Puritan (where a Sheraton hotel was later). She was a burler, which meant she removed imperfections from the navy blue material the mill produced for military use. I remember her coming home with blue hands. Sometimes she had bandages around her fingertips, which were bruised from combing the material with her fingers to pull away imperfections. It was piecework— you got paid by the amount of work completed and she was, of course, encouraged to produce."

The war changed things for many women and they were urged to produce in unexpected ways. Rose Sherman Geller came home after graduating from the University of New Hampshire. "I graduated from college in June of '41 and thought I was going to be the great social worker. I actually had paid rent on an apartment that I was to share with two other girls in Boston on Huntington Avenue, across the street from the New England Conservatory of Music. But all I did was clean the apartment and scrub the floors—never moved in. That was because my brother Louie, who was running Sherman's Furniture, asked at the time, if I didn't have an obligation to the family because they were short of help in the store due to the young men having been drafted. Of course, I started working in the hard-

ware and furniture store and became manager of our second store at 50 Court St. How did I feel about that? Well, there wasn't a choice of feeling.

"We had some women working in the store replacing the men. I did everything. I'd drive the truck with merchandise from the North Plymouth

MANNY VALENTE COLLECTION
During World War II, Plymouth area draftees assembled on the steps of the Registry of Deeds building before being marched off to the railroad depot for induction into military service.

store to take it to the downtown store. I did deliveries, measured linoleum, cut window glass and window shades. I don't remember thinking about the fact I was doing a man's job. The busi-

ness had to go on. And it would be very cold in the store if I didn't shovel coal into the furnace. It was fine— I did what I had to do."

That cold winter Elide Benati was secretary of her high school class. "I loved sports. I was a cheerleader. It's in the yearbook. Our 1944 yearbook was called 'Til Victory.' Before it was always called 'The Pilgrim,' and it was made of leather; ours was made of cardboard. I played softball, basketball and field hockey. In those days cheerleaders cheered all sports. Today there are summer cheerleaders, winter cheerleaders, whatever. See the difference!

"My future husband was a football player and he also played baseball and basketball, so I saw him at everything. But since he was two years ahead of me, he was away at war during most of my high school

CHARLES STASINOS COLLECTION
The Plymouth terminal of the Old Colony Railroad as it appeared during the 1940s.

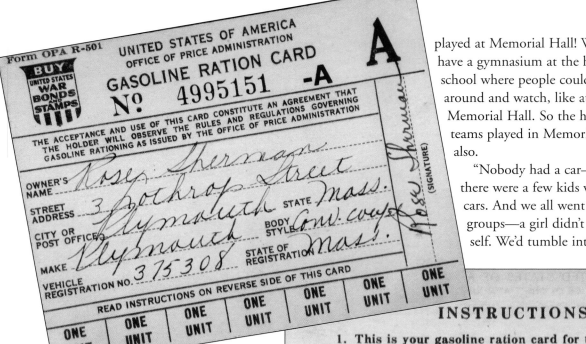

Gasoline ration card issued to Rose Sherman Geller during world War II.

played at Memorial Hall! We didn't have a gymnasium at the high school where people could sit around and watch, like at Memorial Hall. So the high school teams played in Memorial Hall also.

"Nobody had a car—well, there were a few kids who had cars. And we all went around in groups—a girl didn't go by herself. We'd tumble into the car,

INSTRUCTIONS

1. This is your gasoline ration card for the vehicle or boat described hereon. This card must last at least through June 30, 1942, in the rationed area. This card must be presented to your dealer for cancelation of one or more units each time you purchase gasoline.

2. This card can be used only for gasoline delivered into the fuel tank of the vehicle described hereon; or, if a boat, for gasoline to be used therein.

3. The value of the unit may be changed from time to time on announcement by the Office of Price Administration.

4. Your local rationing board alone can make adjustments or issue a different card.

U. S. GOVERNMENT PRINTING OFFICE : 1942—O-455906

the games. That's one thing that was different during my high school years during the war."

Things were different for Aphrodite and Jim Stasinos, Charlie's parents, who had a business downtown. Charlie remembered: "It was called Jim's Restaurant, Jim's Lunch in the early days. It was right across the street from where a drug store later was on Main Street. On the corner there was a hardware store and the next three doors were our restaurant—three different entrances. It was a family restaurant, very busy in the summertime. My father's first restaurant was right next to where the hardware store was on the corner. There was room in the place for three people to stand at the counter. In the summer you could open the window, which was good because of the grill. Then they expanded and expanded. I did everything, from waiting tables to working in the kitchen. I was brought up with it. My mother worked there and frequently took us with her. It was the family business run by my mother, father and my Uncle Charles.

"During the war we got the contract from the Navy to feed the air cadets that were stationed at the Navy air base on South Meadow Road – later the municipal airport. It wasn't much of an airport back then, just a landing strip. They were training to be naval aviators.

"They would bring the air cadets to the restaurant in the morning in two trips. First shift was about 6:30. At lunchtime somebody from the base

years. His name was George Butters but we called him Tim, which was his nickname.

"Dating? It wasn't much! We didn't go out nights. Don't forget, it was wartime and everything was dark. The only entertainment we really had was school functions and the movies—and all sports events. In the summer, we'd go to the beach.

"So the boys we wanted to see, we saw at the games. There were semi-pro teams; they played in Memorial Hall in downtown Plymouth. Yes, Plymouth had a semi-pro basketball team that

I think there were three cars in the whole school, to go to out-of-town games. We couldn't even go on buses—there weren't buses, except for the ballplayers. Busing stopped because of gas rationing. Even the cheerleaders had to find their own way to get to would pick up the box lunches we had prepared. Then at night, they were bused in again for the evening meal at the restaurant. Howard Johnson's on Warren Avenue, up by the country club, had the contract before us and for some reason they changed and we had it for about 18 months. We had two dining rooms and we used both only during the summer. But it was ideal because the Navy people could have some privacy in one of the dining spaces, and we used the other one for our regular customers. It was hard keeping the girls away from the cadets—the girls would come around just to see them.

"The Naval contract helped in another way because it was easier to get supplies. Restaurants had allocations for food, but still meat was hard to get.

"Downtown Plymouth was very active during the war and didn't change until they put in the Southeast Expressway. Before that everyone went through downtown Plymouth, which was the mid-point on the way to the Sagamore Bridge and the Cape. So my father's restaurant was very active too.

"On South Street, approximately where the Pilgrim Pride Apartments were later, on the west side of the street—that was Army barracks and soldiers were stationed there. I would guess there were over 100 soldiers there."

And it seemed that every man wanted to be a soldier. Margie Clausson Burgess told about her grandfather, then in his mid-40s. "My grandfather, Louis Maynard had his hand in many things and was very interested in politics and the news of the world. He kept begging them to take him into the Army, but they told him to go home and grow cab-

bages and he'd help the war effort a lot better. He never gave up. Finally, to keep him quiet they named him civilian in charge of German prisoners at Camp Edwards on Cape Cod. Mostly he stayed at the base and when he did come home on his days off, he would sit in his Morris chair beside his desk listening to the news. He was very good with the prisoners and he was dismayed because when the war was over, that some of them committed suicide."

Other prisoners who had the courage to return went back to a very different Germany, as Louis

> ## "Downtown Plymouth was very active during the war and didn't change until they put in the Southeast Expressway."

Maynard was to learn later. Former German prisoner of war Peter Fischer wrote to him from Munich on Dec. 2, 1946:

My dear Mr. Maynard:

I feel pretty proud realizing that I evidently am the first one whose letter you are answering. It is with a sense of satisfaction and yet with bad conscience that I hear of the many letters that you have received from my former co-prisoners. Bad conscience – because I am somewhat ashamed to be among those who have asked you for a parcel. You must get the impression that those Germans are a nation of beggars.

And yet I think you know yourself that food is not the primary reason for any of us to write that have written you. You will certainly realize that it is in appreciation of the true kindness you have showed us while we were in your country.

And I wish you would take this long letter as proof of the affection of
Peter Fischer

And as the war progressed, Camp Edwards continued to grow to accommodate the increase in military personnel, and it soon became a vital part of life in Plymouth

The Martinelli family befriended a GI stationed at the Camp. He used to hitch rides to Plymouth to visit and became a family friend. Marie said that it was through Joe's visits she became familiar with military activity in the area. Joe was eventually sent to New Guinea and being the letter writer in the family, Marie wrote to him. In one of her letters she told Joe about a clamming excursion with a friend during which she tore her pants.

"So I told him about my clamming trip with Howard and how my pants got ripped. It was because we got stuck in the mud flats with the big fog and couldn't get in the channel; we couldn't see the buoys. I got out and pushed when we hit the mud flat and the boat was zooming out quicker than I could get in, so he grabbed me by the seat of my pants and hauled me in the boat and my pants tore. So when Joe wrote back he said 'Sorry you tore your pants when you were out clamming with Howard.' The officer who was censoring the V-mail (Victory mail) wrote above this line, 'lucky

Howard.' He didn't know Howard was my brother-in-law."

Plymouth was the biggest and most important town near Camp Edwards—and it was important to the townspeople as well. Elide Benati remembered what it was like to shop downtown:

"Food was rationed. You had a ration book with stamps in it and people brought it when they went to the grocery store. My mother and father did the shopping. It was wonderful. We had little stores and we had Broccoli's Market in North Plymouth. They came to your house, took your order and the next day delivered the order to your house!

"We had other stores too in downtown Plymouth. Oh Lord, we had everything—all local stores that had been there for years. There was Sadler's where you bought clothes—women's clothes, Cavicchi's for men's clothing and Puritan Clothing. The department store was Buttner's for needles, thread, and curtains. It was just beautiful.

"Restaurants? I never went out to eat in a restaurant. Never. Up to the ninth grade I never ate in a restaurant. Mumma made everything. We had tortellini and lasagna. We had a speciality of crema, and pastry ravioli with the fruit inside and bowknots that were sweet… No, going out to eat wasn't part of what we did as a

family. There weren't that many restaurants anyway. Not like today—now it's all restaurants and antique shops. In those days, you did all your shopping downtown on a Saturday night when the stores were open."

But Marie Martinelli's favorite time to go downtown was early afternoon. "I would occasionally wait for my mother to leave the Puritan Mill at 4 o'clock. There is a little grassy green area between South Park Avenue and North Park Avenue and I

UNITED STATES OF AMERICA
OFFICE OF PRICE ADMINISTRATION

935311 ER

WAR RATION BOOK No. 3 Void if altered

NOT VALID WITHOUT STAMP

Identification of person to whom issued: PRINT IN FULL

Margie Clausson

(First name) (Middle name) (Last name)

Street number or rural route 156 Sandwich St.

City or post office Plymouth State Mass.

AGE	SEX	WEIGHT	HEIGHT	OCCUPATION
4	F	38 Lbs.	3 Ft. 7 In.	

SIGNATURE Margie Clausson
(Person to whom book is issued. If such person is unable to sign because of age or incapacity, another may sign in his behalf.)

WARNING
This book is the property of the United States Government. It is unlawful to sell it to any other person, or to use it or permit anyone else to use it, except to obtain rationed goods in accordance with regulations of the Office of Price Administration. Any person who finds a lost War Ration Book must return it to the War Price and Rationing Board which issued it. Persons who violate rationing regulations are subject to $10,000 fine or imprisonment, or both.

OPA Form No. R-130

LOCAL BOARD ACTION

Issued by ....
(Local board number) (Date)

Street address ....

City .... State ....

....
(Signature of issuing officer) Book 4

MARGIE BURGESS COLLECTION

Ration book issued to Margie Clausson Burgess during World War II.

would sit on the bench and wait for her to come out and we would walk home together. But once in a while I was able to con her into going downtown and eating supper at Gambini's, which she was very reluctant to do because she was so tired. Occasionally she would succumb and we would go to Gambini's and they had wonderful sundaes—two prices: 15 and 20 cents. One of the 15 centers, which I loved, was vanilla ice cream with some kind of maraschino cherry sauce and you got four or five cherries plopped on top and I would always ask if I could have a deep center.

"Flossie, my friend, worked there and used her influence to get me a job at Gambini's, but I was a terrible waitress. I used to spill coffee into the saucer as I carried it to patrons. The Gambinis were not very accepting of that and gave me my two weeks notice. I didn't feel bad—I didn't like working there."

But Elide Benati seemed to enjoy it. "Gambini's was right on Main Street. It was a nice little place—a working person's place—with an ice cream bar, bakery goods and they served dinners too. I was behind the ice cream counter. The people who worked downtown came in for a quick lunch or dinner—in 20 minutes you were in and out! There was another place like it across the street, Currier's. And there was Smith's, a gift shop. Tip Smith was the owner. He had beautiful gifts for weddings, anniversaries, birthdays—and reasonable too. And they had newspapers. All the newspapers went to Smith's and the boys who had newspaper routes would go there to get their papers to deliver. Everyone went to Gambini's, Smith's and Currier's—everyone! Buttner's sold gifts too, upstairs. Downstairs was a department store.

"On Saturday nights shopping was social. Everyone was downtown shopping. You'd always see people you knew and you'd go get an ice cream cone and visit."

Manny Valente has other memories of downtown: "Often on Saturday mornings you'd see long lines at the meat markets, people waiting with their tokens to buy meat when they had it. Everything was scarce, butter eggs, sugar, and gas of course, But GIs got an allotment of 15 gallons of gas when they came home on furlough. Many of the barbershops closed because there weren't many guys around. Some of the barbers went to the defense plants, or the shipyard in Quincy to barber."

Butter and eggs were hot commodities during the war. Margie Clausson recalls: "Kennedy's Butter and Egg Store was downtown, across the street from Shirley Square, about where Ellis Curtain was later—to the left of it a little. I used to go there with my mother, with the ration books. Sometimes there were lines because butter was in short supply. I guess that's when margarine began. The margarine wasn't like it is now. It came in a plastic bag and was white like lard and had a big bright orange glob in it. We had to squeeze it to mix the color in to make it butter color."

PHYLLIS HUGHES COLLECTION

Ma Emerson in the doorway of her Manomet store.

In Manomet, shopping was a learning experience for young summer resident Phyllis Dale Hughes "I was only seven, but in my family you were sent to the store a lot. There was a little store called Emerson's. Later I worked there. It was a variety store next to the old bowling alley; the post office was in the store. Everybody went there; Ma Emerson ran it. I have a picture of Ma Emerson in the window of that store right next to an ad for cigarettes. She was a remarkable lady. Her daughter and son-in-law worked for her.

"We went there every day to get the Boston newspaper and milk and bread and all the things that spoiled because we had iceboxes. Our icebox was brown; it would be an antique now. There was this wonderful couple named Liz and Frenchie and they actually lugged the ice on their backs up through the sand dunes. They took that ice, big

huge hooks with ice on their backs, to all the people in their homes. They came every other day. I remember it was 25 or 30 cents. We needed to have that ice. And if you wanted to have lemonade, we chipped away with an ice pick, got a big hunk out and made lemonade with it. So you didn't freeze meat; you were lucky when that hamburger arrived—and it was probably black market hamburger.

"When I came down one summer, the first thing I heard was that Ma Emerson's boy had been killed. He was a pilot. I was devastated, as was my whole family. This really hit home for all of us because we knew who the person was."

Two high school classmates of Marie Martinelli and John Russell died in the war. Marie said, "One was Stuart Hatch of the Hatch family—an old Plymouth family. The other was Curt Wilson. I think Stuart died in Normandy."

Death hit very close to home for Elide Benati's family. News of her brother's death is so ingrained in her memory she can recall every detail. "My brother was in college, at Boston University, about a year and half. He thought his draft number would be coming up because the war was escalating. He came home from school and said he didn't want to go into the Army but wanted to be a pilot in the Army Air Force, so he enlisted. Oh, he had such a smile—beautiful teeth—not a cavity in his mouth!

"His plane crashed on Dec. 4, 1944, but we weren't notified until Dec. 16th. In those days everybody knew everybody else in Plymouth. There was a Western Union telegraph office in downtown Plymouth and they got the telegram. Quite a few

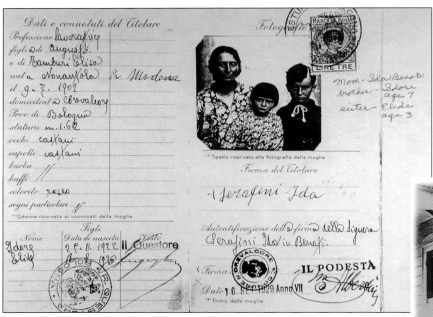

Elide Benati's Italian family passport for immigration to the U.S. in 1929, upper left, included a photo of her mother, herself and brother, Idore. Her brother's naturalization certificate is shown at left, while above, the family posed for a photo at their home on Shaw Court shortly before her brother was killed in a plane crash in his native Italy during World War II.

died from Plymouth and you can see their names on a plaque in front of Memorial Hall. Well, Mr. Crandlemeier was in charge of the telegraph office and he knew my father. Usually someone in authority would deliver the telegram, but they knew us. So Mr.

Crandlemeier sent his son to the Edes company on Water Street, where my father worked. The Edes family lived on Warren Avenue, and the company manufactured copper and zinc and was very prosperous, especially during wartime because of the need for metal. My father worked there for 30 years.

"The telegram was brought to him at the factory. I was 18 years old and working there too. All the men were in the service so they allowed women in. I was working in the laboratory; my father was a sheet metal worker.

"I saw my father come up to the lab with two men holding him. I thought he was hurt. He showed me the telegram; I still have it. We went and read it to my mother: *The Secretary of War asks that I assure you of his deep sympathy…* It changed everything. My mother and father were never the same — never! My brother's name was Idore, but he was called "Mac," short for "Macaroni," a nickname his friends called him in a teasing way. Six feet tall and handsome — their pride and joy. Not that I wasn't — don't get me wrong, but he was to carry the name.

"He was the one to go to college. I wanted to be a teacher, but they couldn't afford to send us both. I'll tell you what my mother did. You won't believe it. Every dime she had, she put away. She paid for my brother's education in dimes. I have a bottle of those dimes she saved — probably worth a lot of money today, but I can't get rid of them. Those dimes were their hopes and dreams."

Hopes and dreams were dispensed regularly at Plymouth's two movie theaters. Manny Valente worked for the Plymouth Theater in North Plymouth, a building that later housed a dry cleaning establishment. "I had a part-time job every

Thursday, folding flyers and stuffing them in envelopes for mailing. They gave the movie schedule for the week. They were mailed to the entire surrounding area: Duxbury, Pembroke, Carver and Kingston.

"Movies cost 10 cents for kids 12 and under and 35 cents for adults—and you saw two movies for that. Our favorite stars were John Wayne, Jimmy Stewart, Humphrey Bogart and Betty Grable. She was a pin-up poster girl; GIs all over the world had Betty Grable's poster on the inside cover of the footlockers that were placed at the end of our bunks. She had beautiful legs and we all envied bandleader Harry James when he married our pin-up girl. You also got the Pathe News, film clips that showed war news. What we knew of the war, we saw in these newsreels. It wasn't real to us then; it was like another movie."

Elide Benati saw the movies at the Old Colony Theater on Main Street Extension in downtown Plymouth. "It's now a professional building overlooking Brewster Gardens. On Saturday or Sunday, we would go off to the movie. I got 2 cents for candy. I would buy Mary Janes because they gave you five for a penny and Sugar Daddies, the lollipop, because they lasted half the movie. If you went on Saturday you saw two movies and a serial. The next Saturday you had to go again so you could see the rest of it because the ending was always the hero falling off a cliff. You were thinking, oh my

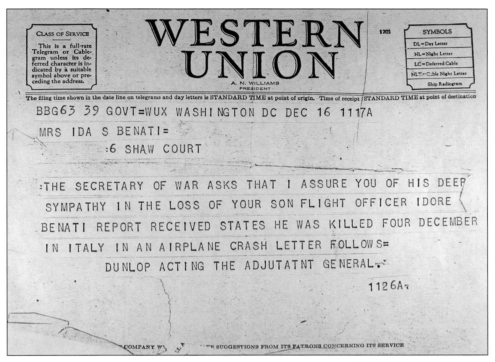

The telegram from the War Department informing the Benati family of the death of their son.

God, I have to know what happened. Kids were sent to the movies to give Mumma and Daddy relief!"

Nevertheless, parents kept a watchful eye on their children's lives. Boundaries were set and firmly drawn. According to Marie Martinelli, "My mother ruled with her eyebrows."

Phyllis Dale had similar memories of her mother. "I do remember there was a hangout down on the beach, a place called 'Playland.' It was an outdoor dance shell where servicemen would go to dance. My mother told us not to go anywhere near that place. We were too young, but to my older sisters she said: 'If anyone here goes near Playland, I'll cut

their legs off.' In other words they'd never walk again.

"When one of my uncles was on leave, my mother was on the beach and saw her brother coming along with this young thing of 13 strutting in a bathing suit. My mother, on the stairs leading down to the beach, called out to him: 'Quentin, do you know how much eight and five is?' Of course, he was the one who became an attorney and he knew legal stuff. We called that girl 'Eight and Five' for the rest of our lives."

Some girls ignored society's rules, Marie Martinelli said, although it wasn't easy. "One of my classmates, in her senior year of high school, was dating a soldier. I don't think he was a local boy, but he received his orders to go overseas and they decided to get married before he left. That was a 'no-no,' for a senior in high school to get married. They didn't want any married students in high school. Even in nurses' training someone had left training to get married, had had two children, just babies, and her husband died. She was living with her parents and wanted to come back into training. There was a long period of assessing whether it was okay for a married student to join our class. For young, innocent virginal students to associate with a mature married person was very much scrutinized. It was a whole different social mindset. They did allow her to return, however. But there were good girls and not so good girls—most of it probably rumored about the not so good girls.

"But I have to give Elspeth Sloane a great deal of credit for wanting to marry her boyfriend before he left to go overseas. It was a decision she made even though she knew she was putting herself in some jeopardy. That was a courageous decision. He did return. But the decision was: Could she stay in school as a married person? This was a small town, you have to remember that. We came from a diverse ethnic background. That, in and of itself, brought a whole different approach to cultural mores."

The culture of the time was patriotic and patriotism was an inherent part of wartime life. Rose Sherman spoke of this. "We had to do something to be of help to our community — something I knew I'd dislike. I became a nurse's aide and began to spend evenings or weekends helping out at Jordan Hospital. I took a course, got certified, and that's what I did—not very glamorous, carrying bedpans. And the evenings when we didn't do that, we went to the American Red Cross, which used the Mayflower Society House on Winslow Street, where we rolled bandages.

"Then there was the Massachusetts Women's Defense Corps; both a motor corps and canteen. I was a canteen driver. We were trained on motors. I could change a tire and help out when a vehicle had a breakdown. We worked in a garage until we learned these things. It was at the Buick garage, later

ROSE GELLER COLLECTION

Rose Sherman Geller as a canteen driver for the Massachusetts Women's Defense Corps during World War II.

the site of the Central Fire Station on Sandwich Street.

"My brother Louie was the Civil Defense warden for Lothrop Street; we had fire wardens for each street. The community was prepared in case of a bomb."

Bombs and guns became part of the

vocabulary. John Russell said. "I enlisted in the Army Air Force with a friend from school because they told us if we enlisted we'd get our choice of where we were going. We wanted to go to Fort Myers, Fla., to train to be gunners. We didn't think anything about it being dangerous. The country needed us."

Marie Martinelli answered the call and went into

nurses' training. "There was a great shortage of nurses—a great shortage of everything. We had to make do for supplies in the hospital (Quincy City Hospital). For example those little wax paper bags that were hung on each bed to throw away your used tissue, bandages, etc., we made those out of newspaper. I could show you how to fold them right now. For medications, we didn't have those small paper cups to put the patient's pills in; there were no paper cups. We used bottle caps from empty bottles—actually, we re-used them."

Preparedness, sacrifice and selflessness became part of community life. "We addressed being at war, pretty much as we did the Depression," Marie recalled. "Everybody was in the same boat and we coped. We were thrifty and didn't waste anything— saved the wrappers from loaves of bread and used them as sandwich wrap. I thought everyone's sandwiches were wrapped in Wonder bread wrapping that had red, white and blue dots all over it. We were all in it together."

Marie tells also of the unwitting sacrifice of some women she didn't know by name. "My entire school experience was walking to and from school. It was during that time that on the way home from the high school, as I walked by the post office in downtown Plymouth, I saw the women who were waiting for their ride to work—the swing shift, 3 to11. They worked at a munitions factory in Hanover. It upset me to see them because their hair and skin were changing color, becoming orange; it was very apparent. It affected me in a very negative way; I was frightened for them. We were not as environmentally aware in those days. But I've often wondered if there were any long-term effects. Every day there were four to six women from Plymouth wait-

44

MANOMET SHORE PATROL

BY GEORGE W. CARTER, JR.

During World War II there were walking beach patrols maintained in Manomet from the Manomet Coast Guard Station at Manomet Point and from a station at Center Hill. The Manomet Point station was a regular U.S.C.G. station, while the Center Hill station was a house either leased or appropriated by the U.S.C.G. The house was on a hill to the south of Ship Pond facing the ocean, between Center Hill Pond and Black Pond. The manning of these stations was accomplished by regular United States Coast Guardsmen and by the United States Coast Guard Temporary Reserves. There were about 10,000 Temporary Reservists in the First Naval District, which covered all of New England except Connecticut.

GEORGE CARTER COLLECTION

George Carter's identification card as a World War II Coast Guard reservist

Patrols to the north and south were dispatched from each station and each station had a tower that was manned as well. The towers were in communication with the First Naval District. The Manomet Station's north patrol walked to Rocky Point where it met an Army patrol. The south patrol met the Center Hill north patrol about half way between the two stations. The south patrol from Center Hill Station proceeded south to the mouth of Ellisville Harbor. On the other side of Ellisville Harbor the Army covered the shore to the Cape Cod Canal.

As a 19-year old U.S.C.G. Temporary Reservist, I participated in the beach patrols in Manomet. While on patrol one carried a Very pistol [for

GEORGE CARTER COLLECTION

George Carter and Ginger patrolling the Manomet shore during World War II.

firing signal flares], side arm, clock, and flashlight (only to be used in an emergency). Each patrol was accompanied by a dog; mine was named Ginger. I recall one occasion when a patrol was saved from walking off a cliff by the dog's refusal to travel farther ahead. In the darkness of the night, the patrol couldn't see that the cliff's edge had been washed away. There were keys located in trees and on posts along each patrol route and the clock was punched at each one of these points. The patrols were four hours in duration, 8 p.m. to midnight and midnight to 4 a.m. Patrols were made regardless of weather conditions.

The shores were also guarded by a number of searchlights and anti-aircraft batteries. When activated at night they outlined the Cape from Manomet to Provincetown. Blimps from South Weymouth [naval air station] also maintained a submarine patrol.

While on a midnight to 4 a.m. tower watch at Center Hill I could make out the outlines of ships coming through the Cape Cod Canal and by the early morning light the bay was filled with ships. There were so many ships, it looked as though you could walk, from ship to ship, all the way to Provincetown.

I remember meeting the south patrol from Manomet one summer evening. Both he and the dog were in the ocean. Although well trained, the dog gave in to its natural instinct and went after a skunk. What I witnessed was an attempted deodorizing process—ultimately unsuccessful!

Marie Martinelli Fehlow as an Army nurse during World War II.

ing for their pick-up ride to Hanover. It wasn't a place I wanted to work! But still, we all did what we had to do and didn't think it extraordinary."

Doing what you had to do and thinking nothing of it, is the way Charlie Stasinos described military service. "Most everyone wanted to go into the service. We felt it was our duty. There was a different sense of commitment than there is today. You took it for granted that you'd do your part."

Finding time to do her part, was exactly what Jeanne Clausson did—this even though she had a dozen or so little foster children at her home on Sandwich Street in addition to her own daughter Margie. "There was a tower up on Stafford Street, Margie recalled, "and my mother was one of the volunteers who used to climb up and sit in that tower to spot enemy planes.

"Also, during the war people were encouraged to become involved. Cigarette packages then had tin foil linings and we peeled them off and kept making them into a ball or block. We saved it for drop-off and collection for re-use by the government.

Patriotism for many included near adoration of President Roosevelt. Pictures of him held an honored place in many homes. Elide Benati said, "Being Democrats, we loved Roosevelt." And Margie Clausson said, "I remember when Franklin Roosevelt died. We were in the kitchen, and I cried because my mother was crying."

Manny Valente said of Roosevelt: "In our house he was thought of as a great president; he could do no wrong. He was the only four-term president."

But there were others whose confidence in the president was tested, Rose Sherman remembered. "We knew a ship (the liner St. Louis out of Hamburg) with hundreds of Jewish refugees had come to this country and was refused entrance by Roosevelt. The president had been considered such a friend before this. Later on he proved to be a friend again. But at the time, we thought Churchill may have persuaded him that if he accepted these refugees, the Germans would attack the United States. Our confidence in him was shattered. And it was the beginning of our understanding of what was going on in Germany. It was a great disappointment. The

United States was known to be the country that accepted everyone. We thought, what happened?"

Mel Klasky was in grade school at the time and loved to play basketball. At the end of the century he said, "There was no discrimination in Plymouth. My father and grandfather before me owned the Plymouth Antiques Centre that I run now, and they felt the same way. In fact a few years after it happened, a kid who played ball with me apologized for not choosing me for some team or other because of my being Jewish. I was surprised and told him that I never thought anything of it—just figured I didn't play well enough to be picked."

Aug. 14, 1945, was a hot, humid partly sunny Tuesday. In the afternoon people began assembling in front of the Central Fire Station on Main Street, awaiting official news from Washington of the Japanese surrender. Recorded music was pumped out over loudspeakers all day with an occasional

> *Patriotism, for many included near adoration of President Roosevelt. Pictures of him held an honored place in many homes.*

broadcast breaking in. At 6:15 p.m. it was announced that the president had received the Japanese message of surrender and an official broadcast would be made shortly.

The *Old Colony Memorial* reported: "Hardly had the news of the surrender been announced…when fire whistles began to blow at Central Station. News broadcasts had several other important announcements to make but it was quite apparent that the crowd had heard the words they wanted to hear. So there was nothing left to do but to abandon the loud speakers at the Central Station, get down onto the street and join the multitudes. Where the people came from in so short a time, one would never know, but in less than 10 minutes time, Main Street in front of the Central Station from Shirley Square to Town Square was just a mass of people.

"The scene soon shifted to Plymouth Rock. Every blade of grass on Cole's Hill was covered by celebrators. Everyone was cheering, shouting and jumping about. When the parade came along with its two bands, bedlam broke loose, all controlled, however, by a piece of mechanism called a microphone. No one got serious until the speaking began. When tribute was paid to those who had died in the war, when Joe Costa of the Legion Band sounded taps on his trumpet, complete silence swayed the crowd."

Margie Clausson was at home on Sandwich Street, when her mother suddenly packed her up and walked with her down to Court Street. Margie says, "They burned Hitler in effigy up in front of the fire station. People were cheering—that's how they celebrated the end of the war."

The Playland dance hall at White Horse Beach c. 1930s.

Margie also recalled her future husband's experience: "Ken was on the train coming down from Boston that day. The people on the train didn't know the war had ended. And they didn't realize the cause of the bedlam they saw as they were passing through the various towns on the train."

In Manomet, Phyllis Dale was very much aware the war was over, "Because of the parade that was going by our house—a group of neighbors banging pots and pans and shouting. We got our own pots and pans and joined them. There were about 300 of us by the time we walked to the Mayflower Hotel. I guess everybody figured they'd never get up there again if they didn't go then because it was an exclusive place. We walked right up the front grassy area, which was huge, and came back down again and walked the circle out Manomet Point Road to what was then Route 3, and back down past the Second Congregational Church. It took several hours and it was wonderful. People cheered along the way and most joined us. It was a very diverse group, all ages; everyone who could took part in it. It's something I'll always remember."

Bob Viella, 10 years old at the time, remembered being in the back garden of his friend, Ann Guidoboni on Suosso Lane and hearing church bells ring. Thinking it unusual for the bells to be clamoring so late in the afternoon, they went around to the front of the house to see what was going on. "People were coming out of their houses, shouting, 'The war's over, the war's over.'" He and Ann followed their neighbors to Court Street and joined the North Plymouth celebration.

"Siever's Lunch, near Broccoli's Market, where Charlie's Hardware was later, was giving away sherbet. There was no ice cream because of the war. And L. Knife grocery across the street was giving away beer. It was a wild time," Viella said.

149

Epilogue

By Peter J. Gomes

Thomas P. 'Tip' O'Neill is famous for his political maxim that "All politics is local," – a phrase now in the lexicon of American political folk wisdom. From his lofty perch as speaker of the U. S. House of Representatives, where he was an intimate part of both party and national politics and third in the line of succession to the presidency itself, Speaker O'Neill never forgot what put him where he was. He never forgot the local dimension of his public life: that constituent services, local issues, and the nourishing of the neighbors and neighborhoods are what returned him to office. In America, from the landing of the Pilgrims to the present day, politics works from the bottom up, and not from the top down.

What is true of politics in America is also true of history, at least in that all history is indeed local and also works from the bottom up, not from the top down. Thus, 'local history' is not the orphan child of 'real' history, but the mother of history itself. From ancient times we begin with our story and the story of our place and from these we construct the larger patterns of meaning by which the history of a people is both formed and preserved.

In architecture, they say "First we shape our buildings, and then they shape us." So, too, with history: first we shape our story, and then our story shapes us. Yet for many, and for a very long time, history was thought to be the lofty enterprise of epochs, great actions, and great personages, the stuff of heroes and legends, far removed from the claims of ordinary people and local circumstance. History was what great men wrote about other great men and the great events for which they bore some responsibility.

'Local history', on the other hand, was almost a pejorative term, whose clearly amateur status removed it from all serious claims to intellectual respectability and academic scholarship. Local history was typically restricted to one locality and made no pretense to philosophical or interpretive insight. It was usually conducted by amateurs far removed from the centers and canons of scholarship, and generally focused on issues and personalities of interest only to the locals.

Genealogy and antiquarianism, memoir and anecdote, together with an obsession with land titles, landmarks, and anniversaries – these pursuits were long regarded as the stock-in-trade of local history, and thus were relegated by professional historians to the second tier of historical scholarship. The fact that these interests tended to be pursued by elite amateurs or eccentric dilettantes only confirmed the low social status of local history.

Long before there was a self-conscious 'profession' of historian in the United States, however, there existed local historians who possessed a sense of purpose and place, and were experts in the matters at hand. Soon these interests were combined into local and independent historical societies, which gave an institutional focus to the history of place and along the way became repositories of artifacts, collections and books.

In the newly formed United States – a country with more future than past — these societies assured a permanent sense of that past without which subsequent professional historians could not have pursued their study of American history. Such institutions were of inestimable value to the study of American history, as Walter Muir Whitehill wrote in 1962 in his classic work *Independent Historical Societies: An Enquiry into Their Research and Publication Functions and Their Financial Future:*

> For periods ranging from 100 to 170 years, these societies, chiefly located along the Atlantic seaboard, have as their chief reason for existence, collected, preserved, made available to scholars, and published source materials of American history. They have done so, without fanfare, from private funds that are astonishingly small

for the results achieved. Their quiet work, which is not dramatic or spectacular in terms of new releases, is as little understood by the man in the street as what goes on in a scientific laboratory. Things of the mind do not lend themselves to sensational pronouncements.

In 1972 when I was preparing for publication my edition of James Thacher's 1832 book *The History of the Town of Plymouth*, I discovered in the stacks of Harvard's Widener Library a copy of the German historian Herman E. Ludewig's 1846 *Literature of American Local History: A Bibliographical Essay*, in which he wrote of the relatively new field of American local history:

> No people in the world can have so great an interest in the history of their own country as that of the U.S. of North America: for there are none who enjoy an equally great share in their country's historical acts.

Ludewig went on to say, "There is no lack of local histories, especially in New England, whose sons may justly be called a 'Documentary people.'" Ludewig was impressed with the American penchant for local history, its capacity to express itself in locally produced volumes, sermons, and essays, and its devotion to the founding of societies and museums for the preservation of the past. (One such society was the Pilgrim Society of Plymouth, founded in 1820 on the bicentenary of the landing of the Pilgrims. The society's museum, Pilgrim Hall, built in 1824, remains the oldest museum in continuous existence in the U.S.)

In 1846 when Ludewig wrote his essay, the study of history, as an intellectual exercise liberated from theology and literature, was a young science whose canons were still evolving under the influence of post-Enlightenment German scholarship. The study and writing of serious history in America was in its infancy. Jared Sparks, the young Harvard clergyman, historian, president of the University from 1849 to 1853, and the David McCullough of his time, made himself both famous and rich through his biographies of the Founding Fathers. In 1839 he was appointed to the MacClean Professorship in History, the first such professorship in any American university; and one might argue that the professional study of American history dates from that time.

Long before 1839, however, history had been the local product of New England, and Plymouth and its local ambitions played a pivotal role in this American historiography. Any student of American history and literature knows of Bradford's *History of Plimoth Plantation*, of *Mourt's Relation*, Winslow's *History*, Nathaniel Morton's *New England's Memorial*, and the other classic texts of New England's sense of its own past, including John Winthrop's *History*, Cotton Mather's *Magnalia Christi Americana*, and, perhaps the most ambitious of them all, Thomas Prince's *Chronological History of New England* in the form of Annals, published in 1736, which purported to begin with the creation.

In 1832, nearly a century after Prince and a little more than 200 years after the landing of the Pilgrims, Plymouth's first local history in the period of the young Republic would be published by Dr. James Thacher, a founder, first secretary, and librarian and cabinet keeper of The Pilgrim Society. Dr. Thacher, a native of Barnstable who had plied his craft as a surgeon in the Revolutionary War, embraced the writing of the history of his adopted town with all the vigor of the local antiquarian who had seen something of the world beyond that of which he wrote. With no apologies for adding to the inflated corpus of Pilgrim history, Thacher observed in his preface to the first edition of 1832:

> Those who have reviewed the numerous local histories produced by learned antiquarians, may imagine that little remains of {the} Pilgrim story for the exercise of another pen, but the gleanings which escape the research, or would not comport with the views of the technical historian, may yet be found to bear a peculiar interest in a memoir of less import, and should not be lost to society. There are, moreover, numerous events and incidents of more recent occurrence, which the antiquarian would lament should be consigned to the shades of oblivion.

Plymouth has not lacked in histories of the Pilgrims and their times. In fact, in a famous essay, historian Samuel Eliot Morison once suggested that the Pilgrim story itself had suffered so much from over-exposure that it was in danger of becoming a cliché. The subject of Plymouth's history since 1692, however, when the colony was absorbed into that of the Massachusetts Bay, has been cultivated almost exclusively by local historians, and Dr. Thacher's name leads all the rest. Thacher was followed by two successors in the Pilgrim Society as historians of the town: William T. Davis, two of whose many works on Plymouth's local history continue to serve as foundational studies (*Ancient Landmarks of Plymouth*, first published in 1883, and *Plymouth Memories of an Octogenarian*, published in 1906); and Arthur Lord, a prominent Boston lawyer, who was president of the Pilgrim Society from 1890 to 1925. Lord received honorary degrees from Dartmouth College and Brown University for his scholarship on the Pilgrims and Plymouth, yet he never yielded his amateur status, and wrote in the classical tradition of the learned gentleman.

After the 1920 celebrations of the Pilgrim Landing tercentenary— the high-water mark in interest in the Pilgrims —curiosity increasingly turned, in Dr. Thacher's words of 1832, to those "numerous events and incidents of more recent occurrence, which the antiquarian would lament should be consigned to the shades of oblivion."

Most of us do not realize that we are living or making history, for we are simply living and doing what we must. It is only when we tell our story to others, and see the context of their stories and ours, that local history becomes the lively and animated thing that it has always been.

In this first volume of a history of 20th century Plymouth, *Ties that Bind*, we proceeded from the beginning of the century to World War II, and have learned how Plymouth mobilized for two world wars, celebrated the tercentenary, coped with industrial problems, developed its identity as a tourist destination, dealt with the Depression, adjusted to an increasingly diverse population with its social separations and integrations, and heard the personal stories and experiences of friends and neighbors. These are among the things now happily rescued from the "shades of oblivion."

BIBLIOGRAPHY

SOURCES CONSULTED

Adadourian, Reverend Haig
Proceedings of the 160th Anniversary Celebration of the Second
Congregational Church, 1898

Barker, Amy
History of the Plymouth Antiquarian Society
Plymouth, MA: The Society, 1959

Bartlett, Robert Merrill
My Corner of New England: Thoughts on Nature and Human Nature
From a Pilgrim House on Cape Cod
Portsmouth, NH: P.E. Randall, 1984
Brims with the rewards of living on the South Shore of Massachusetts. The
author enjoyed over 50 years in his Pilgrim-built house and became one of
the foremost authorities on the Pilgrims.

Bartlett, Robert Merrill
Pilgrim House by the Sea
North Quincy, MA: Christopher Publishing House, 1973

Bittinger, Frederick W.
The Story of the Pilgrim Tercentenary Celebration at Plymouth in the
Year 1921
Plymouth, MA: Memorial Press, 1923

Braddock, Ellsworth
Memories of a North Carver Village
Marion, MA: Channing Books, 1977

Bradford, William
Of Plimoth Plantation
New York: Alfred A. Knopf, 1982

Bradford, William and Edward Winslow
Mourt's Relation; or, Journal of the Plantation at Plymouth
New York: Garrett Press, 1969

Brewster, Ellis
Plymouth In My Father's Time
Plymouth, MA: Pilgrim Society, 1968
An informal collection of pictures and anecdotes, authentically Plymouth,
assembled as some insurance against their loss in the passage of years.

Brown, Dona
Inventing New England: Regional Tourism in the Nineteenth
Century
Washington: Smithsonian Institution Press, 1995

Burbank, A.S.
Guide to Historic Plymouth, Localities and Objects of Interest
Plymouth, MA: Memorial Press, 1928

Cummings, O.R.
Trolleys in the Land of the Pilgrims: the Plymouth and Kingston Street
Railway, the Brockton and Plymouth Street Railway, The Plymouth and
Brockton Street Railway, The Plymouth and Sandwich Street Railway,
1886-1928
Forty Fort, PA: Harold E. Cox, 1992

Daley, Carroll F.
After Kamesit: A Chronical of a Local Habitation and Some Names
Kingston, MA: Pilgrim Publishers, 1974

Davis, William T.
Ancient Landmarks of Plymouth
Boston: Williams, 1883
Traces the transfer of all property, by street name, in the downtown area of Plymouth from 1620 to the late 1800's; also contains an extensive genealogy of nearly every name connected with Plymouth through the 19th century

Davis, William T.
History of the Town of Plymouth
Philadelphia: J.W. Lewis Co., 1985
Covers Plymouth history from pre-Pilgrim times through the 19th century.

Davis, William T.
Plymouth Memories of an Octogenarian
Plymouth, MA: Memorial Press, 1906
Originally a series of sixty-nine front page articles appearing in Plymouth's weekly newspaper from January, 1905 to April, 1906. This book is a valued and classic account of Plymouth life

Dittmar, F. Willard
F. Williard Dittmar Interviews (videorecording)
Plymouth, MA: Plymouth Public Library, 1992.

Douglas, Maude. M.
Brief History of the Ryder Home, 1981-1945
Plymouth, MA: Memorial Press, 1945
Describes the house left to the Plymouth Fragment Society which was to become the Old Ladies Home

Ellis, Ernest Clifton
Reminiscences of Ellisville
Plymouth, MA: Memorial Press, 1973
Rich in details of a bygone era and serves as a valuable addition to the annals of Ellisville; recollections of the oldest resident of the village at the time

Geller, Lawrence D.
Between Concord and Plymouth: The Transcendentalists and the Watsons
Plymouth, MA: Pilgrim Society, 1973
Chapters on Henry D. Thoreau, Ralph W. Emerson, William Ellery Channing II and A. Bronson Alcott.

Geller, Lawrence D.
They Knew They Were Pilgrims, Essays in Plymouth History
New York: Poseidon Books, 1971
Plymouth's post-Colonial history is fruitful ground for studies in social, church and economic history, as well as folklore

Gomes, Peter
"Churches of the Not-So-Standing Order", Pilgrim Society Notes
Plymouth, MA: Pilgrim Society, 1954-1984
A short history of the Methodist, Universalist, Baptist, Episcopal, and the Bethel African Methodist Episcopal Church in Plymouth

Greene, Sarah Pratt McLean.
Cape Cod Folks
Boston: DeWolfe, Fiske & Co., 1904

Griffith, Henry S.
History of the Town of Carver, Massachusetts
New Bedford, MA: E. Anthony & Sons, 1913
An historical review from 1637 to 1910

Hebel, Prof. Dr. Udo
"Historical Bonding With an Expiring Heritage: Revisiting the Plymouth Tercentenary Festivities of 1920-1921", Celebrating Ethnicity and Nation: American Festive Culture From the Revolution to the Early Twentieth Century
New York: Berghahn Books, 2001

Hopkins, Libby O.
Plymouth Beach Book
Plymouth, MA: Manomet Bird Observatory, 1982

Hurd, D. H.
  History of Plymouth County, Massachusetts
    Philadelphia: J.W. Lewis & Co., 1884
    Chapter on Plymouth begins with the arrival of the Pilgrims and
    continues through the late 1800's

Jenks, Frederick A.
  Plymouth, Massachusetts
    Plymouth, MA: F.A. Jenks, 1939
    Interesting potpourri of Plymouth miscellany including chapters on
    historic places and personages.

Karbott, Grace et al
  Manomet In Fact and Fiction
    Plymouth, MA: Manomet Friends of the Library, 1970
    A compilation of stories, news articles, remembrances, letters, and
    pamphlets all about Manomet.

Knox, Robert
  "Trial of the Century"
  Unpublished manuscript, 2001

Longfellow, Henry Wadsworth
  The Courtship of Myles Standish [poem], 1858

Ludewig, Hermann E.
  The Literature of American Local History: A Bibliographical Essay
  New York: R. Craighead, 1846.

Marmein, Phyllis
  Phyllis: A Dancer's Life
    Unpublished manuscript, 1995
    Plymouth Public Library Photoduplication Program

Massachusetts Department of Commerce and Development
  Monograph of the Town of Plymouth
    Boston: The Department. Various years.
    Facts and figures on contemporary Plymouth.

Massachusetts Historical Commission State Survey Team
  Historic and Archaeological Resources of Southeast Massachusetts
    Boston: The Commission, 1982

Mather, Cotton
  Magnalia Christi Americana, Books I and II
    Cambridge, MA: Belknap Press, 1977

Miles, Roger W.
  Old Colony Memorial. Anniversary Issue 1822-1972
    Plymouth, MA: MPG Communications, 1972
    Commemorative volume focuses on the past 150 years of Plymouth history;
    illustrated with photographs, drawings and maps

Morison, Samuel Eliot
  The Ropemakers of Plymouth
    Boston: Houghton-Mifflin, 1950
    A history of the Plymouth Cordage Company from 1824 through 1949
    written by one of America's foremost historians

Morton, Nathaniel
  New England's Memorial
    Boston: Congregational Board of Publication, 1854

Murtagh, William
  Keeping Time: The History and Theory of Preservation in America
    Pittstown, NJ: Main Street Press, 1988

O'Brien, Katharine A.
  The Catholic Church in Plymouth
    Plymouth, MA: Memorial Press, 1936
    Story of St. Peter's, the first Catholic Church built in Plymouth

Old Colony Newspaper [microfilm]
  Plymouth, MA: Memorial Press, 1822-1945

Packard, Winthrop
  Old Plymouth Trails
    Boston, MA: Small, Maynard & Co., 1920
    Woodland walks in and about Plymouth accompanied by illustration

Pilgrim Society
  Proceedings at the Celebration by the Pilgrim Society at Plymouth,
  December 21, 1870
    An account of the ceremonies on the 250th anniversary of the landing of the
    Pilgrims
Pilgrim Society
  Pilgrim Society Notes
    Plymouth, MA: The Society, 1954-1984

Plymouth Collection Vertical File
  Plymouth, MA: Plymouth Public Library
    A specialized collection of newspaper clippings, magazines articles, and
    small pamphlets on Plymouth and the area. This collection is an integral part
    of the library's local history information

Plymouth Cordage Company
  One Hundred Years of Service, 1824 – 1924
    Plymouth, MA: Plymouth Cordage Company, 1924
    History and records of the company plus commemorative addresses offered on
    the occasion of the company's centennial celebration

Plymouth MA Historic District Commission
  Historic Homes of Plymouth, Massachusetts
    Plymouth, MA: The Commission, 1970-

Plymouth Illustrated
    Boston: New England Magazine, 1889
    Articles on Plymouth excerpted from New England Magazine beginning in
    September of 1889.

Plymouth (MA) High Schools
  Plymouth High School Yearbooks
    Plymouth, MA: The Schools, 1921-1945

Plymouth (MA) Redevelopment Authority
  The Bradford Area: A Study for the Preservation and Rehabilitation
  of an Historic Area
    Plymouth Redevelopment Authority, 1980

Plymouth National Bank
  Plymouth 1803-1928
    Boston: Callaway Association, 1928
    Recounts, in diary format, examples of daily life in Plymouth from 1803 to
    1928. Black and white photographs accompany the text.

  Plymouth Yesterday and Today
    Plymouth, MA: The Bank, 1953
    Picture book of familiar Plymouth landmarks as they appeared in 1953 and at
    an earlier date.

Plymouth, Town of
  Annual Reports of the Town of Plymouth, Massachusetts
    Plymouth, MA: The Town, 1865-1945

Plymouth, Town of
  Plymouth Directories
  1896, 1905, 1911, 1915, 1917, 1932, plus others
    A collection of street listings for the town of Plymouth lists businesses and
    each resident with occupation and street address

Plymouth, Town of. Planning Board
  Village Centers Master Plans
    Plymouth, MA: The Town, 1989-1993

Portuguese Pilgrims in New England [videorecording]
    Plymouth, MA: Plymouth-Carver Intermediate School, [197?]

Pratt, Walter M.
  Mayflower Society House
    Cambridge, MA: University Press, 1949
    The story of the Edward Winslow house, the Mayflower Society and the
    Pilgrims.

Prince, Thomas
A Chronological History of New England
Boston: Cummings, Hillgard and Co., 1826

Rezendes, Jerry
A Stroll Through North Plymouth, 1920s-1940s
Plymouth Public Library Photoduplication Program, 1999

Ropemakers of Plymouth [videorecording]
E.D. Dorsey and Plymouth Producers Group, 1979

Rothery, Agnes
The Old Coast Road, From Boston to Plymouth
Boston: Houghton Mifflin, 1920

Russell, Francis
Sacco & Vanzetti: The Case Resolved
New York: Harper & Row, 1986
Retells the 1920 stealing of a local shoe factory payroll and the murder
of a paymaster. The conviction and execution 7 years later of Sacco and
Vanzetti became the American legal affair of the century

Russell, William S.
Guide to Plymouth and Recollections of the Pilgrims
Boston: G. Coolidge, 1846

Sadow, Sue
Can Do (Said Sue)
Denver: Beaumont Books, 1992

Second Church of Plymouth (MA)
The Second Church of Plymouth Congregational at Manomet,
225th Anniversary Year, 1738-1963.
Plymouth, MA: The Church, 1963

Seelye, John D.
Memory's Nation: The Place of Plymouth Rock
Chapel Hill: University of North Carolina Press, 1998

Simmons, James Raymond
The Historic Trees of Massachusetts
Boston: Marshall Jones Company, 1919

Steinway, Ruth Gardner
Plymouth's Ninth Great Lot and the Six Ponds, 1710-1967:
A Chronicle
Kingston, MA: Pilgrim Publishers, 1976

Thacher, James
History of the Town of Plymouth
Yarmouthport, MA: Parnassus Imprints, 1972
History of the town of Plymouth from its first settlement in 1620 to the
present time (1835); with a concise history of the aborigines of New England
and their wars with the English

Thompson, E. S.
History of Plymouth, Norfolk and Barnstable Counties
New York: Lewis Historical Publishers, 1928.
Part I. Plymouth County, covers historical events from pre-Pilgrim times to
the early twentieth century

Travers, Milton A.
The Wampanoag Indian Federation of the Algonquin Nation
Boston: Christopher Pubs., 1961
Fascinating collection of information about the Wampanoag Indian
Federation

Warner, Frances Lester
Pilgrim Trails: A Plymouth-to-Provincetown Sketchbook
Boston: Atlantic Monthly Press, 1921

Weeks, Muriel Holmes Anderson
A Family History
Plymouth Public Library Photoduplication Program, 1975

Whitehill, Walter Muir
Independent Historical Societies, An Enquiry Into Their Research
and Publication Functions and Their Financial Future
Boston: Boston Athenaeum, 1962

AUTHORS AND CONTRIBUTORS

Nan Anastasia, who compiled the material for *As Time Goes By*, is managing editor of the Old Colony Memorial. A graduate of Plymouth-Carver Regional High School and Wheaton College, she worked for the *Patriot Ledger* of Quincy before joining the OCM staff as a reporter in 1984.

James Baker, who wrote *Plymouth: The Tourist Town*, is also the author of *Images of America: Plymouth*, a collection of photographs published by Arcadia Press in 2002, and numerous other works on Plymouth and Pilgrim history. He confesses to "a general fascination with Plymouth history – especially the influence of tourism on the town."

Joan H. Bartlett, author of the *Summer People* stories, is a graduate of Harvard University and the wife of a retired diplomat. She runs a small business helping people write their memoirs and family histories. A summer resident of Plymouth since 1957, she has lived in the town year-round since 1990.

Kathleen Branigan, a graphic artist at Rogers Print & Design in Plymouth, designed this book to have an early 20th century look and feel. A Navy brat who was born in Texas, she is a graduate of George Washington University who has lived in Plymouth since 1978. Prior to joining Rogers Print, she was art director of the *Boston Parents' Paper* for 13 years.

Rose T. Briggs, (1893-1981), who wrote *Life on a Cranberry Bog at the Turn of the Century* in 1975, was born on North Street in Plymouth in 1893. An author, lecturer and artist, she was a director emeritus of both the Pilgrim Society and Antiquarian Society when she died in 1981. "She carried in her veins the lifeblood of old Plymouth," said the Rev. Peter Gomes at her funeral.

George W. Carter Jr., author of *Manomet Shore Patrol*, grew up in Plymouth and worked for the Plymouth Five Cents Savings Bank for 42 years, beginning as a teller and retiring as a senior vice president. A member of the Pilgrim Society, he was a Plymouth call firefighter for 34 years.

John Chaffee, managing editor of this volume, is a retired newspaper reporter and magazine editor. A combat veteran of the Korean War, he is a graduate of Boston University.

Bobbi Clark, author of the story of the Plymouth homefront during World War II, was an Emmy Award-winning television producer in Chicago before moving to Plymouth at the end of the 20th century. A graduate of Emerson College, she is a radio news reporter for WATD-FM in Marshfield.

Wesley Ennis, photography editor of this volume, is a staff photographer for the *Old Colony Memorial*, secretary of the Pilgrim Society, chairman of the Plymouth Historical Commission and a member of the Old Colony Club.

Marie Fehlow, author of *Oak Street School in the 1930s*, is a Plymouth native who left town after graduating from Plymouth High School to become a nurse during World War II. She married a career Army officer and after he retired Marie moved back to Plymouth with her husband, Otto Fehlow, for whom the main meeting room at the Plymouth Public Library is named.

Philip Forman, author of the story about Plymouth's two movie theaters, is a Plymouth native who can trace his heritage back to the Pilgrims. An actor whose interest in films began with his boyhood experiences at the Old Colony theater, his short-film credits include the lead role in both *Smoking* and *When I Was A Boy*.

Karin Goldstein, who wrote six chapters of this volume, is curator of original collections at Plimoth Plantation and a Ph.D. candidate in American studies at Boston University. Former curator of collections at Pilgrim Hall Museum, she is a trustee of the Antiquarian Society.

Peter J. Gomes, provided the bookends of this volume, both a foreword and an epilogue. The Plummer Professor of Christian Morals at Harvard University and minister at Harvard's Memorial Church, the Rev. Gomes, who grew up in Plymouth, is the author of many highly regarded works, including *The Good Book: Reading the Bible with Mind and Heart.*

Herman Hunt, author of A *"Spanish Lady" Plagues Plymouth,* is a retired engineer and very active library volunteer. Recipient of many academic awards, both in high school and college, he said the reason he participated in this local history project was, "My eighth grade history teacher would have insisted on it."

Robert Knox, author of the Sacco-Vanzetti stories, is a correspondent for the Boston Globe and former associate editor of the *Old Colony Memorial.* A graduate of Yale University, he is a published author of poetry and fiction and has won awards from the New England Press Association for arts coverage and editorial writing.

Sharon LaRosa, was the chief copy editor of this volume. A Plymouth reference librarian, she earned a B.A. in art history at Wheaton College and a master's degree in library science at Simmons College. Former editor of a library newsletter, she has traveled extensively in the U.S. and Italy.

Samuel Eliot Morison, (1887-1976) was one of the most distinguished historians of 20th century America. Author of *The Ropemakers of Plymouth,* which was commissioned by the Plymouth Cordage Co., his other works included a 15-volume history of U.S. naval operations in World War II and Pulitzer Prize-winning biographies of both Christopher Columbus and John Paul Jones.

Maggie Mills, whose memories of growing up in downtown Plymouth are excerpted in this volume, has been a staff reporter for the *Old Colony Memorial* for nearly 50 years. Her "Time Lines" and "The Way We Looked…" columns have contributed immeasurably to the history of 20th century Plymouth.

Beverly Ness, author of *Plymouth's Original Town House,* is chairman of the town's 1749 Court House Committee and a reference associate at the Plymouth Public Library. A graduate of UMass-Amherst, she is the author of a 1995 handbook on genealogical resources in Plymouth.

Laurence Pizer, author of *All Plymoutheans Are Immigrants,* has been Plymouth's town clerk since 1992 and is president of the Massachusetts Town Clerks' Association. After earning history degrees from both Brown University and the University of Iowa, he served as director of the Pilgrim Society for 14 years.

Lee Regan, is supervisor of the Plymouth reference library and curator of the library's extensive collection of local history memorabilia. Initiator of the 20th century history project, she grew up in Plymouth, graduated from the local high school and earned degrees at both Bridgewater State College and Simmons College. She has worked for the Plymouth Public Library since 1980.

Sue Sadow, (1896-1996) whose memory of the 1913 Plymouth High School graduation is included in this volume, grew up in Plymouth, graduated from Simmons College and went on to become the first senior citizen to volunteer for the Peace Corps and a nutritionist for the United Nations.

Richmond Talbot, who wrote the story for Plymouth on the dawn of a new century, is one of a fourth generation of his family to live on Mayflower Street in Plymouth. A graduate of Bates College who married the former Annette Sirrico, also of Plymouth, he is the retired owner of a local insurance agency and is now a staff correspondent for the *Old Colony Memorial.*

Alba Thompson, who wrote both *Growing Up Italian in Plymouth* and *First Grade at the Alden Street School,* is a Plymouth native who after World War II became a liaison officer between Gen. Douglas MacArthur's headquarters in Tokyo and the U.S. military government in Seoul, Korea. In 1986 she became the first woman to the elected a Plymouth selectman.

ACKNOWLEDGEMENTS

Preparation of this book would not have been possible without the assistance and support of the following people and organizations who helped us gather information, check facts, find stories and read and re-read manuscripts. While a great deal of their volunteer work is reflected in these pages, much more of what they have contributed will help us prepare Volume II of *Beyond Plymouth Rock*, the story of America's hometown during the 20th century. We regret any inadvertent omissions.

Priscilla Andrews, George Anzuoni, David Arruda, Winifred Avery, Brooks Barnes, Jim & Peggy Baker, Helen Belcher, Marjorie Belcher, Roger Berg, Beverly Booth, Philip Bornstein, Boston Public Library, Mikki Chaffee, Charlotte Clark, Congregation Beth Jacob, Jennifer Conragan, Christine Cook, Ted Curtin, Frederick Darling, Bob Davis, Jim Delano, Mildred Dupuis, Zachary Ennis, John Ferris, Cynthia Buttner Fischer, Peter Forman, William Fornaciari, Annie Foss, Richard Gibbons, Alice Childs Grennell, Bob Hale, Evelyn Hathaway, Marion Hedge, Jeanette Holmes, Joseph Horn, Phyllis Hughes, Herman Hunt, Herb Johnson, Judy Ingram, Marion and Paula Jesse, Doris Johnson, Rodney Randall Joseph, Grace Karbott, Edith LaMarca, David Malaguti, Cyril Leek Marshall, Robert Marten, John Martini, Dr. Barry Meltzer, Saul Meyerson-Knox, Maggie Mills, Thomas Minehan, Enzo Monti, Michael Moskos, New England Historic and Genealogical Society, Newfield House, Inc., Carolee Nielsen, Elaine Nudd, Dinah O'Brien, Phillip O'Connell, Dexter Olsson, Stephen O'Neill, Pilgrim Society, Plymouth & Brockton Street Railway Co., Plimoth Plantation, Plymouth Antiquarian Society, Plymouth Board of Selectmen, Plymouth Cemetery Department, Plymouth County Registry of Deeds and Probate, Plymouth Old Colony Club, Mary Alice Post, Jan Randolph, Sissie Reed, Ellen Remlinger, Jerry Rezendes, Bill Rudolph, Ray Russo, Patti Ryan, Brian Sansoucy, Reed Sibley, Alfred Sitta, Dr. Sam Stewart, Gilbert Tavares, Ken Tavares, Mimi Toabe, F. Steven Triffletti, Florence Van Leuvan, Ruth Walker, Jennifer Walshaw, Bill & Althea Walton, John Warren, Honey Weiss, Gloria Welch, Merrill Welcker, Marilyn White.

Finally, this book could not have been written without the encouragement of the many library patrons who stopped by to offer a quick word of advice, ask about the status and share our enthusiasm.

Our heartfelt thanks to all.

INDEX

Note: Numbers in italics refer to illustrations

A

A & P Supermarket 52
Aimone Family 130
Albertini, Iris 54
Alden Street 124
Alden Street School 97
Alden, Katherine 113
Allerton Street 12
Amendment, 18th 99
Amendment, 19th 42
American Legion 112
American Red Cross 112, 146
American Woolen Co. *See:* Puritan Mills
Amerigo Vespucci Club 52, 71, 76, 100, 105
Anderson, William 82
Angelina Schooner 30
Antiquarian House 79
Armour & Co. 94
Armstrong, John - Police Chief 66
Aron Family 45
Atherton Furniture Co. 94
Atlantic Street 30
Atlas Tack Co. 9
Atwood's Lumber 100

B

Baietti, Elio 100
Baietti Family 54
Baietti, Mary Marvelli 124
Baietti, Vincent (Jelly) 84, 100, 115, 126, 128
Baker, George 18
Barker, LeBaron 82
Balboni, Carol 86
Balboni, Rosa 86
Barbieri Family 134

Barboza, Nellie Youngman 125, 127
Barnes, Brooks 32, 99
Barnes, Susan D. 82
Barrett, William 'Cozy' 1
Bartlett Lane 122
Bartlett Road 59
Bartlett, Joseph 14
Bastoni, Enrico 86
Bastoni, Primo 133
Bavarian Benefit Society 67
Beauregarde, Edgar 137
Bedard Family 53
Beis Jacob Society 44
Belcher, Helen 56, 114, 125, 126
Benati, Elide *See:* Butters, Elide Benati
Benati Family *144*
Benati, Idore 144
Berg Family 43, 44
Berg, Joseph 44
Bert's 138
Beth Jacob Community Center 120
Billings, Hammatt canopy *5, 10, 15, 15, 22, 23*
Billingsgate Shoal 101
Billington Sea 17
Bittinger, Frederick 93
Bittinger, Paul 101, 105, 119
Black Pond 147
Blackmer, Arthur E. 82
Blackmer, M. B., Livery & Boarding Stable *18*
Blackmur, Arnold A. 136
Blake, Earl P. (Sheriff) 79
Blessington, Jean 116, 126, 127, 128
Blessington, Marie 116
Bongiovanni Family 113
Bongiovanni, Adeladi 86
Bongiovanni, Coeli Tarantino 126

Bongiovanni, Pasquale 133
Bongiovanni, Ramo 113, 125, 127, 133
Boot Pond 116
Borgatti Family 54
Borghesani, Gaetano 69
Borghesani, Henry 69
Borghesani, Luigia 69
Borsari, Emma 86
Botieri, Rich 32
Boundary Street 13
Boyden, Mary M. 82
Boyer, Harold 72, 99, 115, 137
Bradford Chair 95
Bradford Joint Co. 7
Bradford Store *114*
Bradford Street 100
Bradford, Muriel 135
Bramhall's Corner 137
Braunecker's Farm 126
Brenner's Paint Shop 132
Brenner, August 132
Brewster Family 8, 20
Brewster Gardens 8, 19, 145
Brewster Spring *25, 27*
Brewster Street 121
Brewster, Ellis W. 1, *122*
Brewster, Lalla Withington 20
Briggs, LeBaron Russell 78
Briggs, Rose T. 1, 15, *39*, 59
Brigida Family 54
Brini Family 75
Brini, Alfonsina 88
Brini, Beltrando 71, 72, 75, 86, 103, 105, 107, 113
Brini, LeFavre *See:* Wager, LeFavre Brini
Brini, Vincenzo 73, 75
Broccoli's Market 142, 149

Brockton and Plymouth Street Railway Co. 9, 10, *28*, 67, 84
Brody Family 44
Bug Light 130
Burbank, A. S. 17, 27
Burbank's, A. S. (store) *22*, 117, 121
Burgess Family 134
Burgess, Jane R. 82
Burgess, Ken 149
Burgess, Margie Clausson 141, 143, 148, 149
Burial Hill 11, 15, 92
burler 139
Burton School 29, 119, *119*
Burns, William *26*
Busi, Joseph 67, 68
Butters, Elide Benati 138, 139, 142, 145, 148
Butters, George 140
Buttner's 142

C

Calhoun, John 32
Calhoun, Mary Jane 32
Camp Edwards 141, 142
Cape Cod steamer 22, 26, 29
Cape Verdeans 41, 57-60
Cappannari Bros. (store) 100, 134
Cappannari, David 38, 54
Cappannari, Mary 55
Cappella, Allen 135
Car Barn #1 84
Carafoli Family 8
Carlier Family 53
Carr, Andrew J. 82
Carter, George *147*
Cash, Mary 73
Cavicchi's clothing store 142
Ceccarelli, Leo 117

Centennial Street 12
Center Hill Station 147
Center Hill Pond 147
Central Fire Station 50, 146, 148
Charlie's Hardware 71, 149
Cherry Court 88
Cherry Street 25, 44, 71, *71*, 72, 73, 76, 92, 132
Chilton Street 9, 121
Chiltonville 17, 74
Christian Science Church 98
Christofori, Esther 74, 86
Christoforo Columbo Club 52
Church of the Pilgrimage 11, 99
Churchill, Charles H. 26
Cingolani Family 121
Citizens Bank 52
Civil Works Administration 115
Civilian Conservation Corps 115, 123
Clark's Island 11
Clarke, G. Herbert 82
Clausson, Jeanne 148
Clausson, Margie
    See: Burgess, Margie Clausson
Cleanist, The 117
Cliff Street 136
Clifford House 17, *28*
Clough's Market 121
Clyfton Street 121
Coast Guard 130
Coast Guard Auxiliary 138
Cobb's Lane 83
Cohen Family 43
Cohen's store 45
Cohen, Harry 119, 122
Cohen, Jacob 119
Cohen, Joseph 45
Cold Spring 119
Cold Spring Club 100
Cold Spring School 98
Cole's Hill 5, 10, *10*, 17, 23, *24*
Cole's Ordinary 15
Collas, John 121

Collas, Nick 121
Collingwood, Martin 112
Colonial Dames of America 8, 92
Columbia Pavilion 17
Commercial Club 26
Committee on Public Safety 65
Company D *See:* Standish Guards
Compass Bank 121
Coolidge, Calvin 77, *77*, *78*, 103
Cooper's Drug Store 120
Cooper's General Store *30*
Cooper, Guy 115, 125
Cordage Terrace 73
Corl, Melvin 88, 89
Cornish School *38*, *119*, 119
Cortelli, Luigi *See:* Knife, Louis
Costa Family 54
Costa Sr., Manuel 130
Costa, Joe 149
Court and Brewster streets 12
Court and Chilton streets 12
Court and Samoset streets 12
Court House, 1749 49. *50*
Court Street
    9, *22*, 45, 88, 112, 117, 119, *131*
Covell, Lewis 68
Cox, Channing 94
Craig, Anne B. 82
Craig, Florence B. 69
cranberry industry 39-42, *40*, 57-60
cranberry pickers *30*, *39*
Crandlemeier, Von J. 144
Curlew Pond 56
Currier's restaurant 6, 19, 142

D

Dale, Phyllis *See:* Hughes, Phyllis Dale
Damon, John H. 82
Danforth, Allen 26
Danforth, William Seaver 26
Daughters of Pocahontas 92
Davis Building *22*
Davis Opera House 12, 30, 50

Davis, Judge Harry B. 82
Davis, William T. 153
Deacon Brothers 94
Depression (Great) 111-115, 123-128
Desmaine, Sabrina *109*
DiCarlo, John 86
DiSalvatori Family 134
Dittmar, Willard 133
Dolan, Mary 54
Donovan, Linda 130
Doten, Charles 65
Douglas, Mabel 98
Downey Construction Co. 52
Downey, Jr., Timothy *21*
Downey, Michael *21*
Duxbury Pier Light 10

E

Eastwood, Frank 82
Eaton, Francis 81
Edes Family 144
Edes Manufacturing Co. 9, 115, 144
Eel River 6
Eel River Beach Club 102, *102*, 116
Eel River Farm 102
Eldridge, William T. 82
Ellis Curtain 143
Ellis Family 14
Ellisville 40, 116
Ellisville Harbor 100, 147
Ellsmore-Nash Band 84
Emergency Relief Act 115, 123
Emerson's store 143, *143*
Emerson, "Ma" Esther 143, *143*
Enemy aliens 66, 74
Excelsior Hook and Ladder No.1 50

F

Farina, Pat 134
Fehlow, Marie Martinelli 126, 137, 142-146, *148*
Ferreira Family 132
Figmic, Minnie E. Burke 120

Fihelly, Arthur 68, *68*
Fiocchi, Margherita 86
Finney, A.K. Construction Co. 110
First Baptist Church *10*, 11,18
First Parish Church 11, 18, *27*, 49
Flockton, William *21*
Forefathers' Day 18
Forefathers' Monument
    See: National Monument to the
    Forefathers
Forest Avenue 126
Forges, The 20, 65, 102
Fort Hill 93
Fortini, Mary 76, 79, 86
Franco-Prussian Veteran Society 67
Francolossi Family 134
Franklin House 116
Franks, William S. 136
Frederick N. Knapp School 31
Freemont Street 84
Frost, Robert 8
Frost, Robert , poem 96
Frumento Family 134

G

Gallo Family 132
Gambini's Luncheonette *112*, 133, 142
Gardner, C. F. 8
Garuti Family 52
Garvin, Beatrice 119
Gascoyne Family 132
Gavoni Family 53
Geller, Louie 146
Geller, Rose Sherman 44, 45, 98, 118, 139, 146, *146*, 148
General Society of Mayflower Descendants 92
German Lutheran Church
    See: Zion Lutheran Church
Glassman Family 134
Goddard, B. F. 18
Gomes, Peter J. *1*, *59*
Gooding, George L. 82
Govoni Family 53, 134

Great Fire (Sept. 12, 1900) 40-41
Griswold, Ruth Dale 101
Guidobone, Abgel 88
Guidoboni, Ann 149
Guidoboni, Dolores 54
Gurnet Point 10, 30, 80, *80*, 94, 95, 101

H

Haire's Restaurant 121
Hamilton Street 138
Hammett, William 81
Hand's shoe store 120
Harding, Warren 8, 18, *93*
Harlow House 92
Harris Hall 35, *132*
Harris, Edward R. 35
Harvey, David O. 6
Hatch, Mercy 99
Hatch, Stuart 143
Healy, Henry *21*
Hedge House 18, 81, *81*, 121
Hedge School 125, 132, 133
Hedge, Thomas 81
Hedges Road 122
Herring Stream *19*
High Cliff 32, 71
High Street 45
Hitchcock, Alice D. 82
Holmes Reservation 6
Holmes Terrace 32
Holmes, Francis C. 63, 64, 82
Holmes, Gideon F. 34
Holmes, Helen 120
Holmes, Jeanette Morton 66, 68, 84, 99
Hornblower, Eleanor 102
Hornblower Family 99
Hornblower, Henry 102
Hornblower, Sr., Ralph 100
Hotel Crescent *26*
Hotel Pilgrim 6, 9, 17, *28*, 84, 95, 100
Howard Johnson's restaurant 141
Howland Court 121
Howland Family 8

Howland House 93
Howland Society 18
Howland Street 121
Howland, Carrold D. 82
Howland, George B. 69
Hughes, Phyllis Dale 143, 145, 149

I

Immigrant monument inscription viii
Improved Order of Red Men 44, 92
influenza epidemic 69-70
International Exposition at Milan 36
Interstate Theater 118

J

Jabez Corner 25, 83, *114*, 115, *135*
Jabez Howland house 18
Janeiro, Aurora 132
Janeiro, Francisco Maria 131
Jennings, Annie 69
Jennings, Ralph K. 69
Jesse Family 132, 134
Jesse Sr., Ted 73
Jesse, Frank 73, 88, 89
Jewish community 43-45
Jim's Restaurant 140
Joe Pioppi's Orchestra 84
John Alden Trolley *28*
Jordan Hospital 21, 25, 27, *70*, 144
Jordan, Eben 20, 70

K

Keene, Flora 97
Keenan Family 121
Keller Family 45
Kennedy's Butter and Egg Store 143
Keough, Bobby 120
Keough, Richard 120
Ketchen Family 119
Ketchen, Billy 119
Ketchen, Miriam 119
King's variety store 121
Klasky, Mel 148
Knapp School *133*

Knapp Street 84
Knife Family 124
Knife, Louis 44, 111, 125, 126
Knife, Louis & Son 94, 149

L

Labor Day festival 67
Lacey's Boatyard 53
Landmark Building 117
LeBaron Alley 6
Legion Band 149
Lend-A-Hand Club 31
Lewis and Clark Exhibition 36
Leyden Street 7, 10, 11, *18*, *37*, 49, 92
Liberty Bonds 66
Lincoln Street 50, 54, 88, 124, 137
Litchfield, Mary P. 82
Little Pond 92
Locatelli Family 121
Lodge, Henry Cabot 77, *77*, 94
Lodi's farm 122
Lombardi Family 134
Long Pond 32, 116
Long Wharf 7, 10, *10*, 23
Longhi, Vincent 86
Lord, Arthur 153
Loring Library 6, 34, 67, 76
Loring Reading Room 131, 132
Loring, Augustus P. 6, 34, 36, 63
Loring, Bunny 120
Loring, Caleb William 34
Loring Family 33
Lothrop House 81, *81*
Lothrop Street 12, 97, 100, 146
Lothrop, Lydia Hedge 81
Lowell, Francis C. 33
Lowell Family 33
Lyceum Hall *22*, 50

M

Mabbett, George & Sons Co. 9, *52*, 65, 94,
111, 114, 115, 127, *134*
Maccaferri Family 44

MacDonald, Susie *70*, 98
MacLean, John D. 69
MacLean, Katherine 69
Main and Leyden streets 5, 11, *22*, 46
Main Street 6, 11, *21*, *25*, *83*, *123*, 148, 149
Main Street extension 46, *46*, 66, 117, 145
Makier Family 132
Malaguti, Lisa 51
Malaguti, Therese 86
Manomet 10, 116, 125, 143, 149
Manomet Coast Guard Station 94, 147
Manomet Life Saving Station 23
Manomet Point 125, 147
Manomet Point Road 149
Manomet Ponds 17
Manomet Post Office 116
Manter's Point 30, 116, 130
Marcella, Maria Rosa 131
Marconi Club 134
Market and Leyden streets 11, 49
Market and Mill streets 9
Market Square 49
Market Street 7, *53*, 122
Markus, Miriam 'Victory' 68
Markus, Myer and Bessie 68
Martinelli, Bruno 110
Martinelli, Elisa 138
Martinelli, Luigi 51
Martinelli, Marie
See: Fehlow, Marie Martinelli
Martinelli, Sylvia 109
Marvelli Family *124*
Marvelli, Lydia 124
Marvelli, Robert 124
Massachusetts Society Sons of the American
Revolution 92
Massachusetts Tercentenary Commission 73
Massachusetts Women's Defense Corps 146
Massasoit statue 92
Mayer, George 125
Mayflower 18, 92
Mayflower Grove 84

Mayflower Hotel 149
Mayflower Society House 146
Mayflower Street 126
Mayflower Worsted Mills 126, 127
Mayflower, yacht 18, 93
Maynard, Louis 141
McCall, Governor Samuel W. 68
McGinnis, Amos 109
McLellan's Store 54
meerstead (the) *11*
Meeting House 49
Mello Family 134
Memorial Drive 82
Memorial Hall 50, 81, 82, *82*, 140, 144
Memorial Press Building 5, 11, 117
Merrick, Dorothy D. 2, 16
Methodist Church 12, 120
Meyer, Louise Fry 102
Middle Street 6, 44, 82, 117
migrant labor 40-41
Mill Village 52, 53, 74, 97
Millar, Helen E. 82
Miller Family 45
Modern Baking Co. 94
Mongan, Edgar 137
Moning, Charles 117, 118
Monti, Enzo 126, 127, 128
Moore's department store 121
Morton Park 5, 92
Morton, Ichabod *31*
Morton, Nathaniel 17
Morton, Tibbie 47
Mullins, Anne 82
Murphy, Rose Marie 130
Myles Standish State Forest 56, 115, 123, 128

N

Nathaniel Morton School 128, 133, 137
National Monument to the Forefathers
 5, 12, 51, 93
National Youth Administration 125
Nazro, William E. C. 34, 36
Nelson Street 138

Nelson Street Park 128
New York, New Haven and Hartford Railroad
 5, 12, 138
nickelodeon theaters 117
Nickerson, Arthur S. 8
Noble, James *21*
North Park Avenue 79, 142
North Plymouth 6, 33, 36, 44, 52,
 73, 88, 100, 117, *131*, 133
North Plymouth post office 13
North Russell Street 119
North Street 6, 12, 92
Number 2 Mill 34, 35

O

O'Brien, Kate 54
Oak Street School 109, *109*, 110
Obery Street 23
Odd Fellows Hall 9, 11, *24, 27*, 50
Old Colony Club 12
Old Colony Laundry 121
Old Colony Memorial
 See: Memorial Press Building
Old Colony Railroad 12, *13*, 17, 26, *139*
 See Also: New York, New Haven &
 Hartford RR
Old Colony Theater 44, 77, 92, 112, 117,
 137, 145
Old Colony Trust 115
Old Curiosity Shop 8, 11, *28*
Old Sandwich Road 20, 25
Orentlicher Family 43
Orentlicher, Simon 45
Ortolani, Clementine 109
Ortolani, Frank 109

P

Padlusky, Ida Sherman 45
Pageant Field 92
Park Avenue 12
Parsons, Willard 79
Patenaude, Jean Whiting 84, 115, 125, 126
Paty, Johnny 110

Peck, Kenneth 118
Pederzani Family 54
Pegg II 101
Pelligrini Family 53
Penn Family 44
Penn, Fannie Brody *43*, 44
Penn, Max *43*, 44
Peoples Market *53*
Perrior Jr., Geoffrey D. 69
Peters, Gertrude J. 69
Peterson, P. J. 8
Pickett, Richard *21*
Pierce, Dr. Helen F. "Nellie" 70
Pig Club 68
Pilgrim Band 27, 82
Pilgrim Hall 1, 12, *18*, 79, 81
Pilgrim Hotel 102, 116
Pilgrim Memorial State Park 92
Pilgrim Progress 92
Pilgrim Sarcophagus 92
Pilgrim Society 11, 12, 17, 152
Pilgrim Spirit pageant 18, 92, 95
Pimental, Manuel "Barney" 117, 118, *118*
Pimental, Richard "Mousey" 118
Pina Family 134
Playland 145, *149*
Pleasant Street 44
Plimoth Plantation 19, 102
Plymouth Alms House 11
Plymouth and Brockton Street Railway Co. 84
Plymouth and Kingston Street Railway Co.
 17, *28*, 83
Plymouth and Middleboro Railroad Co. 12
Plymouth and Sandwich Street Railway Co.
 10, 30, 84
Plymouth Antiquarian Society 18, 81, 82
Plymouth Antiques Centre 148
Plymouth Beach 6, 7, 9, 17, 130
Plymouth Beach: breakwater construction 30
Plymouth Board of Public Welfare 111, 115
Plymouth Boat Yard 138
Plymouth Boys Club 82

Plymouth Cooperative Bank 113
Plymouth Cordage Auditorium 132
Plymouth Cordage Band 36
Plymouth Cordage Co. 6, 9, 12, 33, *33*, *35*,
 37, *61*, *62, 63*, 94, 95, *108*, 111, 114,
 115, 127, 131, *132*
Plymouth Cordage Co. strike 61-64
Plymouth Cordage Co. wages 61-62, 112
Plymouth Cordage Men's Club 36, 132
Plymouth Country Club 6, 102
Plymouth Courthouse *86*
Plymouth Day 93
Plymouth downtown *129*
Plymouth Electric Light Co. 6, 10, 31, 94
Plymouth Fire Dept. *21, 31*
Plymouth Foundry 123
Plymouth Fragment Society 112, 125
Plymouth Gas Light Co. 94
Plymouth Golf and Tennis Association 6
Plymouth Golf Links 12
Plymouth Hackney Stud Fire Dept. 30
Plymouth Harbor 10, *24*
Plymouth High School 48, 114, 124, *127*,
 133, 137
Plymouth Honor Roll 73
Plymouth Industrial Park 126
Plymouth Light Station 80, *80*
Plymouth Long Beach 94
Plymouth Lumber Co. 136
Plymouth Marine 138
Plymouth Memorial Building
 See: Memorial Hall
Plymouth Mills 9
Plymouth National Bank 68, 111, 115
Plymouth Philharmonic Orchestra 137
Plymouth Point Beach Pier 10
Plymouth Police Station 119
Plymouth population 27
Plymouth Post Office 46
Plymouth property tax rate 1900 29
Plymouth Public Library 1, 6, 120
Plymouth Redevelopment Authority 2

Plymouth Rock   5, 8, 10, 15, 19, *23*, 73, 92

Plymouth Rock House (Hotel) 5, 10, 17, 100

Plymouth Savings Bank   26

Plymouth School Committee   119

Plymouth Stove Foundry Co.   9

Plymouth Tercentenary Committee   94

Plymouth Theater   112, 117, *117*, 144

Plymouth waterfront   *5, 12-13, 15*

Plymouth Yacht Club   6, *9*, 10

Policow Family   45

Poluzzi Family   54

Portland Storm   17

Portuguese immigration   57-60

Portuguese Society   95

Post, Mary Alice Janeiro   132

Powderhouse Memorial   92

Priscilla Beach   32

prohibition   99-101

Public Works Administration   124

Puritan Clothing Co.   44, 133, 142

Puritan Mills   7, 9, 52, *52*, 82, 94, 111, 112, 127, 138, 142

Q

Quartz grocery store   97

R

Ragazzini, Arthur   131

Railway Express freight terminal   136

Randall, Mildred   110

Raymond & Beaman   6

Reagan, Thomas   *21*

Red Cross Society   65, *66*

Regan, Lee   75

Registry of Deeds   124, 138

Resnick Family   43

Resnick, Bill   112

Resnick, David   43

Resnick, Louis   43

Rezendes Family   54

Rezendes, Jerry L.   118, 136

Rice Family   45

Ripley & Bartlett Tack Manufacturing Co.   9

Robbins Ice Co.   56

Robbins Lane   12

Robbins Lumber Yard   12

Robbins Road   100

Robbins, Captain C. H.   7

Robinson Iron Works   *24*

Rocky Hill Road   10, 84

Rocky Point   76, 94, 147

Rogan, Terese   120

Romano Family   134

Roosevelt, Franklin   114, 148

Ropewalk Court   132

Route 3 (old)   125

Ruggiero Family   134

rumrunning   99-101

Russell Library   31

Russell Mills Pond   122

Russell Street   49, 121

Russell, Allen Danforth   1

Russell, Andrew L.   119

Russell, John   138, 143, 146

Russell, William G.   21

S

S.S. Pierce Co.   94

Sacco, Nicola   *88*

Sacco and Vanzetti   71-76; 85-91; 103-107

Sacco-Vanzetti funeral procession   *105*

Sacco-Vanzetti memorial plaque   *106*

Sacco-Vanzetti supporters   *103*

Sadler's clothing store   142

Sadow Family   43

Sadow's woman's shop   66, 120

Samoset House   12, *16*, 17, 95, 121

Sampson, Everett   *21*

Sandwich Street   45, 84, 93, *137*, 146, 148

Saquish Beach   101

Saquish Head   10

Saquish Neck   10

Scagliarini, Adelaide   133

Scagliarini, Anita Fiocchi   101, 126, 134

Schneider Family   134

Schwartz, Dr. Phillip   97

Scott, Manuel   *21*

scrip   115

Sears, Jennie Mazzilli   98

Seaside   13

Seaview Street   133

Second Congregational Church   149

Seven Hills Road   126

sewing project (WPA)   124

Sgarzi, Amedeo   38

Sharp, Eunice E.   1

Shaw Court   138

Shaw, Dr. John Holbrook   70

Sherman Building   45

Sherman Family   *45*

Sherman's Furniture   139

Sherman, Abraham   45

Sherman, Carleton   122

Sherman, Ida   122

Sherman, Leon   *28*

Sherman, Orrin   122

Sherman, Rose *See:* Geller, Rose Sherman

Sherman, Sarah Toabe   44, 45

Ship Pond   32, 147

Shipman, Wayne   54

Shirley Square   29, 112, 119, 121, 143

Shoman, Bobby   45

Shoman, Samuel   45

Shriber Family   *43*, 44

Shwom Building   45

Shwom Family   45

Siever's Lunch   149

Sinclair Refining Co.   94

Sloane, Elspeth   146

Smith's gift shop   142

Smith's Lane   132

Smith, Charles A.   6

Smith, Tip   142

Soares Family   132

South Meadow Road   140

South Park Avenue   121, 142

South Plymouth   136

South Pond Road   6

South Russell Street   49

South Street   45, 134, 141

Sparrow House   113, 128

Spencer, Angie Hathaway   *109*

Spooner Street School   133

Spooner Family   33

Spooner, Bourne   61

Spring Hill Restaurant   *25*

Spring Lane   122

St. Louis World's Fair of 1904   36

St. Mary's Church   71, 132

St. Peter's Church   12, 120

Stafford Street   148

Standish Avenue   12

Standish Guards   7, 65, *65, 66*

Standish Guards Armory   11

Standish Mills *See:* Standish Worsted Co.

Standish Worsted Co.   9, 65, 94, 111, 123, 127

Standish, Winslow Brewster   11, 18

Stasinos, Aphrodite   140

Stasinos, Charlie   138, 148

Stasinos, Jim   140

State Pier   94, 121

Station Street   13

Stein Family   45

Stein, Ken   73

Steinberg, Jacob   45

Stephens Field   101, 125

Stoddard & McLean   7

Stoddard, Isaac N., & Son   6

Stone and Webster   84

Stone Estate   76

Stone, Charles   84

Store Pond   *133*

Stringer Family   121

Strocchi Family   53

Stump Town   97

suffrage   42

Sullivan Family   134

Summer Street   6, 45, 113, 122

Suosso Lane   71, 105, 149

T

Taddia Family   134
Talbot Sr., Richmond   126, 128
Talbot, Harry   7
Tassinari Family   8
Taylor Avenue   125
temperance movement   99-101
Temperance Society   99
Tercentenary Celebration   8, 18, 19, 92, *93*,
                                      94, 95, 96
Teves, Marion   *57*
Thacher, James   1, 15, 152
Thompson, Alba Martinelli   73, 74, 98
Toabe hardware store   44
Toabe, Max   43
Toabe, Michel   *44*, 45
Toabe, Mitchell   44, 45, 68, 100
Toabe, Sarah See: Sherman, Sarah Toabe
Torrent No. 4   50
Town Brook   5, 8, 11, *11*, 15, 19, 46, 92, 127
Town House   11, 44, 50, *50*, 115
Town Square   11, *29*, 49, 93, 115
Town Tree   93
Training Green   31, 68, *134*, 135
trolleys   *28, 83*, 83-84, *135*

U

Unitarian Universalist Church
    See: First Parish Church
United States Coast Guard Temporary Reserves
                                            147
Universalist Church   10

V

Vacchino Family   53
Valente Family   54
Valente's Florist   71
Valente, Manny   117, 138, 143, 144, 148
Valeriani Family   132
Vallerville   23, 100
Vanzetti Trail   76

Vanzetti, Bartolomeo   64, *71, 75, 88*
Vanzetti, Luigia   107, *107*
vaudeville   117
Ventura's Restaurant   88
Venturi Family   121
Vermiere Family   53
Victory gardens   68
Viella, Antonio   74
Viella, Bob   74, 149
Viella, Margaret Christofori   74
Village Landing   52
Vine Hills Cemetery   31

W

Wager, Lefevre Brini   75, 88
Ward, Helen   *97*
War Saving Stamps   66
Warren Avenue   9, 84, 116, 130, *135*,
                                  141, 144
Warren Cove   9, 14
Washington Street   126
Water Street   5, 8, 11, *51*, 53, 82, 84,
                              121, 125, *134*
waterfront renovations   92
Waterman, Dr. Isadore   45
welfare   111
Wellingsley School   135, *136*
West Plymouth   12
Western Union   143
Weston's Stable   23
Weston, Horace C.   2
Weston, Jane Brenner   132
Westwood Road   53
Whipple Jr., Sherman   7
Whipple, Margaret   7
Whipple, Sherman   65, 93
White Horse Beach   32, 125, *149*
White Horse Beach Hotel   32
White, James   123
Whiting, William   47
William Harlow House   92
Wilson, Anne   120

Wilson, Curt   143
Winokur Family   45
Winslow and Brewster streets   *134*
Winslow Street   10, 146
Winslow-Warren House   *29*
Winslow, Edward   81
Withington, Sherman Whipple   *102*
Wixon, Lincoln   121
Women's Christian Temperance Union   99
Wood Street   52
Woolson, Doris Gerard   66, 111, 112, 126
Woolworth's   54
Works Progress Administration   124
World War I homefront   65-68
World War II:
    Army barracks   141
    casualties   143-144, *145*
    draftees   *139*
    lookout tower   148
    Navy air base   140
    rations   *140, 142*
    shore patrols   147
    victory celebration   149

Z

Zammarchi, Adaline Vincina   69
Zammarchi, Baby   69
Zammarchi, Eugenio   69
Zavalcofsky Family   134
Zion Lutheran Church   13, 30, 38, 99, *131*
Zucchelli Family   121

TIES THAT BIND

The editorial team that produced this book poses in front of Plymouth's monument to post-Pilgrim immigrants, which was dedicated in Brewster Gardens, Oct. 6, 2001. From left, Karin Goldstein, Kathleen Branigan, Wesley Ennis, John Chaffee, Beverly Ness, Sharon LaRosa and Lee Regan.

Inscribed on the base of the monument are these words from the Rev. Peter Gomes:

To the enduring memory of those immigrant settlers of Plymouth who as latter day Pilgrims from many cultures and countries over the course of three centuries helped build upon these shores a robust and hospitable community. At great personal sacrifice, they established new homes in a new world and, by their hard work, enriched and transformed this town of their adoption. Precious to a grateful posterity is the remembrance of their lives and labors.